Campaign '96

Recent Titles in the
Praeger Series in Political Communication
Robert E. Denton, Jr., *General Editor*

Campaign '96

A Functional Analysis of Acclaiming, Attacking, and Defending

William L. Benoit,
Joseph R. Blaney, and P. M. Pier

Praeger Series in Political Communication

Westport, Connecticut
London

Library of Congress Cataloging-in-Publication Data

Benoit, William L.
    Campaign '96 : a functional analysis of acclaiming, attacking, and
defending / William L. Benoit, Joseph R. Blaney, and P.M. Pier.
      p. cm.—(Praeger series in political communication, ISSN
1062–5623)
    Includes bibliographical references and index.
    ISBN 0–275–96361–6 (alk. paper)
    1. Political oratory—United States.   2. Television broadcasting
of campaign debates.   3. Presidents—United States—
Elections—1996.   I. Blaney, Joseph R.   II. Pier, P. M.
III. Title.   IV. Series.
PN4055.U53B45   1998
808.5'1'088329—dc21   98–15646

British Library Cataloguing in Publication Data is available.

Library of Congress Catalog Card Number: 98–15646
ISBN: 0–275–96361–6
ISSN: 1062–5623

First published in 1998

Praeger Publishers, 88 Post Road West, Westport, CT 06881
An imprint of Greenwood Publishing Group, Inc.

Printed in the United States of America

The paper used in this book complies with the
Permanent Paper Standard issued by the National
Information Standards Organization (Z39.48–1984).

10 9 8 7 6 5 4 3 2 1

Contents

Series Foreword

Those of us from the discipline of communication studies have long believed that communication is prior to all other fields of inquiry. In several other forums I have argued that the essence of politics is "talk" or human interaction.[1] Such interaction may be formal or informal, verbal or nonverbal, public or private, but it is always persuasive, forcing us consciously or subconsciously to interpret, to evaluate, and to act. Communication is the vehicle for human action.

From this perspective, it is not surprising that Aristotle recognized the natural kinship of politics and communication in his writings *Politics* and *Rhetoric*. In the former, he established that humans are "political beings (who) alone of the animals (are) furnished with the faculty of language."[2] In the latter, he began his systematic analysis of discourse by proclaiming that "rhetorical study, in its strict sense, is concerned with the modes of persuasion."[3] Thus, it was recognized over twenty-three hundred years ago that politics and communication go hand in hand because they are essential parts of human nature.

In 1981, Dan Nimmo and Keith Sanders proclaimed that political communication was an emerging field.[4] Although its origin, as noted, dates back centuries, a "self-consciously cross-disciplinary" focus began in the late 1950s. Thousands of books and articles later, colleges and universities offer a variety of graduate and undergraduate coursework in the area in such diverse departments as communication, mass communication, journalism, political science, and sociology.[5] In Nimmo and Sanders's early assessment, the "key areas of inquiry" included rhetorical analysis, propaganda analysis, attitude change studies, voting studies, government and the news media, functional and systems analysis, technological changes, media technologies, campaign techniques, and re-search techniques.[6] In a survey of the state of the field in 1983, the same authors and Lynda Kaid found additional, more specific areas of con-cerns such as the presidency, political polls, public opinion, debates, and advertising.[7] Since the first study, they have also noted a shift away from the rather strict behavioral approach.

A decade later, Dan Nimmo and David Swanson argued the "political communication has developed some identity as a more or less distinct domain of scholarly work."[8] The scope and concerns of the area have further expanded to include critical theories and cultural studies. Al-though there is no precise definition, method, or disciplinary home of the area of inquiry, its primary domain comprises the role, processes, and effects of communication within the context of politics broadly de-fined.

In 1985, the editors of *Political Communication Yearbook: 1984* noted that "more things are happening in the study, teaching, and practice of po-litical communication than can be captured within the space limitations of the relatively few publications available."[9] In addition, they argued that the backgrounds of "those involved in the field [are] so varied and pluralist in outlook and approach . . . it [is] a mistake to adhere slavishly to any set format in shaping the content."[10] More recently, Swanson and Nimmo have called for "ways of overcoming the unhappy consequences of fragmentation within a framework that respects, encourages, and ben-efits from diverse scholarly commitments, agendas, and approaches."[11]

In agreement with these assessments of the area and with gentle en-couragement, in 1988 Praeger established the series entitled "Praeger Se-ries in Political Communication." The series is open to all qualitative and quantitative methodologies as well as contemporary and historical stud-ies. The key to characterizing the studies in the series is the focus on communication variables or activities within a political context or di-mension. As of this writing, over seventy volumes have been published and numerous impressive works are forthcoming. Scholars from the dis-ciplines of communication, history, journalism, political science, and so-ciology have participated in the series.

I am, without shame or modesty, a fan of the series. The joy of serving as its editor is in participating in the dialogue of the field of political communication and in reading the contributors' works. I invite you to join me.

Robert E. Denton, Jr.

NOTES

1. See Robert E. Denton, Jr., *The Symbolic Dimensions of the American Presidency* (Prospect Heights, IL: Waveland Press, 1982); Robert E. Denton, Jr., and Gary

Woodward, *Political Communication in America* (New York: Praeger, 1985; 2d ed., 1990); Robert E. Denton, Jr., and Dan Hahn, *Presidential Communication* (New York: Praeger, 1986); and Robert E. Denton, Jr., *The Primetime Presidency of Ronald Reagan* (New York: Praeger, 1988).

2. Aristotle, *The Politics of Aristotle*, trans. Ernest Barker (New York: Oxford University Press, 1970), p. 5.

3. Aristotle, *Rhetoric*, trans. W. Rhys Roberts (New York: The Modern Library, 1954), p. 22.

4. Dan Nimmo and Keith Sanders, "Introduction: The Emergence of Political Communication as a Field," in *Handbook of Political Communication*, ed. Dan Nimmo and Keith Sanders (Beverly Hills, CA: Sage, 1981), pp. 11–36.

5. Ibid, p. 15.

6. Ibid, pp. 17–27.

7. Keith Sanders, Lynda Kaid, and Dan Nimmo, eds., *Political Communication Yearbook: 1984* (Carbondale, IL: Southern Illinois University, 1985), pp. 283–308.

8. Dan Nimmo and David Swanson, "The Field of Political Communication: Beyond the Voter Persuasion Paradigm," in *New Directions in Political Communication*, ed., David Swanson and Dan Nimmo (Beverly Hills, CA: Sage, 1990), p. 8.

9. Sanders, Kaid, and Nimmo, *Political Communication Yearbook: 1984*, p. xiv.

10. Ibid.

11. Nimmo and Swanson, "The Field of Political Communication," p. 11.

Preface

We take up three topics here. First, we sketch our functional approach to political campaign discourse (which is elaborated in Chapter 1). Second, we describe the purpose and scope of our investigation. Finally, we acknowledge those who have helped, directly and indirectly, with this project.

A FUNCTIONAL APPROACH TO CAMPAIGN DISCOURSE

Campaign discourse generally has one goal: to persuade citizens to vote for one candidate instead of an opponent (of course, a few candidates may campaign to champion an issue as well). Because each vote is a *choice between competing candidates*, persuasive attempts to win votes are inherently comparative. When voters are fortunate, this means picking the best of two good candidates; at other times, it means selecting the lesser of two evils. A candidate need not be perfect to elicit votes: each voter chooses to cast his or her ballot for the candidate who appears *preferable* on whatever criteria are most important to that voter.

This goal of appearing to be the preferable candidate prompts political campaign rhetors to develop and present messages designed to make them appear *better* than their opponent(s). Candidates can accomplish this goal by engaging in (1) *acclaiming* (self-praise: lauding one's own positive qualities or accomplishments) and (2) *attacking* (*kategoria*: criticizing opposing candidates as possessing negative qualities or having performed objectionable actions). If attacked, candidates may also choose to engage in (3) *defending* (*apologia*: responding to criticisms from others). Thus, political campaign messages can serve three fundamental functions: acclaiming, attacking, and defending. Each of these kinds of messages has the potential to help make a candidate appear more desirable than his or her opponent(s), especially if the message which acclaims, attacks, or defends concerns a topic of particular concern to voters. Of course, candidates may choose to employ combinations of these strategies. In particular, politicians may directly compare their records (or proposals, or character) with those of their opponents, simultaneously praising self and attacking opponent.

Although this point is never developed as extensively as we do in this treatise, other scholars have made generally similar observations. Jamieson (1996), for example, wrote that "from the country's first contested election, strategists have offered voter advertising that venerated their candidate and vilified his opponents" (p. ix). Popkin (1994) noted that "each campaign tries hard to make its side look better and the other side worse" (p. 232). Smith (1990) observed that "in no other profession [besides politics] do people pursue and defend jobs by publicly boasting and attacking others" (p. 107). Thus, acclaiming (boasting) and attacking (but not defending) are viewed as common features of political campaigns.

Those who study political advertising routinely distinguish between positive and negative spots (see, e.g., Devlin, 1989, 1993; Kaid & Davidson, 1986; Kaid & Johnston, 1991). Trent and Friedenberg (1995) even observed that televised political ads perform all three of these basic functions: extol the candidates' own virtues; condemn, attack, and question their opponents; and respond to attacks or innuendos. So, political communication scholars recognize that political television spots acclaim and attack—and some even acknowledge the existence of defensive advertisements. However, this common distinction between positive and negative political advertisements is rarely applied to other important forms of campaign discourse, like acceptance addresses or keynote speeches. Furthermore, research analyzing televised campaign commercials does not incorporate Trent and Friedenberg's observation, analyzing political advertisements into defensive as well as positive and negative spots.

PURPOSE OF THIS STUDY

This book develops a functional theory of political campaign discourse using the three concepts of acclaiming, attacking, and defending. We also distinguish between messages that focus on *policy*, or issues, and *character*, or image, and we analyze both policy and character into finer subdivisions (policy: past deeds, future plans, and general goals; character:

personal qualities, leadership ability, and ideals). Then, we apply our functional approach to a variety of forms of campaign discourse (primary and general election debates; primary and general election televised advertisements, talk radio appearances, speeches, and free television remarks) in the 1996 presidential campaign.

To accomplish this purpose, we begin Part I by advancing a theory of the functions of political campaign discourse (Chapter 1). We then describe the method we will utilize (analyzing acclaims, attacks, and defenses on policy and character) to analyze the 1996 presidential campaign. We also discuss three preliminary studies undertaken to develop our functional approach (Chapters 2 and 3). Then, several chapters describe the results of our analysis of the 1996 presidential campaign, grouped into sections on the primaries (Part II), the nominating conventions (Part III), and the general election campaign (Part IV). Finally we discuss the implications of our findings for the 1996 campaign and for political campaign communication generally (Part V).

This investigation has multiple strengths. First, it analyzes several different kinds of messages (spots, debates, talk radio appearances, speeches, free television time utterances). Previous research on presidential campaigns, especially book-length treatments, has a tendency to focus almost exclusively on television spots and debates. While we agree that these two forms of messages deserve analysis, we believe other message forms merit scholarly attention as well. Second, our study analyzes these messages for all three functions—acclaiming, attacking and defending. As noted above, defense is rarely investigated in presidential campaign studies, and acclaims (positive messages) and attacks (negative messages) are usually studied only in television spots. Third, our study analyzes these messages on both policy and character grounds. Again, prior research on policy (issue) and character (image) is usually limited to studies of television spots. While no single study could reasonably purport to provide a *comprehensive* analysis of anything as complex as a presidential election campaign, our investigation provides an extensive analysis of many of the key messages employed in campaign '96.

We have developed six specific research questions designed to guide our analysis of the messages in Campaign '96.

1. How often do the major candidates employ each of the three functions of political campaign messages (acclaiming, attacking, defending)?

2. Do the candidates devote more utterances to addressing policy considerations (issues) or character concerns (image)?

3. How many utterances are devoted to the three forms of policy utterances (past deeds, future plans, general goals) and the three forms of character remarks (personal qualities, leadership ability, and ideals)?

4. To what extent are these messages targeted to the candidates, the parties, or both?

5. How do candidates elaborate their utterances in the discourse?

6. Which candidates devoted more utterances to the issues of most importance to voters?

Use of a standard set of questions will help us to generate similar insights to the varied campaign message forms we investigate.

We continually write about "political campaign communication" to remind readers of our focus. There are many forms of political discourse—like the State of the Union Address—that are not instances of *campaign* discourse; we do not include them in our discussion. The concept of the "permanent campaign" (Blumenthal, 1980) suggests that officeholders may never completely stop campaigning, so every message articulated by a politician is a campaign message to a certain extent; but we focus on messages that are explicitly devoted to seeking office. Similarly, there are other forms of campaigns besides political, such as commercial advertising campaigns; we do not address those persuasive messages (arguably, some of these campaigns are aimed at least in part toward swaying political officeholders, but they are not generally aimed at securing a candidate's election to office). It would be possible to extend our functional analysis to other kinds of campaigns (analyzing how advertisers acclaim their own products, attack their opponents' wares, and defend their products from such attacks), but we do not take up that task here.

DID CAMPAIGN '96 MATTER?

We have selected the 1996 presidential campaign to illustrate this functional theory of political campaign discourse. Some readers may wonder if recency is a sufficient rationale for studying this campaign because Bill Clinton led the race from start to finish. Benedetto (1996) reported that "one common thread in all independent national polls since spring is that none found Dole ahead" (p. 8A). In fact, the closest point occurred when Dole narrowed the gap to come within seven points of Clinton after he received the "bounce" from the Republican National Convention. However, while a Clinton win might have looked as if it was inevitable, that is simply not the case.

First, President Clinton did not look invincible after the off-year elections of 1994. In fact, although Clinton led Dole from the end of January through election day, trial heats by Gallup as late as January 12–15 reported Dole leading Clinton (Gallup Poll, 1996, p. 3). Second, although Clinton led in the polls, this does not mean that all of the respondents who reported that they favored him were actually *committed* to voting for him. Exit poll data from 1996 reveals that 11% of voters decided in the last three days before the election; an additional 6% in the last week, and 13% more in the last month (AllPolitics CNN/*Time*, 1996). A 30% shift in the polls from these undecided voters could have reversed the outcome of the campaign. Third, large leads have disappeared during prior presidential campaigns. For example, in 1988, Michael Dukakis led George Bush by 17% in July (Lichter & Noyes, 1995) only to lose in November. In 1992, George Bush had appeared unbeatable after Desert Storm but still managed to lose to Clinton in November. Other races had seen large leads almost completely evaporate: "Like Nixon in 1968, Carter [in 1976] took a commanding lead and saw it shrink to a point where he nearly lost the election" (Diamond & Bates, 1993, pp. 243–44). A large early lead cannot be assumed to guarantee a victory in November. Nor should one assume that an election can be won without an important struggle during the campaign. We will argue in our conclusion that our analysis shows that Bill Clinton's messages were, on certain grounds, better developed than Bob Dole's messages.

Furthermore, we want to directly address the notion that campaign messages do not affect election outcomes. First, while it is clear that a portion of the electorate simply votes for their party's nominee, the power of political parties has diminished sharply since 1968 (Trent & Friedenberg, 1995). The White House has swung back and forth from Republican to Democrat five times in the ten campaigns from 1960–1996—and not because of huge vacillations in party affiliation during those years. Exit poll data from 1996 indicated that neither party accounted for even 40% of all voters, and 26% said they were independent (AllPolitics, CNN/*Time*, 1996). Party affiliation is undoubtedly an important factor in deciding presidential elections, but it is undeniable that party affiliation does not *determine* the outcome of presidential elections today.

Second, we recognize that elections can be greatly influenced by voters' perceptions of the state of the economy and foreign affairs. In 1996, we faced no all-encompassing foreign crisis (e.g., no Vietnam War or oil embargo) and the domestic economy was in relatively good shape. However, this does not mean that Clinton's reelection was a foregone conclusion. Agenda-setting research has confirmed that news stories on the economy (i.e., unemployment and inflation) influence public perceptions of the importance of these issues. However, recent research found that on the topics of energy and inflation (although not unemployment) *presidential speeches had considerably more impact than televised news stories* on public perceptions of the importance of an issue. Strikingly, the *actual figures on unemployment and inflation had no appreciable effect on public opinion* (Iyengar & Kinder, 1987). Although this study was not concerned with voting or campaign messages, it strongly suggests that voters' perceptions can be influenced more by what the candidates say about the economy than the economic figures themselves—or what the news media says about those figures (the "facts" do not speak for themselves). We will argue later that Clinton effectively took advantage of the economic situation in his campaign discourse.

Third, there is no doubt that incumbency is a potentially significant factor in political campaigns (see, e.g., Dover, 1994). Incumbents, especially presidential incumbents, are extremely well-known (compare, for example, voters' knowledge of Governor Bill Clinton in early 1992 with their knowledge of President Bill Clinton in 1996). Incumbents can obtain network (and front-page) news coverage with a press secretary's telephone call. Presidents are among the most newsworthy individuals in the nation (see Trent & Trent, 1995; Trent & Friedenberg, 1995). Not surprisingly, several sitting Presidents (e.g., President Nixon in 1972; President Reagan in 1984) have been reelected. Furthermore, George Bush was a sitting vice president when he defeated Michael Dukakis in 1988. However, Gerald Ford in 1976, Jimmy Carter in 1980, and George Bush in 1992 all lost elections while sitting in the Oval Office; these examples provide incontrovertible evidence that incumbency is no guarantee of reelection.

Finally, we are accumulating research demonstrating that campaign messages do influence election outcomes. Some studies report significant correlations between money spent on television spots and election outcomes (Joslyn, 1981; Palda, 1973). For example, Wanat (1974) found that, for election winners, broadcast spending correlated highly (.56) with voting outcomes. McClure and Patterson (1974) reported that in the 1972 campaign, "Exposure to political advertising was consistently related to voter belief change" (p. 16; see also Patterson & McClure, 1973). Mulder (1979) reported that exposure to ads in a Chicago mayoral campaign correlated significantly with attitudes (see also Atkin & Heald, 1976). Benoit and Wells (1996) summarized evidence that presidential debates can facilitate learning in viewers and can influence voting intention as well. So, these studies establish the fact that campaign messages can and do influence voting. Thus, campaign communication merits scholarly attention, and the 1996 presidential campaign in particular is worth studying.

WHAT ABOUT ROSS PEROT?

We would also like to note that we believe Ross Perot's importance in 1996 was greatly diminished from 1992. One indication of this change can be seen in the decision of the Commission on Presidential Debates to recommend Perot be included in the 1992 presidential debates but not in the 1996 encounter (Lewis, 1996a, 1996b). Also, Perot garnered 19% of the popular vote in 1992 but only 8% in 1996. For this reason we decided to focus our attention on the nominees of the two major parties (and our analysis of the 1996 Republican primaries focused on the major contenders there as well). Undoubtedly there is a great deal to be learned from studies of the campaigns of Ross Perot, Ralph Nader, Harry Browne, and others; however, we wanted to limit our investigation to a manageable project and focus on the principal contenders.

SUMMARY

We develop a functional theory of political campaign communication, arguing that such discourse can be understood as acclaiming, attacking, and defending on topics of policy and character. We illustrate this theory through an examination of a variety of messages (debates, television ads, talk radio, speeches, free television remarks) throughout the 1996 presidential primaries, the nominating conventions, and the general election. We limit our focus to the two major party candidates, Bill Clinton and Bob Dole (and to Dole and his opponents in the Republican primaries). This investigation is designed both to illustrate our functional theory of political discourse and to provide insight into the 1996 presidential campaign.

ACKNOWLEDGMENTS

We would like to thank several people for their contributions, direct and indirect, to this project.

William L. Benoit: Pamela Benoit (1997) has written the first treatment of acclaiming in the communication literature (and the most extensive treatment of this topic in any discipline). Something was missing in the initial study of attack and defense in the 1992 presidential debates (Benoit & Wells, 1996), and Pam's research supplied that missing piece. Although we take her ideas in a different direction, they were indispensable to our project. She also is very supportive of my research and writing—whether that entails monopolization of the TV and VCR for videotaping campaign-related programming, subscribing to the *New York Times* during the campaign, or buying a political communication library for research and teaching.

Jennifer Benoit is always an inspiration for me. She, too, put up with my demands for the TV and VCR. It is very satisfying to have such a bright and fun daughter with whom I can discuss my ideas. I remember watching political ads with her and being delighted—but not surprised—

when she turned to me and correctly noted: "That one was both positive and negative, wasn't it?" We also watched parts of the presidential debates together.

Suzy Shuster of Fox News graciously provided us with a videotape compilation of all of the "Voice of the People" statements. The DNC (Democratic National Committee) and the RNC (Republican National Committee) each sent three of their commercials (Clinton's and Dole's campaign staffs, on the other hand, both promised to send copies of their ads after the end of the campaign, but apparently were too busy wrapping things up to follow through). Dr. M. J. Smythe has been supportive as Chair of the Department of Communication. My students in Comm 373, Political Campaign Communication, listened patiently while he tried out some of the ideas we develop in this book. Bill Wells initiated our study of the 1992 presidential debates, and would have been a part of this project if he hadn't been writing his dissertation (analyzing the 1976, 1980, and 1984 presidential debates) as we worked on it—and even then he participated in our preliminary analysis of nomination convention acceptance addresses from 1960–1996. Of course, my co-authors have been very important to this project; they are truly co-authors who made substantive contributions to this project and not simply research assistants. They worked hard on this research even as they pursued their doctoral degrees and taught their courses.

Joseph R. Blaney: I would like to thank my wife, Lauri, and our daughter, Maggie, for their encouragement throughout this project. I would also like to thank my mother, Ellen Blaney, who continues to teach me. It goes without saying that I am grateful to Dr. William L. Benoit, my mentor, and P. M. Pier, my colleague, for the opportunity to work on this project with such dynamic people.

P. M. Pier: I would like to thank Dr. Bill Benoit and Joseph Blaney for their friendship and inspiration throughout the project. In addition, I would like to thank my husband, John Atkinson, for his understanding, support, and words of encouragement. My gratitude and love go out to EuGene and JoAnne Pier for their guidance and enthusiasm during this project. I would like to thank Don Stanton, Carol Gaede, Sandra Weiser Matthews, and Wallace Bloom for inspiring me to pursue my academic goals. Finally, thanks to Krista Holloway for seeing me through to the end.

Part I

Introduction

Chapter 1

Overview: A Functional Theory of Political Campaign Discourse

In this chapter we develop our functional theory of political campaign persuasion. Then we discuss several advantages of our functional approach to studying political discourse. A functional analysis is particularly appropriate for analyzing political campaign discourse. Such rhetoric is clearly conceived and implemented as a means to an end: winning the election. In the case of presidential campaign discourse, the prize is control of the most powerful political office in the world. Political campaign rhetoric is without question instrumental, or functional, in nature. While discourse may profitably be understood from other perspectives (e.g., as epistemic or ontological), the functional approach is well suited for understanding political campaign discourse.

THE FUNCTIONAL THEORY OF POLITICAL CAMPAIGN DISCOURSE

The functional theory of political campaign discourse is built upon several key assumptions. Specifically, we advance five propositions that form the underpinning for this theory. Each proposition will be discussed separately in this section.

Voting Is a Comparative Act

The decision facing voters—for whom should I cast my vote?—is a choice, an inherently *comparative* judgment. No candidate is utterly perfect; no candidate is completely and irreparably flawed. At times voters face the happy situation of choosing between two desirable contenders; at other times voters are forced to select the lesser of two evils. The point is, a voter chooses to vote for that candidate who appears *preferable* to him or her, on whatever criteria are most salient to that voter.

This proposition that voting is a choice between competing candidates is becoming increasingly important as political parties decline in influence. As Popkin noted, "Today, in an environment of diminishing party loyalty, campaigns and candidates exert a greater influence on voters than they did in the elections of 1940 and 1948" (1994, p. 12). In the past, the party nominee was often selected at the convention. Levine notes that in the past "Presidential hopefuls generally did not even need to campaign in primaries, which were relatively few in number" (1995, p. 56). For example, in 1968, Hubert Humphrey was nominated despite the fact that he had not won a single primary (indeed, he had not campaigned in any primary; see Levine, 1995). This situation led to divisive convention struggles broadcast on the national television networks. To prevent contentious conventions, both parties expanded their reliance on primaries and caucuses for selecting their nominees. In 1968, there were only sixteen Republican and seventeen Democratic primaries (Crotty & Jackson, 1985). In 1992, there were primaries in 39 states (Trent & Friedenberg, 1995).

The increased importance of political primaries has been a very important development, because one unintended consequence is the decline in importance of political parties and the concomitant rise in importance of individual candidates (and their political consultants). While some voters still cast their votes for the candidate who represents his or her respective party, the individual candidates, and their apparent preferability to voters, are increasingly important determinants of election outcomes. Simple party loyalty is exerting less influence on voting decisions; the individual candidates and their messages are filling the void left by the diminishing role of party identification. So, voters choose between the available, competing candidates, and not just by party loyalty.

Candidates Must Distinguish Themselves from Opponents

The fact that candidates must appear preferable to voters means that it is important for candidates to distinguish themselves from each other. As a candidate, if you fail to establish clear differences between yourself and your opponent, there is no reason for any citizen to vote for you instead of for your opponent. As Popkin explains, "Somehow, candidates manage to get a large proportion of the citizenry sorted into opposing camps, each of which is convinced that the positions and interests of the other side add up to a less desirable package of benefits" (1994,

p. 8). All candidates in races for contested offices must offer distinctions between themselves and their opponents.

Establishing clear distinctions between candidates is often difficult, because the outcome of general election campaigns turns out to hinge on which major party candidate can attract the undecided, independent, and weakly leaning voters. Today, the strongly partisan voters of neither major political party constitute a majority of voters. The number of independent voters has increased from 22.6% in 1952 to 38.0% in 1992 (Weisberg & Kimball, 1993). Therefore, competing candidates in any given race often find themselves in the position of appealing to the *same group(s) of voters* as their opponent, and both candidates are often forced take fairly similar stands on the issues that matter to those voters. This means candidates often sound alike, adopting virtually identical stands on some issues that are important to many voters. In March 1996, the *New York Times* joked that the Clinton-Dole race would pit the "center against the middle" (Toner, 1996, p. 4.3). So, candidates often appear similar on some topics as a result of their attempts to appeal to the same group of undecided voters. Still, if voters are to have a basis for choosing one candidate instead of another there must be some points of distinction between the contenders that are salient to voters.

Candidates have only two broad options for differentiating themselves from their opponents: they may contrast their character, or they may contrast their policy stances (of course, they can use both options together). One candidate may attempt to portray himself or herself as a forceful leader. Another may want to create the impression that he or she is compassionate. In 1996, for example, Bob Dole argued that he was truthful (and implied clearly that Bill Clinton was not). The candidates may choose to disagree on policy issues, like national defense, abortion, education, immigration, taxation, and social welfare. Bob Dole stressed his proposed 15% tax cut in the 1996 campaign, while Bill Clinton talked about connecting classrooms to the information superhighway. Candidates need not differ on every point of comparison, but they must differ sufficiently to enable voters to choose one contender over the other.

Of course, which topics are important to voters varies by campaign. In the aftermath of Watergate, some voters felt betrayed, and character (especially honesty and integrity) seemed paramount. Foreign policy is more important when it seems to impact voters more directly (e.g., during the Mideast oil embargo; when the Vietnam War was being broadcast on television). Also, if the economy appears strong (and no foreign crisis looms), presumption means that incumbents probably enjoy a substantial advantage. On the other hand, if the economy seems weak, presumption may tend to favor change and challengers. Regardless of which issue seems most important to voters, candidates must establish enough of a distinction between themselves to allow voters to choose among the contenders.

Political Campaign Messages Are Important Vehicles for Distinguishing between Candidates

We cannot and should not rely on the news media to provide voters with information on which to base their voting decisions. Research from the 1972 and 1984 presidential campaigns has revealed that more issue information is available from televised political advertisements than from network news. Patterson and McClure (1976) concluded that in 1972 "during the short period of the general election campaign, presidential ads contain substantially more issue content than network newscasters" (p. 23). After the 1984 election, Kern reported that "by a ratio of 4 to 1, Americans received the majority of their information about candidate positions on the issues from ads rather than the news" (1989, p. 47). Nor is this situation limited to television spots. In their study of the 1992 presidential campaign, Lichter and Noyes (1995) found that "The candidate's own speeches actually discussed policy issues far more frequently and in considerably more detail than did either print or broadcast [news] reports" (p. xvii). So, the candidates' campaign discourse provides more information about issues than print or electronic news media.

Furthermore, there are differential effects on voter learning as a consequence of these differences in information sources. Patterson and McClure (1976) found that "during the 1972 presidential campaign, people who were heavily exposed to political spots became more informed about the candidates' issue positions. . . . On every single issue emphasized in presidential commercials, persons with high exposure to television advertising showed a greater increase in knowledge than persons with low exposure" (pp. 116–17). Similarly, Lichter and Noyes (1995) reported that "voter knowledge does not increase from exposure to day-to-day TV coverage, and increases modestly with day-to-day newspaper reading. Voters do learn from TV coverage of live campaign events, such as convention speeches and debates" (p. 101). Thus, voters receive more issue-related information from campaign messages (in these studies, from political advertisements and campaign speeches) than from the national news media.

There are at least three reasons for this finding. First, news tends to concentrate on the "horse race" aspects of the campaign: who is ahead in the polls? which states are being actively contested by the campaigns? will one candidate attack the other? who is advising and managing the campaign? who will be included in a presidential debate? etc. The answers to these questions may be news, but they simply do not help voters decide which candidate should be elected president. As Patterson (1980) concluded, "In its coverage of a presidential campaign, the press concentrates on the strategic game played by the candidates in their pursuit of the presidency, thereby de-emphasizing the questions of national policy and leadership" (p. 21). In fact, after studying the 1976 campaign, he reported that "The election's substance . . . received only half as much coverage as was accorded the game" (p. 24). The news of the campaign as a contest between competing candidates tends to drown out the news of the substance of the campaign.

Second, campaign news is only one story topic among many. The network news runs for 30 minutes, but subtracting commercials, stories on noncampaign topics, and horse-race coverage leaves little time to actually contrast the candidates' views on policy questions. Especially in the latter phases of a campaign, political ads, direct mail, and presidential debates provide more issue information to viewers than the news.

Finally, the news media is more likely to focus on short sound bites from candidates than on the more extended quotations that facilitate thoughtful consideration of issues. Hallin (1992) found that in 1968, the average quotation from candidates in the news was 43 seconds long. After 20 years, candidate quotations had shrunk to a mere 9 seconds long (see also Adatto, 1993). If the news only presents short quotations from candidates, the candidates have no choice (if they wish to be heard on the news at all) but to offer sound bites to the news media.

During the same time period, journalists also spoke in shorter increments. However, they spoke in political news stories almost twice as frequently in 1988 as in 1968: "Journalists inserted their voices more often, by an increment of .17 times per report per year" (Steele & Barnhurst, 1996, p. 191). Furthermore, the length of a political news story decreased by about 20% (Hallin, 1992) and the number of political news stories dropped by 20% from 1968–1988 (Steele & Barnhurst, 1996). Thus, the news presents fewer political stories, the stories tend to be shorter, stories spend far less time quoting the candidates, and the stories feature journalists themselves more frequently. The upshot of these factors is that voters must look elsewhere for information contrasting presidential candidates: We simply cannot rely on network news for comprehensive coverage of the candidates' viewpoints.

This discussion may sound as if it is an indictment of the news media, but it is not intended that way. We believe that it is not reasonable to expect the news media to excel at the task of informing the electorate about candidates' issue stands and their other qualities. The purpose of the news, by definition, is to report what is "new" to voters. As Patterson points out, "Policy problems lack the novelty that the journalist seeks. . . . The first time that a candidate takes a position on a key issue, the press is almost certain to report it. Further statements on the same issue become progressively less newsworthy, unless a new wrinkle is added" (1994, p. 61). In 1996, the first time Dole proposed a 15% tax cut, that was news. However, later discussions just were not as newsworthy as the initial announcement—even if they contained more specifics about his plan. Thus, we should not expect the news media to provide the electorate with information that distinguishes the candidates and helps them cast their votes. At times the news media may convey useful information about the candidates; however, given the fact that this is not their purpose, we cannot count on them to comprehensively inform the electorate.

Candidates, scholars, and voters should all recognize this situation, and its clear implication: political campaign messages are the best places for voters to obtain information that distinguishes the candidates, information that can be used by voters to decide which candidate is preferable. Popkin (1994) argued that "Campaign communications . . . increased the accuracy of voter perception; misperceptions were far more likely on issues that were peripheral to the campaign." In fact, he concluded that "exposure to communication was the strongest single influence on accuracy of perceptions" (p. 39). Clearly, political campaign communication—television spots, stump speeches, pamphlets, presidential debates, interviews, and the like—are important sources of information about the candidates, about their character and policy or issue stands.

In 1996, the television networks started to offer free television time to the leading candidates in the general election. Fox broadcast one minute clips from Clinton and Dole addressing the same question (Moore, 1996). CBS gave Clinton and Dole two and a half minutes each for four days in late October (Mifflin, 1996). PBS's "Democracy Project" gave each candidate time (on alternating weekdays) from October 17 to November 1. We applaud these efforts to offer candidates an opportunity to address the same topics at the same time, facilitating the ability of voters to choose which candidate is preferable (and we analyze three sets of free television time messages in Chapter 13).

Presidential debates, which have become a standard part of the presidential campaign in recent years, permit the candidates to present their own views; unfortunately, in our opinion, the format for these encounters is really more of a joint press conference than a debate. As a result, debates are too often dominated by topics prompted by questions from journalists rather than by the topics the candidates choose to address (or the voters would like to hear discussed). Still, debates do provide voters an opportunity to contrast the leading candidates, speaking on the same topics at the same time.

Of course, this does not mean that we naively believe that candidates offer a thorough discussion of every issue, or that they present voters with an unbiased view of themselves and their opponents. Strategic ambiguity can be useful to political candidates. Some issues (like the specific details of proposals to balance the federal budget) are so complex that discussion becomes unwieldy. Clearly it is in the candidates' best interests to present themselves in a favorable light, and to portray their opponents in an unfavorable light (ad watches are trying to curb excessive deception in political advertising). This can easily lead to inaccuracies, omissions, and misrepresentations of the issues. Nevertheless, voters must rely on candidates' campaign messages for much of the information they have about the candidates; it is a mistake to assume that the news media provides a comprehensive understanding of candidates' policy positions.

Some scholars, however, are not convinced that political campaigns matter. Lichtman (1996) identifies a set of thirteen "keys" which "predicts elections on the basis of historical conditions alone, without the use of candidate-preference polls or reference to the strategy, tactics, or events of campaigns" (p. xi). He claims that his system can "account for or predict the outcomes of all thirty-four elections since 1860" (p. xii). His thirteen keys are the following:

KEY 1   Incumbent-party mandate: After the midterm elections, the incumbent party holds more seats in the U.S. House of Representatives than it did after the previous midterm elections.

KEY 2   Nomination-contest: There is no serious contest for the incumbent-party nomination.

KEY 3   Incumbency: The incumbent-party candidate is the sitting president.

KEY 4   Third party: There is no significant third-party or independent campaign.

KEY 5   Short-term economy: The economy is not in recession during the election campaign.

KEY 6   Long-term economy: Real annual per-capita economic growth during the term equals or exceeds mean growth during the two previous terms.

KEY 7   Policy change: The incumbent administration effects major changes in national policy.

KEY 8   Social unrest: There is no sustained social unrest during the term.

KEY 9   Scandal: The incumbent administration is untainted by major scandal.

KEY 10   Foreign or military failure: The incumbent administration achieves a major failure in foreign or military affairs.

KEY 11   Foreign or military success: The incumbent administration achieves a major success in foreign or military affairs.

KEY 12   Incumbent charisma: The incumbent-party candidate is charismatic or a national hero.

KEY 13   Challenger charisma: The challenging-party candidate is not charismatic or a national hero. (p. 3)

Lichtman asserts that if eight or more of these factors are true, the incumbent party will win; and if six or more are false, the incumbent party will lose. There is no question that he has included key elements among these keys: whether the nomination is contested, how the economy seems to be doing, the presence of social unrest or foreign policy failures, and the charisma of the competing candidates.

However, he goes on to make the striking argument that "The fact that the outcome of every election is predictable without reference to issues, ideology, party loyalties, or campaign events allows us reasonably to conclude that *many of the factors most commonly cited in explaining election results count for very little on Election Day.*" He also asserts that "Despite the hundreds of millions of dollars and months of media attention lavished on them, *general-election campaigns don't count*" (p. 5, emphasis added). Lichtman concludes that "effective government, not packaging, image making, or campaigning" (p. 159) is what matters. Although we do not endorse packaging (by which we mean development of misleading images of candidates), and we do not stress the importance of image over issue, we reject Lichtman's claim that campaigns don't matter, based on the evidence he presents for his claim, as well as evidence we offer to the contrary here in this book (e.g., the preface, Chapter 10 on general television spots, or Chapter 12 on presidential debates). We also argue that several of his keys are in fact influenced, if not determined, by campaign messages.

First, even if his keys can predict election outcomes, that does not prove other factors are in fact irrelevant. For example, it might be possible to predict a child's success in school from such factors as parents' income, the number of books in the child's home, or amount of time parents read to their child. Such a prediction would not constitute proof that the child's studying or the teacher's instruction did not matter.

Second, the keys to the White House is an empirically-derived set of factors (developed out of pattern recognition work), not a conceptually or theoretically-driven model. Any empirically-derived system is limited by the campaigns that constituted it. A new election could easily turn on another factor that wasn't important in previous years. Lichtman assumes that because this system explains past elections, it will also explain all future ones. However, the situation facing presidential candidates is changing. For those who agree that campaigns matter, new technology (e.g., for targeting television spots, tracking polls, and distributing information on the World Wide Web) alters what candidates can do and what means are available to them. Another factor that seems important is the shift away from partisan party loyalty as the number of independent voters continues to rise. The tremendous amount of soft money available to recent campaigns is yet another important factor. If the situation facing candidates changes in important ways—and we've identified just three differences—then the "keys" to the White House will change, and the keys that may have explained past elections are unlikely to work so well in the future.

Third, most of these keys are subjective, so his assertion that the keys explain all those elections is questionable. For example, how does the analyst determine whether there has been a "serious" contest for the incumbent party nomination (Key 2)? Key seven asks whether the incumbent administration has produced "major changes in national policy." How does one know if a change was major or minor? "Changes" is plural: how many major changes must an incumbent administration enact to consider this key fulfilled? In the eighth key, what qualifies as "social unrest" and how long must it persist to be count as "sustained"? The ninth key is scandal. In 1996, some would have said Clinton sustained at least one major scandal, but others would reject this assessment of affairs. How can one be sure if there was a major scandal or not? Keys 10 and 11 both speak of "major" successes or failures in foreign or military affairs. How serious must they be to count as "major"? The last two keys use "charisma" (not an objectively quantifiable characteristic) and "hero." Again, consider one of the candidates from 1996. We don't know anyone who would deny that Bob Dole was a hero during World War II. But it is not obvious that everyone considered him a hero in 1996 (isn't there a difference between *being* a hero and *having been* a hero?). So, was Dole a hero in the 1996 campaign or not? Most of the keys are so subjective that they do not neatly and decisively account for all campaign outcomes.

Lichtman brushes aside the criticism that the keys are subjective, asserting that using the keys "merely requires the kind of informed evaluations that historians invariably rely on in drawing conclusions about past events" (p. 14). We do not find this dismissal compelling. Astonishingly, Lichtman admits that one of the co-authors of this approach predicted a Bush victory in 1992 because that writer (DeCell) judged that only four keys weighed against Bush. Lichtman's own forecast, made later in the year, guessed that six keys weighed against Bush and Lichtman predicted a Bush loss. Clearly, when two co-authors using the same approach judge the keys differently and make conflicting predictions, this system is subjective and not as predictive as Lichtman would have us believe. Lichtman admits that five elections (1888, 1892, 1912, 1948, and 1992) "hinge on the calling of a single key" (p. 16). This system is far too subjective to function as evidence that other factors are irrelevant. Furthermore, we argue that campaigns do matter. As mentioned above, the preface, Chapter 10 (on general campaign television spots), and

Chapter 12 (on presidential debates) all present evidence of the impact of campaign messages (see also Holbrook, 1996).

More importantly, voters' perceptions—perceptions shaped by the candidates—have been shown to be more important than the "facts" themselves. As mentioned earlier, research has found the public's view of which issues are important is shaped most by presidential speeches, secondarily by media agenda-setting (news stories), and not at all by the actual state of the economy (Iyengar & Kinder, 1987). Lichtman admits that the recession key "depends primarily on whether there is the widespread *perception* of an economy mired in recession during the election campaign" (p. 32, emphasis added). Surely these public perceptions are influenced by campaign discourse about whether there is a recession. Similarly, he recognizes that "charisma is most likely to be determined during the general-election campaign" (p. 47). It seems likely that perceptions of the candidates' charisma are shaped, if not determined, by the candidates' campaign messages. It is reasonable to assume that campaign discourse influences the voters' perceptions (of whether there are scandals, of policy initiatives, of foreign policy successes or failures, of the short- and long-term state of the economy), thus *indirectly* influencing the keys. We noted earlier that campaign messages contain more policy information than the news media (Patterson & McClure, 1976; Kern, 1989) and that voters do in fact learn from campaigns, so Lichtman should not assume that campaign messages are irrelevant to voters' perceptions of domestic or foreign policy. Far from being irrelevant, campaign discourse is therefore an integral, if indirect, part of the keys to elections.

Lichtman asserts that "Presidential elections are primarily referenda on the performance of the incumbent administration during the previous four years" (p. 1). We agree that the incumbent's past deeds are one very important factor in the election—or at least how that candidate and the opponent *characterize those past deeds in campaign discourse* is important (and the challenger's deeds play a role as well). However, we also believe that elections are referenda on the next term, and *what each candidate promises to do—and how they characterize their opponent's promises—in their campaign discourse (future plans, general goals)* are other important factors in the election. Furthermore, we agree that character (roughly equivalent to Lichtman's notion of charisma) can be important, but it too is influenced by campaign discourse. We strongly reject his claim that campaigns (and television, and money) don't matter in election outcomes. We reject Lichtman's implicit assumption that voters learn information needed to turn the keys from *sources other than campaign messages* (and recall from our discussion above that we cannot assume the media will provide voters with sufficient issue or policy information). Campaigns, and the messages that constitute them, matter a great deal in presidential elections.

The Key Functions of Political Campaign Discourse Are Acclaiming, Attacking, and Defending

Of course, it is not enough simply for candidates to be distinctive in their messages, even on the issues that matter most to voters in that election year; a candidate must appear to be different from his or her opponents *in ways that will attract voters*. For example, a statement like "I am the only candidate to have been convicted of influence-peddling" would surely distinguish that candidate from his or her opponents, but it would not make the candidate more electable.

This need for a candidate to appear preferable to voters means that all political campaign discourse has three potential functions. First, a candidate's message may *acclaim*, or engage in self-praise. This praise may focus either on policy stands or on character of the candidate, as discussed later. Emphasizing positive attributes of one candidate tends to make that candidate appear preferable (for voters who value that attribute) to his or her opponent(s). One way to increase the likelihood that voters will perceive a candidate to be preferable is for that candidate to produce discourse that acclaims, or emphasizes, his or her desirable points.

Second, a candidate's discourse may *attack*, or criticize the opponent. Again, attacks may focus on either the policies or the character of the opponent, as discussed later. Stressing an opponent's negative attributes tends to make that opponent appear less enticing (for voters who value that attribute). Attacks can therefore improve a candidate's relative position by reducing his or her opponent's desirability.

Of course, a candidate may choose not to attack his or her opponent. It is well known that many voters dislike, sometimes intensely, mudslinging (Stewart, 1975) and some politicians may not wish to appear to engage in character assassination. However, this does not necessarily mean attacking is ineffectual. Some political campaign attacks may hurt both sponsor and target, so the key question in deciding to use them may be who will suffer a net loss if a candidate attacks. Furthermore, some people believe that a sitting president ought not attack because that makes them appear less "presidential." Incumbency has its advantages, and challengers may need to attack more to overcome presumption (Trent & Friedenberg, 1995; Trent & Trent, 1995). Furthermore, there is evidence that voters tend to consider policy attacks more acceptable than character attacks (Johnson-Cartee & Copeland, 1989), so some attacks might be more likely to backfire than others. Clearly, attacking is an option in a political campaign—even if some candidates choose not to use it—and it is capable of altering voters' perceptions of which candidate appears preferable.

Third, if attacked by an opponent, a candidate's persuasive communication can *defend* himself or herself against that attack. Because an opponent's attacks can address either policies (issues) or character (image), a candidate's defense can concern either topic. A timely and apt defense may prevent an attack from making the candidate appear less preferable, or it may partially or completely restore a candidate's preferability reduced by an attack (for those voters who value the attribute criticized in the attack).

As with attack, we recognize that a given candidate may decide not to respond to an attack with a defense. It might seem to place him or her on the defensive; a candidate may not wish to "dignify" an opponent's charges with a response. However, the fact that some candidates may not choose to engage in political campaign self-defense does not deny that defense is an option that inheres in the situation facing a candidate for elective office. Furthermore, when one chooses to respond, the defense should not be delayed. In 1988, "Michael Dukakis failed to respond quickly and effectively to the initial Republican attacks" (Levine, 1995, p. 293), suggesting that defense can be an important campaign function.

Of course, some voters may not accept a candidate's statements at face value. Candidates may not always address the most prominent concerns of voters, and that will inevitably diminish the impact of the message. Furthermore, we should not assume that a single message will make a voter choose the candidate presenting or sponsoring the message. However, the messages that each voter does attend to during the course of an election (along with other predispositions, like party affiliation for some voters) gradually shape his or her decision about how to vote.

Smith (1990) acknowledged the importance of two of these functions from the candidates' perspective when he explained that only in politics "do people pursue and defend jobs by publicly boasting and attacking others" (p. 107). Sabato (1981) made a similar point from the standpoint of voters' decision making when he explained that there are five possible ways of voting: "for or against either of the party nominees or not voting at all" (p. 324). Acclaiming provides the basis for voting for either candidate. Attacking (if not successfully defended against) provides the basis for voting against either candidate. (While we do not want to stray from our main point, it is interesting that Ansolabehere and Iyengar [1995] have argued that attacks in some political spots may be intended to decrease voter turnout when it is believed that more of those who are discouraged from voting would have voted for the opponent, indicating that attacks might influence the fifth "way" of voting as well.)

Similarly, scholars who investigate televised political advertising often distinguish between positive and negative spots (see, e.g., Devlin, 1989, 1993; Kaid & Davidson, 1986; Kaid & Johnston, 1991). Trent and Friedenberg (1995) even observed that televised political ads perform all three of these basic functions: extol the candidates' own virtues; condemn, attack, and question their opponents; and respond to attacks or innuendos. So, political scholars have recognized that political television spots acclaim and attack—and a few have even acknowledged the existence of defensive advertisements. However, this common distinction between positive and negative political advertisements is rarely applied to other forms of campaign discourse. Furthermore, few scholars acknowledge the existence of defensive television spots.

One exception to the generalization that most writing on the functions of political messages is limited to television can be found in research on presidential debates. Benoit and Wells' study of the 1992 presidential debates concluded that "all three presidential candidates engaged in copious persuasive attack and defense during the course of the debates" (1996, p. 110). A limitation of this work is that its analysis did not conceptualize acclaiming as a distinct function, but folded it in with defense (specifically, as bolstering and corrective action). Still, it demonstrates the importance of these functions in political campaign discourse.

Thus, while writers do not always describe all three of these functions, political communication scholars in general acknowledge the importance of these goals of political campaign discourse. These functions have been studied in research on televised political advertisements (acclaiming and attacking) and in research on presidential debates (attacking and defending).

Recognition of these important functions of political discourse is not limited to political communication scholars. Politicians and their advisors also recognize this fundamental principle. For example, Haldeman offered this advice on the reelection campaign to President Nixon on June 23, 1972 (quoted in Popkin et al. [1976] p. 794n): "Haldeman: getting one of those 20 [percent] who is an undecided type to vote for you on the basis of your positive points is much less likely than getting them to vote against McGovern by scaring them to death about McGovern." Thus, Haldeman recognized that Nixon could seek votes by praising himself (stressing Nixon's positive points) or by attacking his opponent (frightening them about his opponent). Similarly, Vincent Breglio, who worked on Ronald Reagan's 1980 campaign, explained that "It has become vital in campaigns today that you not only present all the reasons why people ought to vote for you, but you also have an obligation to present the reasons why they should not vote for the opponent" (1987, p. 34). So, political campaign advisors recognize that candidates can praise themselves or attack their opponents.

Thus, it seems reasonable to approach political campaign discourse as utterances that *acclaim* the preferred candidate, *attack* the opponent(s), and *defend* the candidate from opponent's attacks. We do not argue that these three political campaign communication functions occur with equal frequency; nevertheless, they are all options that candidates can use, and we argue that they all occur to some extent in political campaign discourse. We also argue that a *complete* understanding of political campaign communication must consider all three functions.

Important recent works on the functions of political campaign communication include Jamieson's book *Dirty Politics*, Pfau and Kenski's *Attack Politics*, and Felknor's *Political Mischief*. Unfortunately, none of these works are intended to explore acclaiming, or self-praise, in persuasive political campaign messages. Still, they are useful works and we will discuss them when we describe our method in Chapter 2.

Scholarship on televised political advertising offers other lists of functions of political discourse. For example, Devlin (1986; 1987) discusses several functions of political ads.[1] However, we argue that our three functions are more basic. For example, one of the functions Devlin lists is raising money. Surely a candidate must tout his or her desirable qualities (and/or attack his or her opponent) in order to convince donors to contribute. Furthermore, the money raised must be used to produce acclaiming, attacking, or defending messages to get the candidate elected. Another function identified by Devlin is reinforcing supporters. Surely supporters are reinforced by stressing the good qualities of the candidate (and, quite possibly, the negative qualities of the opponent). Thus, we offer these activities—attacking, acclaiming, and defending—as the three *fundamental* functions of political advertising.

Similarly, Gronbeck discusses a number of instrumental and consummatory functions of presidential campaigning (1978). Some of these functions sound much like uses and gratifications for the audience. Of course, we agree that it is important to know how auditors make use of campaign discourse. However, those sorts of functions supplement, rather than compete with, our analysis of campaign functions because we explicitly privilege the viewpoint of the candidate's purposes in our analysis.

A Candidate Must Win a Majority (or a Plurality) of the Citizens Who Vote in an Election

This proposition may sound so simple that it is not worth mentioning. However, several key tenets of campaigning are implicit within this proposition. First, a candidate need not persuade everyone to vote for him or her. Only those citizens who actually vote matter. As mentioned earlier, Ansolabehere and Iyengar (1995) argue that some candidates use negative television advertisements in order to depress voter turnout, hoping that those who might not vote are more likely to favor the candidate's opponent. The net effect, if true, would increase the candidate's share of the votes actually cast in the election.

Second, a candidate need not persuade everyone who participates in the election to vote for him or her; only a majority (or plurality) of those voting is enough. In many cases, the hot issues are dichotomous: a candidate can either be for abortion (perhaps with some limitations) or against it (perhaps with some exceptions); a candidate can either favor an assault weapons ban or not; a candidate can either support restrictions on cigarette advertisements aimed at teens or not. Candidate stands on such choices simultaneously attract some voters and repel others who care about that issue. To win the election, a candidate does not have to try to accomplish the impossible task of convincing every voter that he or she is preferable. The candidate need only persuade a sufficient number of voters that he or she is the better choice.

Third, in a presidential election, a candidate only needs to persuade enough of those who are voting in enough states to win 270 electoral votes. This leads candidates to campaign more vigorously (e.g., spend more on airing political advertising; schedule more speeches and political rallies) in some states than others. It also can influence which issues candidates decide to stress, and which to ignore (as well as what position they might take on the issues they do address).

The claim that a candidate only needs to obtain the support of part of the electorate is a very important proposition. As suggested, it is unreasonable to expect every eligible voter to prefer a given candidate. Given the fact that we enjoy a diverse electorate and an increasingly complex political environment, candidates must make choices that increase preferability among some voters while decreasing preferability among other groups of voters (although candidates may attempt to use strategic ambiguity to lessen this effect). This means that audience analysis is essential to effective political campaigning (and the rise of public opinion polls by the campaigns themselves attests to the importance of this proposition).

Audience analysis helps candidates make two important decisions in their campaigns. First, presidential candidates must decide which states to contest. Kaid reports that "The 1992 campaign saw spot buys in selected markets reach new heights. The Clinton campaign particularly used this strategy on a national basis" (1994, p. 124). A candidate who uses national advertising buys spends money in states that he or she is almost certain to carry as well as in states he or she is virtually certain to lose. Bill Clinton used spot media buys to maximize his advertising in states that were close (Devlin, 1993).

Second, candidates must also decide which topics to emphasize in their messages—as well as which position to take on various issues. The candidate must persuade a majority of those who are voting that he or she is preferable on the *criteria that are most important to those voters.*

These considerations suggest five specific strategies for maximizing a candidate's likelihood of winning. First, a candidate can try to increase the election day turnout of voters who tend to prefer that candidate. A decision that one candidate is preferable to another does the candidate no good if that person does not actually vote.

Second, a candidate can try to persuade undecided voters to support him or her. The number of independent voters has increased over time, as noted above, as the importance of parties has declined. It is reasonable to conclude that much of a general election campaign does not concern committed partisans (who will almost certainly vote for their party's nominee) but focuses on the undecided.

Third, a candidate can try to entice those who lean slightly toward his or her opponent to switch allegiance. As suggested above, candidates are unlikely to sway committed partisans, but some of a candidate's support may be weak and susceptible to persuasion. Political candidates can try to steal away soft support from their opponents.

Fourth, a candidate can try to firm up support from those who lean slightly his or her way. Candidates are unlikely to lose the support of strong partisans, but some adherents are less firmly committed. Candidates can try to shore up their own soft supporters and prevent defections.

Finally, candidates may try to discourage voter turnout from those who do not support him or her. This strategy flies in the face of democracy. We would argue that it is unethical. However, it is a possible option, and Ansolabehere and Iyengar (1995) have argued that some negative political advertisements are designed to do just this.

This analysis also explains why observers at times accuse candidates of "running to the right (or left) in primaries and to the center in the general election." To secure their party's nomination, a candidate must convince the majority of strong partisans that he or she is preferable to *other party members* on the issues that matter most to committed party members. For Republicans, this means emphasis of issues to the right of the political spectrum; for Democrats, it means a focus on issues to the left of the political spectrum. However, in the general election the party's nominee can take for granted the votes of most committed party members. In order to win the election, the candidate must appeal to *other groups of voters*—undecided, independent, and those who weakly lean to one's opponent—and who often have different concerns from committed partisans. Candidates must then address different issues and take positions that lie more in the middle of the political spectrum. This suggests that political campaigns during the primary should differ in significant ways from campaigns during the general election.

We hasten to add that the foregoing analysis is not meant to imply that all voters take a rational approach to voting: gathering, weighing, and integrating as much information as possible to assure that they make the most rational decision. On the contrary, as Popkin (1994; see also Downs, 1957) argues most effectively, many voters take information shortcuts. Many voters do not seek out information about the candidates (or wait until just before the election to do so). Voters do not fit information they possess about the candidates into mathematical formulas in order to determine their vote.

Nevertheless, the precepts we outlined should hold true generally, regardless of a given voter's degree of involvement in the election. Giving a voter information about a candidate's desirable qualities or issue stands has a tendency to increase that candidate's apparent preferability somewhat. Giving a voter information about an opposing candidate's undesirable qualities or issue stands tends to decrease the opponent's apparent preferability to some extent. Defending against an attack should help restore a candidate's apparent preferability. The effects of these three kinds of messages should be more important when they address topics of particular concern to voters. Although the effect of individual messages may be small and depend upon how much attention voters accord them, and although some voters may have strong party preferences, the cumulative effect of such information over time may influence voters' decisions—especially undecided, independent, and weakly leaning voters.

This also explains why basic themes are, and should be, repeated throughout the campaign. For those voters who pay attention throughout the campaign, repetition serves to reinforce the candidate's message with those auditors. On the other hand, it puts out a relatively constant message so that voters who only pay sporadic attention to the campaign will pick up on the campaign theme when they do happen to notice a campaign message.

ADVANTAGES OF THE FUNCTIONAL APPROACH

Our approach offers several distinct advantages over existing studies of political campaign communication. We believe that televised political spots may be the most intensely studied forms of campaign discourse, so we will develop this claim initially by contrasting our method with previous research on political advertising. Our method begins where many analyses of televised political advertisements begin, by conceptualizing them as negative (attacking) and positive (acclaiming) messages. However, although they are not as common as attacks and acclaims, some political television spots defend, and our approach acknowledges the existence of defensive political spots. For example, a television spot for Nixon in 1960 began by explaining that in this advertisement, "President Eisenhower answers the Kennedy-Johnson charges that America has accomplished nothing in the last eight years." It then featured Eisenhower, who declared that "My friends, never have Americans achieved so much in so short a time," clearly and directly denying the accusation. We do not believe that a spot like this is adequately understood by describing it as negative (even though it rejects the opposition) or as positive (even though it touts past deeds). It takes an attack by an opponent and explicitly rejects that attack. Thus, by looking for defenses as well as attacks and acclaims we provide a more complete understanding of the messages we analyze.

Second, many studies classify political spots as concerned with policy (issues) or character (image). Our analysis extends by analyzing both policy and character into finer subdivisions than does most current research (as we describe in Chapter 2, we divide policy into past deeds, future plans, and general goals; we divide character into personal qualities, leadership qualities, and ideals). This allowed us to discover in Chapter 10, for example, that Bill Clinton's television spots acclaimed his past deeds and his future plans, and that his ads attacked Bob Dole's past deeds and his future plans. In sharp contrast, Bob Dole's ads acclaimed his future plans (but rarely praised his past deeds), and his spots attacked Bill Clinton's past deeds (but rarely criticized his future plans). An analysis that lumped all policy or issue ads together, without distinguishing between past deeds and future plans, could not have detected the places where Bob Dole could have acclaimed (his past deeds) and attacked (Clinton's future plans), but rarely did so.

Third, because many television spots contain many different utterances, we do not classify entire ads as *either* positive (acclaiming) *or* negative (attacking), as is the case in most previous research. Some political ads are entirely positive or entirely negative, but many are mixed, and that mix is not always 50/50. For example, in 1980, Gerald Ford recorded a television spot supporting Ronald Reagan's bid to unseat Jimmy Carter:

Ford: This nation will be better served by a Reagan Presidency *rather than a continuation of the weak and politically expedient policies of Jimmy Carter*. For the future of our country, a change of leadership is mandatory. Cast your vote for Ronald Reagan.

Announcer: The time is now for strong leadership: Reagan for President.

In this excerpt, we italicized the attacks and left the acclaims in plain type. An analysis that classifies this spot as *either* positive *or* negative clearly provides an incomplete understanding of this spot. Accordingly, we analyze and classify *each utterance* in a given commercial, providing a more precise picture of *the degree to which* a political spot is positive, negative, or defensive. Note that a few analyses include a third option: positive, negative, and comparative (both positive and negative). However, we know that not every ad that combines acclaims and attacks divides them evenly (e.g., some have 25% or 10% acclaims and 75% or 90% attacks). Using three categories is a bit better than using two, but our approach of categorizing each remark as acclaiming, attacking, or defending is still superior.

Fourth, we discovered that (especially during the primaries) campaign advertisements that attack may have several different targets (for example, in 1996, Republican primary spots targeted the other Republican candidates, the Washington establishment, and President Clinton). Surely it makes a difference whether, for example, Steve Forbes' television advertisements attack Bill Clinton, Bob Dole, or Pat Buchanan. However, previous research tends to overlook this aspect of political spots (for that matter, there is very little research on primary spots at all).

We combined both function (acclaim, attack, defend) and topic (policy, character). Many studies of political spots examine one aspect or the other, but not both. Again, our approach is more complete than other research in the literature on political campaign communication.

Finally, we apply this analysis to a variety of political campaign messages in addition to televised political advertisements: primary debates, talk radio appearances, nominating convention speeches, general election debates, free television time, and radio addresses. Research has not studied these messages from the functional perspective (that is, as positive and negative messages, or as acclaiming, attacking, or defending). General election debates have been studied, but analyses of primary debates are less common. Benoit and Wells' (1996) literature review indicates that no one has studied campaign debates from the standpoint of attack and defense. Their study, not informed by the functional theory of campaign discourse, lumped acclaiming utterances in with defense remarks (bolstering, corrective action).

Similarly, there is considerable research on nominating convention keynote and acceptance speeches. However, Benoit, Blaney, and Pier (1996) reviewed the literature on nominating convention keynote speeches, finding that the functional approach has not been used to analyze keynotes before. Wells, Pier, Blaney, and Benoit (1996) examined the research on nominating acceptance addresses, again finding that the functional approach has not been used to analyze these speeches previously. Free television time was tried for the first time in 1996, so no research could have been conducted on these kinds of messages in previous years. Nor have we found research on the 1996 messages. Our literature review did not locate previous research on campaign radio addresses. So, our functional approach extends work done on positive and negative political spots to aid in the understanding of these other forms of campaign messages.

SUMMARY

We have articulated the five propositions that underlie the functional theory of political campaign discourse. We have argued that our approach has advantages compared with previous research on political communication. In the next two chapters we will describe our method and our procedures in more detail.

Thus, our approach to studying 1996 presidential campaign spots is superior to previous approaches to studying presidential ads. Moreover, we apply our method to other kinds of campaign messages—speeches, talk radio appearances, free television time—that have not even been studied as acclaims and attacks, or as concerned with issues (policy) and images (character). Thus, we provide an analysis of the messages in campaign '96 that has great breadth (diverse message forms) and depth (detailed analyses of each message).

NOTE

1. Other authors have addressed the question of the functions of political campaigns at different levels of abstraction. For example, candidates need to raise money to finance their campaigns. Ultimately, though, a candidate obtains donations by convincing potential donors that he or she is preferable to other candidates. Of course, the reasons given to potential donors to convince them to contribute to a given candidate may not be identical to the reasons given to citizens to vote for that candidate.

Chapter 2

Method: Acclaiming, Attacking, and Defending

In this chapter, we describe the method used to investigate the three functions—acclaiming, attacking, and defending—of political campaign communication in the 1996 presidential campaign. First, we describe our approach to analyzing the content of political campaign messages: policy considerations and character of the candidates and parties. These two topics are illustrated through excerpts from political campaign discourse on each of the three functions. Second, we discuss each of the three functions themselves: acclaiming, attacking, and defending.

TOPICS FOR POLITICAL CAMPAIGN COMMUNICATION

We divide message content into two broad categories: policy considerations and character (of candidate and/or party). These terms correspond to the relatively common differentiation between issues and image. However, the word "issue" has two meanings in this context. First, it can refer to discourse that concerns policy questions. Second, it can have a broader referent, concerning any question on which disputants (including political candidates) can disagree. Because candidates can, and do, disagree about character (e.g., how important should this topic be in the campaign? what kind of character do the candidates possess?), that makes image an issue. Furthermore, one can speak of the image a candidate projects on policy, or the issues. Thus, we prefer to write about policy considerations rather than issues, and about character (of the candidates and their parties) rather than image.

Furthermore, we want to acknowledge that image and issue, or policy and character, are inexorably intertwined (see, e.g., Friedenberg, 1994; Hinck, 1993; Leff & Mohrmann, 1974; Levine, 1995; McGee, 1978; Rosenthal, 1966; Rudd, 1986; Stuckey & Antczak, 1995; West, 1993). For example, Benoit and Wells (1996) argue that "candidates' images are intimately tied to their actions, the policies they embrace, and the stand they take (however vague) on the issues" (pp. 26–27). Devlin (1995) explains that "I make no distinction [between image and issue ads] because issue ads really do create image impressions on the part of the viewer, and image ads can convey substantive information" (p. 203). Furthermore, it is possible to argue that voters cannot decide how to vote on the basis of an objective understanding of a candidate's stand on the issues; instead, voters make decisions based on their perceptions, or images, of the candidates' policy stands. Still, we find it useful to distinguish between discourse that focuses primarily on policy considerations, and utterances that are addressed mostly toward character.

Topics for Political Campaign Acclaims

It can be argued that there are three potential grounds for making a voting decision: party, issues, and image. As Levine (1995) recognizes, "The relative importance of issues, images, and partisanship varies with the context of the specific presidential election and the candidates. But the influence of issues in the presidential race is more and more important" (p. 107). The state of the economy, possible foreign affairs crises, and incumbency are other important variables discussed in the preface. Candidates occasionally switch parties, but policy and character are better sources for inventing a wide range of arguments for voters to prefer one candidate over another. As we argued in Chapter 1, major party candidates ordinarily can count on the votes of committed partisans, but to win elections they must use policy and character to win the votes of the undecided and independent voters. Thus, we focus on policy (issue) and character (image), because these are more open to use (exploitation, manipulation) in political campaign messages.

As indicated in Chapter 1, we divide each potential topic area into three subdivisions: policy (past deeds, future plans, and general goals), character (personal qualities, leadership abilities, and ideals). This typology is displayed in Table 2.1.

Previous studies have investigated the topics of political acclaims in three different campaign contexts: television commercials from 1980–1992 (Benoit, Pier, & Blaney, 1997), nominating convention keynote speeches from 1960–1996 (Benoit, Blaney, & Pier, 1996), and nomination acceptance addresses from 1960–1996 (Wells, Pier, Blaney, & Benoit, 1996). We shall provide examples of the topics used in political acclaims from these studies.

Table 2.1
Topics for Acclaiming, Attacking, and Defending

Policy Considerations (Issues)

    Past Deeds

    Future Plans

    General Goals

Character (Image)

    Personal Qualities

    Leadership Ability

    Ideals (Principles, Values)

Policy Considerations (Issues). Acclaims in televised political advertise-ments may address policy considerations. Policy utterances are divided into past deeds, future plans, and general goals.

In 1988, George Bush touted his *past deeds* in a television advertise-ment: "Over the past six years, eighteen million jobs were created, in-terest rates were cut in half. Today, inflation is down, taxes are down, and the economy is strong." More jobs, lower inflation, lower taxes, and a strong economy are important policy achievements, worthy of self-praise. This kind of utterance, typical of a campaign message, gives vot-ers reasons to prefer Bush.

Similarly, in 1968, Daniel Inouye's keynote address praised the accom-plishments of Democrats, stressing past deeds:

And since 1963, President Johnson has proposed and Congress has enacted more than 40 major new laws to foster education in our country. Since 1963, our Gov-ernment has tripled its investment in education and in the past four years alone we have invested twice as much as was spent in the previous 100 years. (p. 711)

Inouye recounts successful legislative initiatives on education, and boasts of the historic accomplishments of the Democratic Party in this area. The obvious implication of this campaign utterance is that the Democratic candidate is preferable to the opponent.

Voters also want to know what candidates propose to do in the future. Michael Dukakis stressed his future plans in one of his television spots: "Mike Dukakis wants to help. His college opportunities plan says that if a kid like Jimmy has the grades for college, America should find a way to send him." Dukakis has proposed a plan to provide America's youth an opportunity to attend college. This acclaim is presented as a desirable proposal, and as a reason to vote for Dukakis in the election.

In 1992, George Bush's nomination acceptance address attacked Congress for "pork barrel projects that waste your money." He proposed a future plan to correct this problem, the line-item veto: "So I ask you, the American people, give me a Congress that will give me the line-item veto" (p. 708). Bush rather directly asserts that the line-item veto will allow him to curb wasteful government spending, a desirable outcome. This is a reason to vote for Bush on election day.

However, some policy positions are given only the broadest outlines. Sometimes candidates take positions on issues without describing specific plans. It is possible that this occurs at least in part to take advantage of strategic ambiguity (see, e.g., Eisenberg, 1984; Putnam & Sorensen, 1982; Rudd, 1989; or Williams, 1980). More people are likely to agree with a general goal of, for example, balancing the budget than with more specific plans of tax increases or spending cuts.

For example, in the 1988 campaign, George Bush stressed his goals in a television commercial: "I will not allow this country to be made weak again. I will keep America moving forward, always forward, for an endless enduring dream and a thousand points of light." While not discussing any specific plans, he outlines his general goals as a reason to elect him president.

In like manner, Republican keynote speaker Katherine Ortega described President Reagan's goals in 1984: "President Reagan is a candidate who can and will achieve peace without caving into Soviet threats" (p. 12). Peace without appeasement is presented as a desirable goal, a reason to reelect Ronald Reagan.

Character (Image). Messages from candidates can also acclaim on the basis of the candidates' (and their parties') qualities. We divide political campaign acclaims into praise of personal qualities, leadership ability, and ideals.

In 1992, a television spot sponsored by Bill Clinton mentioned one of his positive personal qualities: "I care so much about people." Surely this characteristic is desirable in a president. However, this is a personal quality, one that will help him be a desirable president, but it does not concern Clinton's leadership ability per se.

In support of Lyndon Johnson, the 1964 keynote by John Pastore proclaimed the personal qualities of the Democratic nominee: "These months confirm the wisdom of our fallen leader, and the vision of President Kennedy lives on in the character, in the capability, and in the courage of the teammate of his choice" (p. 708). While calling on the memory of President Kennedy, who selected Johnson as vice president, Pastore emphasizes Johnson's character, ability, and courage (if Pastore had only commented on Johnson's ability, this would have been an example of an acclaim focused on leadership ability rather than personal qualities).

In one television advertisement in 1988, George Bush is characterized as an experienced leader. The narrator proclaims that "Perhaps no one in this century is better prepared to be President of the United States" than Bush. His unparalleled experience qualifies him to be leader of the free world and is a reason to elect him president.

Similarly, Phil Gramm celebrated George Bush's leadership ability in his 1992 keynote speech: "*Leadership is the difference*. It has changed the world and it has brought us more than peace; George Bush's leadership has brought us victory" (p. 721; italics in original). Although this utterance contains a fairly clear reference to Desert Storm (the victory), Gramm's emphasis is on how that provides evidence of Bush's leadership ability.

Another characteristic possessed by candidates concerns their ideals, principles, or values. Michael Dukakis stressed his ideals in the 1988 campaign, suggesting in a television spot that he would be "a president who fights for you," the common people. Unlike Bush, who allegedly fights for the privileged few, Dukakis values ordinary people (most voters).

A politician may also praise the ideals of his or her political party. Walter Judd announced in his 1960 keynote speech that "The Republican Party stands for liberty" (p. 649) a clear declaration of ideals, not policy. Praise of party on grounds of ideals is evident in this passage.

Topics for Political Campaign Attacks

Although some studies suggest that voters resent political attacks (e.g., Merritt, 1984; Stewart, 1975), they are common features of political campaigns. Some attacks are reprehensible, especially when they fabricate evidence or are deliberately misleading. However, acclaims are just as reprehensible as attacks when they fabricate or mislead. We argue that while attacks can be misused, they are not inherently inappropriate. We assume that, in general, the more information available to voters the more likely they will make a better decision. Hence, if a candidate has weaknesses (and no one is perfect), voters can use that information to make a more informed decision. Thus, it is not wrong for one candidate to expose the weaknesses of an opponent (again, we do not condone intentionally misleading or false messages).

Research on negative political advertising suggests that people may share the view that some kinds of attacks are appropriate while others are not. Johnson-Cartee and Copeland (1989) generated a list of topics found in negative political ads, grouped them into ten categories, and asked respondents to rate them as fair or unfair. The topics clustered into two groups, labeled "Political Issues" (political record, stands on issues, criminal record, and voting record) and "Personal Characteristics" (personal life, marriage, family, religion, medical history, and sex life). At least 83% of respondents rated each political issue as a fair topic for an attack; no more than 36% rated any of the personal characteristics as an acceptable topic for political attack. This reveals that there was general, albeit not universal, agreement on which topics are fair for an attack. It also suggests that respondents did not condemn political attacks wholesale, but believed that attacks on some topics were more acceptable than on others.

Furthermore, even if voters profess to despise negative appeals, that does not prove they are ineffectual or that politicians eschew them. Kaid and Johnston (1991) found that 71% of the ads from 1960–1988 were positive and 19% negative. However, the number of negative ads varied over time: negative spots spiked at 40% in 1964, dropped to 22–28% in the 1970s, and increased to 35–37% in the 1980s. Negative appeals are a large component of political campaign advertising; they may be a substantial portion of other forms of campaign discourse as well. Our functional analysis of political campaign discourse argues that attacks can help candidates appear to be preferable by reducing the appeal of opponents. Clearly, they merit scholarly attention. As with acclaims, we will illustrate our approach to investigating the topics available for political attacks from these studies.

Policy Considerations (Issues). Political campaign attacks that concern policy may be divided into utterances on past deeds, (relatively specific) future plans, and general goals. One consideration that at least some voters make, when deciding how to cast their vote, is how well have the candidates performed in office in the past (Fiorina, 1981). Presumably, if a candidate has a record of failures or mistakes in past office, there is a risk that similar problems will occur if that candidate is elected to the presidency.

For example, a Bush/Quayle 1988 television advertisement criticized Michael Dukakis's past deeds: "As Governor, Michael Dukakis vetoed mandatory sentences for drug dealers. He vetoed the death penalty. His revolving door prison policy gave weekend furloughs to first degree murderers not eligible for parole. While out, many committed other crimes like kidnaping and rape." The spot explicitly discusses past actions that Dukakis took as Governor of Massachussets: a veto of mandatory sentences for drug dealers, a veto of the death penalty, and his prison furlough policy. These are characterized as undesirable, as mistakes or errors in judgment for which Dukakis deserves the blame. The implication in this message is clear that Dukakis's past record is considered bad, and that therefore he should not be elected president.

In his nominating convention keynote speech of 1992, Phil Gramm attacked past deeds done by Democrats: "We have not forgotten that the last Democrat in the White House so decimated defense that on any given day, 50% of our combat planes couldn't fly and our ships couldn't sail, for lack of spare parts and mechanics" (p. 721). This was a clear reference to defense procurement policies of the Carter administration. The president, as commander in chief, is ultimately responsible for the state of the armed forces (although one might wonder if congressional appropriations or defense bureaucracy have a role to play in equipment readiness). It should be obvious that Gramm's point is that when the Democratic Party controlled the executive branch, the president had failed to keep our airplane and naval ships in a state of readiness, and that we should not risk impairing our defense readiness by electing another Democratic president.

Of course, one's past deeds are not the only evidence citizens might consider when deciding how to vote. Candidates make promises or announcements about the future plans they intend to pursue if elected. Opponents can attempt to indict those future plans. In another television commercial in the 1988 campaign, Michael Dukakis warned viewers against George Bush's future plans: "George Bush wants to give the wealthiest 1% of the people in the country a tax break worth $30,000 a year." Giving the wealthiest people a $30,000 tax break is a fairly specific future plan, and one that many voters (the other 99%) might find offensive and a reason to vote for Dukakis instead of Bush.

In 1972, President Nixon's nomination acceptance address criticized the Democrats for their future plans to cut the defense budget: "Our opponents have proposed massive cuts in our defense budget which would have the inevitable effect of making the United States the second strongest nation in the world" (p. 709). He alludes to the disastrous consequences of such proposed action, giving viewers a reason to reject his opponents.

Criticism of opponents may also proceed on more general grounds. Michael Dukakis also criticized Bush's general goals in a 1988 television spot: "Mr. Bush does not object to the wave of merger and of speculation that has put our companies and our country itself on the auction block." Here, Dukakis criticizes Bush's policies on foreign investment in the United States. Dukakis does not mention any particular executive orders or other acts of Bush; rather he attacks Bush's policy generally. However, there is no question that the advertisement suggests that this general policy is bad for America: surely we don't want to sell our country and our companies to foreign investors.

Ronald Reagan, in his 1984 nomination acceptance address, characterized his opponents' general goals: "Our opponents are openly committed to increasing your tax burden.... They will place higher and higher taxes on small businesses, family farms, and every other working family" (p. 708). He strongly suggests that his opponents' goals are mistakes.

Thus, political campaign attacks often concern policy questions. When policies are addressed, the attacks may focus on past deeds, future plans, or general goals. In all three cases, the opponent's policy is characterized as inappropriate or mistaken, and the implication is that the candidate who espouses such wrongheaded policy should not be elected president.

Character (Image). Of course, political campaign attacks also may focus on undesirable qualities of opposing candidates (and of their political parties). Some might immediately think of mudslinging and character assassination when the idea of attacking on personal qualities or character arises. Of course, there is little question that political campaigning can quickly degenerate into a series of demeaning insults and slurs. Research mentioned earlier by Johnson-Cartee and Copeland (1989) reported that most people thought policy attacks were more fair than personal attacks. As noted above, some attacks are inappropriate. However, we believe that attacks on some of the qualities of candidates are not necessarily unfair (see, e.g., Cragen & Cutbirth, 1984).

First, as mentioned earlier, candidates often make promises and announcements of actions they intend to take if elected. Although at times circumstances may change, it seems reasonable for Bill Clinton to remind voters that George Bush asked us to read his lips when he promised "no new taxes" and later raised them. Similarly, we have no problem with Bob Dole reminding voters that Bill Clinton promised middle-class tax relief but raised taxes in his first term instead. If a candidate does not appear to behave consistently, this may create legitimate concerns about the candidate's agenda and what he or she is likely to do if elected.

Perhaps most importantly of all, no candidate can possibly anticipate all of the issues that might arise in the next four years. Nor can a candidate possibly address all of the contingencies that might arise in any given area. Thus, it is impossible for any candidate to provide a complete description of his or her policy stands for all issues that might arise during the coming term in office. Voters who cast votes based on future policy actions must, therefore, be able to trust that the candidate will consistently apply his or her political philosophy to issues that might arise. Thus, voters—even those who primarily vote on policy grounds— must *trust* their candidates to implement their avowed policies. There can be little doubt that character considerations have a legitimate role in the selection of our president.

This being the case, political attacks do address qualities of the candidates and their parties. We divide these topics into three areas: personal qualities (e.g., honesty, compassion) leadership ability (e.g., experience), and ideals (values, principles). We will illustrate each of these potential topics for political attacks from past research.

After being the target of negative television spots by George Bush (especially on crime and on the Massachussets furlough program), Dukakis in a 1988 commercial characterized Bush's personal qualities: "The real story about furloughs is that George Bush has taken a furlough from the truth." By saying Bush took a "furlough from the truth," Dukakis is suggesting that Bush is a liar, a very unflattering personal quality for anyone, let alone a presidential candidate. This attack may not only reduce Bush's apparent desirability, but it may also undermine his statements (people may wonder if he is telling the truth in other utterances).

Political parties can have qualities as well as candidates. Mark Hatfield's 1964 keynote address described the qualities of the Democratic administration, suggesting it was fearful and distrustful: "Time and time again this administration has revealed distrust of us all . . . the administration's fear of the people is demonstrated by its lack of confidence in the capacity of the individual to manage his own affairs" (p. 653). He does not point to any specific policies of the Johnson administration in making this accusation, but rather describes its feelings or relationship toward the people in a negative light.

In 1988, some of Michael Dukakis's television advertisements featured actors pretending to be Bush/Quayle campaign advisors. One simulated reluctant testimony, reflecting unfavorably on the vice-presidential candidate's leadership potential: "Suddenly, the words 'President Quayle' even make me nervous." Clearly, this ad was attacking Dan Quayle's qualifications to lead the nation. No specific policy questions were mentioned; only his leadership ability was attacked.

Similarly, Bill Bradley's 1992 keynote speech attacked George Bush's leadership ability: "Tonight in America, wages are flat, unemployment is up, the deficit grows, and health care and college costs skyrocket. What did you do about it, George Bush? You waffled and wiggled and wavered" (p. 655). Bradley did not discuss the Bush administration's specific policies on wages, employment, the deficit, or health care and college costs. His focus was clearly on characterizing Bush's leadership as inconsistent and ineffectual.

Dukakis also presented a negative characterization of his opponent's ideals in a televised political spot: George Bush is a man who "fights for the privileged few." These kinds of campaign advertisements attack the qualities of the candidates, giving voters a reason they might use to vote against the target and for the sponsor.

Thomas Kean, in his 1988 Republican keynote, criticized the ideals of the Democratic Party, asserting that "Liberal Democrats believe that Washington should manage dreams for all Americans" (p. 8). No specific policy is addressed in this attack. However, it is clear that Kean is describing a Democratic philosophy of, in his view, unwarranted intrusion into voters' lives.

Topics for Political Campaign Defense

Our analysis so far suggests that defense may be most common in the directly confrontational nature of political debates. Benoit and Wells (1996) found considerable defense in the 1992 presidential debates. Their method did not divide utterances according to whether they concerned policy or character, so we do not have examples of defense on past deeds, future plans, and so forth. Furthermore, we found even less defense in our analyses of presidential spots, keynote addresses, and acceptance addresses: defenses accounted for only about 1% of the utterances in each type of campaign message. Accordingly, we will not illustrate defenses on each of the potential topics.

Summary

Thus, we divide the candidates' campaign utterances into policy considerations (issue) and candidate/party qualities (character or image). We subdivide policy discourse into that which concerns past deeds, future plans, and general goals. We subdivide qualities into personal qualities, leadership ability, and ideals (values, principles). This scheme has been applied to analyze political campaign discourse in several contexts: televised political spots, nominating convention keynote speeches, and nominating convention acceptance addresses.

Of course, other kinds of divisions are possible. One could, for example, divide policy discourse into domestic and foreign policy utterances. It would also be possible to add finer distinctions to our topical system. Other research has delved into the question of what specific personality traits (e.g., honesty, compassion) are important in evaluating the character of a presidential candidate (see Trent & Friedenberg, 1995). Perhaps future research into the functions of political campaign discourse will extend our theory in these directions.

ANALYZING THE FUNCTIONS OF POLITICAL CAMPAIGN DISCOURSE: ACCLAIMING, ATTACKING, AND DEFENDING

In this section we describe our approach to analyzing discourse to identify the three functions of political campaign discourse. Strategies for acclaiming, attacking, and defending will be described separately.

Acclaiming

Pamela Benoit offers the first analysis of the speech act of acclaiming, or self-praise, in the communication literature (1997; see also Schlenker,

Table 2.2
Strategies for Acclaiming

Enhance Desirability

  Extent of Benefits

  Effects on Audience

Enhance Credit

  Overcame Obstacles

  Hard Work

  Modesty

1980). This kind of utterance is intended to enhance the reputation of the speaker. We extend this notion, applying it to political campaign discourse. In most situations, actors must balance competing constraints: enhancing one's image and avoiding the appearance of immodesty. It is not clear to us, however, that the modesty constraint is as strong in political discourse as in other realms.

Benoit analyzed self-presentational discourse in three settings: Nobel Prize acceptance addresses; statements by athletes who had broken a record, won an award, or won a game/championship; and utterances at Mary Kay success meetings. We focus more on *topoi* for acclaiming: what kinds of claims can candidates (or their proponents) make about their suitability for office. We offer a tentative typology of kinds of acclaiming strategies in political discourse, displayed in Table 2.2.

Attacking

Somewhat more work has been done on persuasive attack. In rhetoric, Fisher acknowledges the existence of such discourse by identifying subversion, creating a negative image, as one of the four motives of communication (1970), but he does not develop this analysis in detail. Ryan (1982, 1988) advanced another basic statement on persuasive attack (*kategoria*), but he offers a more general set of *stases*, not a more specific list of *topoi* for persuasive attack.

In the literature on political communication, two books consider persuasive attack. First, Pfau and Kenski's *Attack Politics* (1990) offers "a theoretical and empirical examination of the role and impact of the attack message approach in modern political campaigns" (p. xv). While they provide an interesting and useful analysis of such messages, their goal is not to provide a set of *topoi* for constructing persuasive attacks. Their analysis concerns three very general options: attacking first, counterattacking, and prevention (a refutation strategy).

Second, Jamieson's *Dirty Politics* (1992) devotes a chapter to "Tactics of Attack." She identifies two major approaches, identification (association) and apposition (contrast: "to make their candidate's name a synonym for everything the electorate cherishes and to transform the opponent into an antonym of those treasured values," p. 47). Each process is further divided into verbal and visual aspects. Verbal identification is subdivided into personal (image) and policy identification. She also offers an interesting discussion of the importance of television and highlights inherent differences between television and both print and radio political advertising. However, this analysis, while clearly useful and relevant, is quite general (association and contrast being its two tactics). It does include medium (verbal, visual) but, again, does not have as its goal the development of a set of *topoi* or strategies for persuasive attack.

Felknor (1992) published an interesting study of political attack: *Political Mischief*. He observes that "negative campaigning has been practiced since 1796, and is likely to occur with some frequency as long as the United States holds free elections" (p. 29). His work provides some useful historical background and many examples of negative campaigning, but is not intended to provide a conceptual framework for describing forms of persuasive attack.

A theory of persuasive attack (Benoit & Dorries, 1996; Benoit & Wells, 1996) has been developed to fill this void in the literature. We sketch the basic tenets of this theory and briefly illustrate the strategies of attack.

A persuasive attack contains two elements (although either one could be implicit): an offensive act and attribution of responsibility for that act to the target or accused (see Pomerantz, 1987). First, the accused must believe that this act would be perceived negatively by a salient audience. The act can be an offensive deed, a word, or even an undesirable cognition. This action can be an act of commission or omission. Second, the accused must be perceived as responsible for the wrongful deed. Responsibility may appear in a variety of forms. The target of the attack may have actually committed the act, or may have encouraged, provoked, or suggested the act, or in some way permitted it to occur. Some persuasive attacks are quite simple (e.g., "He is a thief"), while others elaborate either offensiveness (e.g., "It is bad enough that he stole the money, but he stole *from the Church*," or "This was no mere dip into the till but a massive embezzlement of over a half a million dollars") or responsibility (e.g., "Given the fact that she has done this before, it is no mere accident"). A variety of discursive strategies are available for em-

Table 2.3
Strategies for Attacking

Increasing Negative Perceptions of the Act

    Extent of the Damage

    Persistence of Negative Effects

    Recency of Harms

    Victims Are Innocent/Helpless

    Obligation to Protect Certain Groups

    Inconsistency

    Effects on Audience

Increasing Perceived Responsibility for the Act

    Intended to Achieve Outcome

    Planned the Act

    Knew Consequences of Act

    Accused Committed Offensive Act Before

    Accused Benefited from Offensive Act

Source: Benoit & Wells (1996), p. 38.

bellishing or developing these two essential components of a persuasive attack (see Table 2.3).

Increasing Negative Perceptions of the Act. When a rhetor chooses to elaborate the offensiveness of the alleged act, there are at least seven discursive strategies available. Each will be briefly discussed in this section.

Frequently, images are damaged by the extent of the effects of the offensive act under consideration. For example, Jim and Tammy Bakker were charged with embezzling $10 million from their ministry ("TV Ministry," 1988). This is no minor theft, but (allegedly) a massive plundering of their ministry. Their alleged theft was for literally millions of dollars.

A second strategy for increasing the offensiveness of an offensive act is to stress persistence of negative effects. Hilts noted that the danger to the environment from the *Exxon Valdez* oil spill was expected to last at least ten years (1989). Harms that last longer appear to be more offensive, and probably do more damage to the actor's image, than temporary ones.

The more recent an offensive event, the more potential impact it has with an audience. Furthermore, people sometimes mend their ways. This is surely the reasoning behind the statute of limitations in the law, which does not punish criminals once a certain number of years has passed since the crime was committed. Given that both newspapers and electronic media (with its live coverage of news as it happens when possible—like the trip of O.J. Simpson's white Ford Bronco through Los Angeles) stress the "current" in current events, more recent acts often seem particularly offensive.

One can also increase the offensiveness of an act by emphasizing the fact that its victims are innocent, helpless, or especially vulnerable. The cartoon character promoting Camel cigarettes, Joe Camel, came under especially severe attack for allegedly appealing more to children than adults (Goodman, 1992). Thus, when victims are young, old, relatively helpless, or otherwise innocent and/or vulnerable, the offensiveness (and resultant damage to the accused's image) is exacerbated.

In some cases, people (or organizations) are seen as having a special obligation to certain groups. When one hurts those to whom one owes a special obligation, the offensive act seems even worse. Almost 2,000 scoutmasters who were suspected of molesting Boy Scouts were thrown out—"but some simply went elsewhere and continued to abuse scouts" ("Scouts Files," 1993, p. 12A). Sexual molestation is terrible whenever it occurs, but when scout leaders violate the trust we place in them, the accusations can seem even worse, and the damage to their image may be even greater.

Another way of intensifying an accusation is through charges of inconsistency. A prostitution sting operation arrested St. Louis prosecutor George Peach, who had been a "strong supporter of sting operations to net prostitution arrests" ("Prostitution Sting," 1992, p. 3A). It is bad enough that he was arrested for committing a crime, but his apparent hypocrisy made things look even worse.

It is possible to heighten a persuasive attack by relating the negative effects directly to the audience. For example, after a Government Accounting Office report found that prescription drug makers charge 60% more for certain "best-selling brand-name" drugs in the United States than in England, Representative Henry Waxman explained that "These numbers translate into real costs to real people, particularly the elderly, who purchase 34 percent of the drugs" ("Same Drugs," 1994, p. 7A). This message functions to intensify the attack by relating the consequences of the charges directly to members of the audience.

Increasing Perceived Responsibility for the Act. In addition to, or instead of, elaborating offensiveness, rhetors may choose to stress blame. There are five rhetorical strategies for increasing the actor's apparent responsibility for an act (see Table 2.3). Again, these will be briefly discussed in this section.

We may be willing to forgive those who accidentally do wrong, but those who intend their offensive acts are judged more harshly. Judy Moriarty was the first Missouri Secretary of State ever to be impeached. She allegedly illegally permitted her son to file for elective office after the deadline had passed. This was no accident, or oversight, because it was alleged that Moriarty "did purposely cause and direct or did knowingly allow" the late filing ("Interim Secretary of State," 1994, p. 1A). When we intend to commit wrongdoing, the likelihood that we will be held accountable for that action is high, and the damage to our reputations should be more severe.

Some acts are not only intentional but actually premeditated or planned beforehand. After the tragic Pittsburgh plane crash, USAir was accused of "trying to milk more use out of the engines on ill-fated Flight 427 by running them on shorter flights rather than giving them an overhaul." It was not an oversight that maintenance was delayed on this plane, but a calculated cost-cutting strategy: "USAir aimed to save $1 million per plane and gain an extra two years before an overhaul" ("Flight 427," 1994, p. 3A). It seems likely that such allegations would increase apparent responsibility for the offensive act, and concomitant damage to the accused's image.

An actor who knows the likely consequences of an act is likely to be blamed more than one who did not know what to expect from an action. A story concerning the revelation that a safer cigarette had been developed but never marketed asserted that Ligget and Meyers Tobacco Company "knew about the dangers of tobacco for more than 30 years, despite industry denials of any proven link between smoking and disease" ("Safer Cigarette," 1992, p. 4A). Thus, responsibility for ill effects is heightened when perpetrators know the consequences of their actions.

When an offender commits an offensive act for the first time, it is easier to excuse them. However, when a person or organization has committed the offensive act before, they are more likely to be blamed. When Show-Me Furniture announced their second "going-out-of-business" sale, Wright suggested it might be false advertising. "This isn't the first time that Show-Me Furniture has told the public it was going out of business" (1993, p. 1A). The fact that they apparently had attempted to deceive the public in the same way before places the blame squarely on the store.

When the actor benefits from the offensive act, it is easier to blame the perpetrator. Representative Dan Rostenkowski was accused of paying himself for "a Chicago office that appears to be vacant." His selfish motive was self-evident, and there is little question about whether he appears responsible for this apparent misuse of government funds ("Congressman Paid Self," 1992, p. 5A). He wasn't diverting funds to help widows, but for his personal benefit.

Defending

Of the three forms of discourse studied here, the most research by far has examined persuasive defense, or *apologia*, or accounts, or image repair. Several approaches have been developed for explaining verbal self-defense, some developed in communication/rhetoric and some in sociology. The works of Burke (1970), Ware and Linkugel (1973), and Scott and Lyman (1968) each present several verbal image restoration strategies, but each theory includes options neglected by the others. Benoit (1995a) developed a typology of image repair strategies that is more complete than those currently available in the rhetorical literature (see also Benoit, 1995b, 1997a, 1997b; Benoit & Anderson, 1996; Benoit & Brinson, 1994; Benoit & Czerwinski, 1997; Benoit, Gullifor, & Panici, 1991; Benoit & Hanczor, 1994; Blaney & Benoit, 1997; Brinson & Benoit, 1996; or Kennedy & Benoit, 1997).

Jamieson's book *Dirty Politics* (1992) analyzes responses to attacks that she found in her analysis of political campaigns. She describes ten potential responses: counterattack (responding to one illegitimate attack with a like response), inoculation, forewarning of impending attack, reframing (providing an alternative and more favorable interpretation of the attacking message), taking umbrage (expressing outrage at the attack), using humor to reframe the attack, using credible sources to rebut the charges, using the press's credibility to rebut the charges, disassociation, and admitting mistakes and asking forgiveness. Like other inductively derived lists (see, e.g., Benoit, 1982), this one includes strategies at more than one level of abstraction. For example, some concern the content of the response (e.g., counterattack, inoculation, forewarning, reframing, disassociation, admission), some concern the source of evidence used in the response (credible sources, media credibility), and two options seem to concern the tone of the response (taking umbrage, using humor). Nevertheless, these are potentially useful strategies, and several of them are quite similar to the categories of persuasive defense discussed next (e.g., counterattack is the same as attacking accuser; ask forgiveness seems to be the same as mortification; disassociation seems quite similar to differentiation or denial; some of the illustrations of reframing seem to include denials). Gold (1978) as well as Trent and Friedenberg (1995) also discuss political apologia.

The analysis of persuasive attack developed earlier suggests that there are two key elements in such discourse: (1) the accused must be linked to, or seen as responsible for, an act; (2) that act must be viewed as

Table 2.4
Strategies for Defending

Denial

    Simple Denial

    Shift Blame

Evade Responsibility

    Provocation

    Defeasibility

    Accident

    Good Intentions

Reduce Offensiveness of Event

    Minimization

    Differentiation

    Transcendence

    Compensation

Mortification

Source: Benoit (1995a), p. 95.

Note: Three categories are omitted: bolstering and corrective action are considered acclaims
(Table 2.2) and attack accuser is considered an attack (Table 2.3).

offensive by the audience. The theory of image restoration keys on this
analysis of persuasive attack and offers five broad categories. Denial and
evasion of responsibility address the first component of persuasive attack, rejecting or reducing the accused's responsibility for the act in question. Reducing offensiveness and corrective action, the third and fourth
broad categories of image restoration, concern the second component of
persuasive attack: reducing offensiveness of the act attributed to the accused. The last general strategy, mortification, attempts to restore an image not by disputing the charges, but by asking forgiveness. Each
strategy will be discussed briefly in this section (see Table 2.4).

    Denial. A person accused of wrongdoing may simply deny committing the offensive action (see Ware & Linkugel, 1973). One may deny the act occurred, or that the accused performed it. Brinson and Benoit (1996) add a third option: the rhetor may admit performing the act but deny that it has any harmful effects. Whether the accused denies that the offensive act occurred, denies that he or she performed it, or denies that the act is harmful, such denial, if accepted by the audience, should help restore the image of the rhetor.

In 1991, Pepsi-Cola accused its chief competitor, Coca-Cola, of requiring its other accounts to pay higher prices, thereby subsidizing Coke's largest customer, McDonald's (see the example below of attacking accuser). Coke replied by denying Pepsi's charges. A letter from C. A. Frenette, senior vice president and general manager, stressed that charges that Coke increased prices for some customers but not all "were absolutely false," and that price increases were "universally applied; there were no exceptions" (1991, p. 24). Here, Coca-Cola directly and unequivocally rejected Pepsi-Cola's charges as false: Coke simply did not do what Pepsi had alleged.

A related option is for the rhetor to attempt to shift the blame. Burke (1970) labeled this option victimage. After the *Exxon Valdez* oil spill, L. G. Rawl, chair of Exxon, attempted to shift blame for delays in the cleanup. He "blamed state officials and the Coast Guard for the delay, charging . . . that the company could not obtain immediate authorization on the scene to begin cleaning up the oil or applying a chemical dispersant" (Mathews & Peterson, 1989, pp. A1–6). If this version of events was accepted, it should absolve Exxon of guilt for delays in the cleanup (although not for the spill itself).

Evade Responsibility. Another general image repair strategy is attempting to evade or reduce responsibility for the offensive act, which has four versions. Each will be discussed briefly.

Claiming that an act was provoked by another, prior offensive act may lessen responsibility for that act. Scott and Lyman (1968) suggest that the accused can claim that his or her action was merely a response to another's offensive act and that this behavior can be seen as a reasonable reaction to that provocation (they called this strategy scapegoating, but we rename it provocation to avoid confusing it with shifting the blame). If accepted, this rhetorical strategy may shift some or all of the responsibility from the rhetor, helping to repair his or her image.

The strategy of defeasibility alleges a lack of information about or control over important elements of the situation (Scott & Lyman, 1968). The rhetor claims that because of this lack of information or control, he or she should not be held completely responsible for the offensive act. If accepted, this claim should reduce the responsibility of the accused for the offensive act and help repair the damaged reputation. For instance, a busy executive who missed an important meeting could attempt to justify his or her behavior by claiming that "I was never told that the meeting had been moved up a day." If it is true that the meeting was changed and the executive wasn't informed, he or she lacked crucial information that excuses the absence.

We have a tendency to hold people responsible for factors that are reasonably considered to be under their control (Scott & Lyman, 1968). If the accused can convince the audience that the act in question happened accidentally, he or she should be held less accountable, and the damage to his or her image should be reduced. For example, in response to accusations that Sears had overcharged its auto repair customers in California, Chair Brennan characterized the auto repair mistakes as "inadvertent," rather than intentional ("Sears to Drop," 1992, p. 5B).

In this strategy, the audience is asked to reduce the accused's responsibility for the wrongful behavior because it was done with good intentions (considered by Ware & Linkugel, 1973, to be part of denial). Those who perform improper actions while trying to accomplish good are usually not held as accountable as those who intend to do bad. When Sears was accused of overcharging customers, Brennan declared that "we would never intentionally violate the trust customers have shown in our company for 105 years" (1992, p. A56). Thus, Sears claimed good intentions in its auto repair operations.

Reduce Offensiveness of Event. Rather than deny or reduce responsibility for an act, a rhetor who is accused of wrongful actions can try to reduce the perceived offensiveness of that act. This general image repair strategy has six versions: bolstering, minimization, differentiation, transcendence, attacking one's accuser, and compensation.

A persuader may use bolstering to strengthen the audience's positive feelings toward the accused, in order to offset the negative feelings connected with the wrongful act (Ware & Linkugel, 1973). Rhetors may describe positive characteristics they have or positive acts they have done in the past. Following the *Valdez* oil spill, Exxon attempted to use bolstering as part of its image repair effort. Chair Rawl declared that "Exxon has moved swiftly and competently to minimize the effect this oil will have on the environment, fish, and other wildlife" (1989, p. A12). If accepted, this claim should help repair Exxon's image.

A second possibility is to try to minimize the negative feelings associated with the wrongful act. If the audience comes to believe that the act is less offensive than it first appeared, the amount of damage to the rhetor's reputation should be reduced (Scott & Lyman, 1968). After the *Valdez* oil spill, Exxon officials tried to downplay the extent of the damage. For example, R. W. Baker explained that "On May 19, when Alaska retrieved corpses of tens of thousands of sea birds, hundreds of otters, and dozens of bald eagles, an Exxon official told National Public Radio that Exxon had counted just 300 birds and 70 otters" (1989, p. 8). This represents an attempt to portray the damage as less serious than it appears.

Differentiation is another way to reduce the offensiveness of an act. Here the rhetor attempts to distinguish the act he or she performed from other similar but more offensive actions (Ware & Linkugel, 1973). In comparison, the act performed by the rhetor may seem to the audience to be less offensive, reducing the negative feelings toward the rhetor. President Nixon decided to order troops into Cambodia during the Vietnam War. He attempted to differentiate his military offensive from an invasion of another country: "This is not an invasion of Cambodia. The areas in which these attacks will be launched are completely occupied by North Vietnamese forces" (1970, p. 451). He referred to a map of Southeast Asia in which the North Vietnamese strongholds were marked, saying, "The sanctuaries are in red, and you will note that they are on both sides of the border" (p. 450). Thus, he attempted to differentiate his use of military troops as a continuation of existing policy (attacking the North Vietnamese), not as a new offensive or invasion.

Transcendence attempts to place the act in a more favorable context (Ware & Linkugel, 1973). Nixon also attempted to justify his military offensive in Cambodia by using transcendence. He declared that "We take this action not for the purpose of expanding the war into Cambodia but for the purpose of ending the war in Vietnam, and winning the just peace we desire" (1970, p. 451). Here Nixon justifies his action on the basis of higher goals ("ending the war," "winning a just peace"), transcending the specific action taken.

If the rhetor can damage the credibility of the source of allegations (attacking one's accuser), damage to the rhetor's image may be limited (Scott & Lyman, 1968). Pepsi-Cola attacked Coca-Cola in advertisements aimed at retail outlets (*Nation's Restaurant News*). One Pepsi advertisement claimed that Coke's pricing policies treated other accounts differently (and worse) than McDonald's: "This year, while Coke required national accounts like you to absorb a per-gallon price increase, we hear there was no change to McDonald's net price." To make sure the implications were clear, the ad stressed that "Coke's pricing policy is requiring you to subsidize the operations of your largest competitor" (Pepsi-Cola, 1991, p. 34). Here the persuasive attack on Coke is quite clear.

In using compensation the rhetor offers to reimburse the victim to help mitigate the negative feeling arising from the act. This payment can be goods or services as well as monetary reimbursement. If the compensation is acceptable to the victim, the negative affect from the wrongful act should be eliminated or reduced, improving the rhetor's image. For example, a group of disabled people were denied admittance to a movie theater. An official later apologized and offered them free passes to a future movie ("Rebuffed Moviegoers," 1992). Clearly the passes were intended to help compensate them for the offensive act.

Corrective Action. Another general image restoration strategy is corrective action, in which the rhetor promises to correct the problem. This action can take the form of restoring the state of affairs existing before the offensive action, and/or promising to prevent the recurrence of the offensive act. In 1993, AT&T experienced a breakdown in long distance service to and from New York City. Chair Allen relied heavily on corrective action. For example, he announced that "We have already taken corrective and preventive action at the affected facility" in New York City. He also announced that AT&T planned "to spend billions more over the next few years to make them even more reliable" (1993, p. C3). Thus, he not only promised to correct the problem at the New York City switching plant, but to prevent future problems.

Mortification. Another general strategy for image restoration is to confess and beg forgiveness, which Burke labels mortification (1970, 1973). If the audience believes the apology is sincere, they may pardon the wrongful act. Another part of AT&T's response was to apologize, or engage in mortification. Allen offered explicit apology: "I apologize to all of you who were affected, directly or indirectly" (1993, p. C3). Thus, he accepted responsibility for the offensive act and directly apologized to those affected by it.

Three changes were made in the list of defensive strategies used in this analysis (see Table 2.4) for purposes of coding, reflecting the fact that it was developed before typologies for persuasive attack or defense. First, utterances that would have been treated as bolstering or corrective action in analyses of defense have been considered to be instances of acclaiming (covered in Table 2.2), and as a result these two categories were omitted (or, more accurately, transferred and elaborated into acclaiming strategies). Second, one of the methods for reducing offensiveness of an accusation is attacking one's accuser. Because there is a separate typology for persuasive attack (displayed in Table 2.3), attack accuser was omitted from the list of defensive strategies (and elaborated into a separate list of attacking strategies).

SUMMARY

We have described our basic method, analyzing utterances into acclaims, attacks, and defenses. We also analyze whether the discourse concerns policy or character, and subdivide each topic into three components (past deeds, future plans, and goals on policy; leadership ability, personal qualities, and ideals on character). We reviewed past research on these functions of discourse. The next chapter will describe the specific procedures we employed to apply this method to the messages we analyzed from the 1996 presidential campaign.

Chapter 3

Procedures: How We Analyzed Campaign '96 Messages

We began by obtaining copies of a variety of forms of persuasive discourse from the 1996 presidential campaign. Whenever possible, we obtained both transcripts and videotapes of the messages we studied. From the Republican primary, we selected three sets of texts: television advertisements, primary debates, and primary talk radio appearances. From the party nominating conventions, we also chose three sets of texts: keynote speeches, acceptance addresses, and speeches by the candidates' spouses. From the general campaign, we picked four sets of texts: television advertisements, debates, radio addresses, and free television time. In each application chapter we will discuss the details of the texts we analyzed.

We began our program of research with three preliminary studies: nominating convention keynote speeches from 1960–1996 (Benoit, Blaney, & Pier, 1996), nominating convention acceptance addresses from 1960–1996 (Wells, Pier, Blaney, & Benoit, 1996), and presidential general election television spots from 1980–1996 (Benoit, Pier, & Blaney, 1997). We started with keynote speeches. As a group, we read, analyzed, and discussed several keynote texts, one after another, to develop and refine our analytic categories. Once we had agreed on how we would analyze the 1996 campaign messages, we established our procedures.

One important decision concerned whether to use the traditional analytic approach of dividing the texts among the authors and testing for intercoder reliability on a small sample. We decided against taking that approach. It has the undeniable advantage of efficiency (if a study has but a single author, he or she has no choice but to use two or more coders). If two people are analyzing a group of texts, each coder needs to analyze but 60% of the texts. Forty percent of the texts are analyzed by one of the two coders and 20% are analyzed by both. Their results are compared, resulting in a figure representing intercoder reliability, say for instance 90%. What this means is that in the 20% of the texts analyzed by both coders, they agreed 90% of the time and disagreed 10% of the time. However, they have no idea which of the two divergent "readings" of the text ought to be adopted in the 10% of the cases in which they disagreed. Further, in the 80% of the texts analyzed by a single author (40% by each), they simply assume that the agreement is probably the same as in the 20% they both analyzed (in this case, 10%). Of course, if the texts coded by both authors are selected at random, the intercoder reliability is probably 10%, but that is not certain.

Instead of following this procedure, we divided the texts so that each message was independently read and analyzed by two authors. After analyzing the texts separately, the two authors met and discussed every coding decision. When disagreements arose, they were resolved by discussion (Burgoon, Pfau, & Birk, 1995, used coders to classify stimulus messages, using discussion to achieve consensus). Thus, we achieved 100% agreement on every coding decision for every text we analyzed (see Benoit, Pier, & Blaney, 1997). We believe this procedure, though more time-consuming, has several distinct advantages over the more traditional approach.

First, we achieved 100% agreement between two authors on each and every analytic decision in our analysis. We did not have to settle for lower levels of intercoder agreement. Second, we achieved this rate of agreement on every text we analyzed. We did not take a sample (like 20%) and extrapolate our rate of intercoder agreement on that sample to the remaining texts. Third, our procedure meant that all authors had read very carefully a substantial portion of the texts. This made each author familiar with a large proportion of the texts we analyzed, making it easier for each of us to understand the texts and our analysis of them.

Fourth, our discussions of each text, comparing our separate readings, provided a much richer understanding of the texts. A similar procedure was followed by Collier and Collier (1986) in their analysis of films. Each author viewed the films they analyzed separately. Then the authors met and discussed their individual analyses in a joint viewing. They explain the advantage of this approach: "These discussions clarified details, raised important questions, and defined conclusions, and the interplay of ideas sharpened our examination of the evidence and the precision of our analysis. On a conceptual level, these joint viewings were the most productive stages of the research" (p. 177). Similarly, our discussion not only increased our confidence in our analytic decisions (because each analytic decision was corroborated by two authors and because two authors analyzed the entire corpus, not just a subsample), but it allowed insights to arise that had not become apparent during our preliminary (individual) analyzes.

Furthermore, it is important to keep in mind that this issue concerns intercoder *reliability*, not validity. Ideally, a high figure for intercoder reliability is important because of "the assurance it provides that data are observed independently of the measuring event, instrument, or person" (Kaplan & Goldsen, 1965, pp. 83–84). Similarly, Weber (1985) explains that "high reproducibility" or intercoder reliability "measures the consistency of shared understandings or meanings" (p. 17). However, when low figures for intercoder reliability are obtained, the literature advises more training for the coders: "What is to be done when intercoder agreement figures are below an acceptable level? Research directors may continue to train their coders, redefine and tighten categories, or adjust the number of categories for which a single coder is responsible" (North, Holsti, Zaninovich, & Zinnes, 1963, p. 49). It should be obvious that the more coders are trained (to correct their "errors" and produce consistent codings), the less their responses represent the way other people would analyze the texts. Holsti, Loomba, and North (1968) go so far as to recommend that "the investigator may want to run experiments to identify and eliminate judges [coders] deviating consistently from the group" (p. 657). Sepstrup (1981) recognizes that "High intercoder reliability only indicates that two or more persons have successfully been 'educated' to uniform perception" (p. 139). Thus, a high figure for intercoder reliability does not prove that other, untrained people would produce the same analysis of those texts. It does not assure that the coding represents an intersubjective or generalizable view of the texts.

Furthermore, another study in this research program, analyzing presidential television spots, was not co-authored. This meant that the issue of coding reliability had to be treated in the more traditional manner (Benoit, 1998). Two coders independently analyzed 20% of the texts using the same procedures outlined here. Cohen's *kappa* for coding themes as acclaims, attacks, and defenses was .98; the figure for classifying themes as policy or character was .71; *kappa* for classifying policy themes as past deeds, future plans, or general goals was .84; and the figure for coding character utterances as personal qualities, leadership ability, or ideals was .72. Fleiss (1981) explains that *kappas* of .75 or above are excellent, from .40 to .75 are good, and .40 or less are poor. These coding procedures, used in a related study, provided reliabilities that are good to excellent when more traditional procedures are used. Thus, we have confidence in the reliability of our analysis.

In our view, the best argument for the value of a coding system is to provide copious examples of excerpts from the text illustrating how the categories were actually operationalized during the coding process. This allows readers to see for themselves what decisions the coders were making as they analyzed the texts; it permits readers to see what kinds of utterances were coded into each of the categories. This does not mean we fail to recognize the importance of consistency in interpreting texts (after all, we achieved 100% exact agreement in our analyses). Obviously, we do not want to base our conclusions on inconsistent or idiosyncratic analyses of texts. Nor do we reject the use of multiple coders and the calculation of figures for intercoder reliability. However, we believe that there is a tendency to take a standard practice in textual coding—use of multiple coders who work independently and never discuss their coding decisions—and enshrine it as the only acceptable approach. We are confident that our procedures, while different from conventional practice, have produced a sound and legitimate analysis of the texts we study and have certain clear advantages over that standard approach.

As mentioned in the preface, we developed six particular research questions that guided our analysis of selected messages in the 1996 presidential campaign.

1. How often do the major candidates employ each of the three functions of political campaign messages (acclaiming, attacking, defending)?
2. Do the candidates devote more utterances to addressing policy considerations (issues) or character concerns (image)?
3. How many utterances are devoted to the three forms of policy utterances (past deeds, future plans, general goals) and the three forms of character remarks (personal qualities, leadership ability, and ideals)?
4. To what extent are these messages targeted to the candidates, the parties, or both?
5. How did candidates elaborate their utterances in the discourse?
6. Which candidates devoted more utterances to the issues of most importance to voters?

In order to answer these questions, we established a six-step analytic procedure. First, we unitized the messages into themes, or utterances that address a coherent idea. Because naturally occurring discourse is enthymematic, themes vary in length from a phrase to several sentences. Sometimes candidates expressed their ideas in only a few words. For example, in the 1996 Clinton/Gore television advertisement "Economic Plan," the announcer tells viewers:

Ten million new jobs. Family income up $1,600 [since 1993]. President Clinton cut the deficit 60%, signed welfare reform requiring work, time limits. Taxes cut for fifteen million families.

We identified five themes here: new jobs, family income, federal deficit, welfare reform, and tax cuts. The rule we followed was to break each part of a passage into a separate theme whenever we would have considered that part to be a theme if that part of the utterance had appeared alone. Themes varied in length (these are among the shortest themes we found in our analysis of campaign '96, incidentally), but each one addressed a coherent idea about the candidates and/or their parties.

Second, each theme was classified as an acclaim, attack, or defense according to these rules:

Themes that portrayed the candidate and/or the candidate's party in a favorable light were considered *acclaims*.

Themes that portrayed the opposing candidate or political party in an unfavorable light were considered *attacks*.

Themes that repaired the candidate's and/or party's reputation (from attacks by the opposing party) were considered *defenses*.

The five brief themes identified in the passage above were all considered acclaims. Other utterances were not analyzed. For example, at times campaign discourse describes events without attributing credit or blame to either candidate or party. Only utterances that acclaimed, attacked, or defended were analyzed.

Third, the target of the acclaim, attack, or defense was identified. In the excerpt above, we considered Bill Clinton to be the target. Usually, potential targets were the candidates, the parties, or both. However, in the primaries, candidates quite frequently attacked one another (as well as the presumed nominee of the opposing party). Furthermore, primary candidates at times attacked the Washington political establishment. Nominating conventions are a celebration of the party as well as the candidate (and vilification of the opposing party and its candidate). Thus, we looked to see if convention speakers directed their remarks toward the candidates, the parties, or both. However, in the general election campaign the target was virtually always one of the two candidates, Bill Clinton or Bob Dole (and rarely their respective parties). Thus, we do not discuss the target during the general campaign.

Fourth, a judgment was made about whether the theme primarily concerned policy or character, according to these rules:

Themes that concerned governmental action (past, current, or future) and problems amenable to governmental action were considered *policy* themes.

Themes that concerned characteristics, traits, abilities, or attributes of the candidates (or their parties) were considered *character* themes.

Table 3.1
Importance of Policy and Character to Voters in the 1996 Campaign

	June 20-25	Sept. 12-17	Oct. 19-22
Positions on the Issues	65%	65%	65%
Personal Character and Values	25%	27%	24%

Source: NBC News/*Wall Street Journal*.

Policy themes were further divided into utterances that concerned past deeds, future plans, and general goals. Character themes were further divided into utterances that addressed personal qualities, leadership ability, and ideals (see Table 2.1). The passage quoted earlier concerned policy, and Clinton's past deeds in particular.

Fifth, the theme was analyzed to see if it was elaborated with one of the strategies portrayed in Tables 2.2–2.4.

Finally, we wanted to know to what extent the two candidates devoted time to the topics most important to voters (see Benoit & Wells, 1996, who used this procedure as part of their analysis of the 1992 presidential debates). First, we located public opinion poll data on what topics were most important to voters during the 1996 presidential campaign. We decided to use two sets of questions asked in several NBC News/*Wall Street Journal* polls. The first set of questions (used on three dates) asked respondents, "Which one of the following two qualities is more important to you in determining your choice of a presidential candidate—the candidate's position on the issues, or the candidate's personal character and values?" The results of this poll are summarized in Table 3.1. The results of our fourth step, where we determined whether an utterance concerned policy or character, will be used in connection with these poll data.

Additionally, we located a second set of questions that were also from NBC News/*Wall Street Journal* polls. These questions asked respondents (on five dates), "Which of the following issues will be most important to you personally in your voting for Congress and president this year?" Possible answers were jobs and the economy, education, the budget deficit, taxes, Medicare and health, crime and drug abuse, and (once) welfare. The results are summarized in Table 3.2. The final step in our data analysis began with those themes identified in step four as concerned with policy (past deeds, future plans, and general goals). These utterances were classified into one of the seven areas from the list in the public opinion poll questions (and an eighth possibility, "other"—the candidates, of course, discussed other policy issues as well, like campaign financing, the environment, foreign aid, and national defense).

We illustrate our procedures with a brief discussion of two passages. These have already been unitized into themes, the first step. This excerpt is taken from Mario Cuomo's 1984 Democratic keynote address:

Think about it: What chance would the Republican candidate have had in 1980 if he had told the American people that he intended to pay for his so-called economic recovery with . . . the largest Government debt known to humankind? (p. 648)

We decided that this passage was an attack because it attempted to *create or reinforce an unfavorable impression* of President Reagan. Then we agreed that the target of the attack was *the Republican candidate, Ronald Reagan*, rather than the party as a whole or both Reagan and the Republican Party. Next, we decided that this utterance addressed a *policy question* (the state of the economy) rather than his character. Specifically, we decided that this was an attack on Reagan's *past deeds*. Then we agreed that this attack was elaborated by emphasizing the extent of the alleged problem ("largest Government debt known to humankind"). Finally, we decided that this passage concerned the *budget deficit*.

Contrast the previous quotation with the following passage in Mark Hatfield's 1964 Republican keynote address:

The Republican Party is committed to a set of principles. This commitment is an act of unwavering faith in the American people in the cause of freedom, in the eternal principles of morality. (p. 652)

This theme is considered to be an instance of an acclaim because it attempted to create or reinforce a favorable impression (commitment to *freedom and morality*) of the target. The target was the *Republican Party* as the first sentence reveals, rather than its specific candidate (Barry Goldwater). Instead of focusing on particular policy questions or issues, this acclaim addressed the ideals (freedom, morality) on which the Republican Party is founded. Because this passage does not deal with policy, it was not classified as dealing with one of the issues listed in Table 3.2 (step six).

We begin each analytical chapter by reproducing sample messages or excerpts from sample messages. For example, Chapter 5 on televised Republican primary advertisements starts with the texts of several of the spots we analyzed in this chapter. Frequently we referred to these sample messages to illustrate our findings in that chapter, although we quote other passages at times as well. While we developed numerous tables of numerical data, we made a determined effort to keep our conclusions

Table 3.2
Importance of Issues in the 1996 Campaign

	March 1-5	May 10-14	August 2-6	September 12-17	October 19-22	Rank
Jobs and Economy	33%	31%	24%	33%	22%	1
Education	16%	17%	23%	18%	20%	2
Budget Deficit	16%	17%	23%	18%	12%	3*
Medicare and Health	9%	10%		14%	15%	4*
Welfare			11%			5
Taxes	9%	10%	10%	9%	9%	6
Crime and Drugs	8%	6%	7%	9%	9%	6

*Note that in the last month the importance of the Budget Deficit dropped to less than Medicare and Health.

Source: NBC News/Wall Street Journal.

grounded firmly in the texts we analyzed by using frequent excerpts from the texts to illustrate our conclusions (copious use of illustrative excerpts also provides evidence for the appropriateness of our coding of the texts).

SUMMARY

Thus, this study applies the functional theory of political campaign discourse to a variety of texts—from primaries, conventions, and the general campaign—used during the 1996 election. We examine their use of acclaiming, attacking, and defending. We divide utterances into those addressing policy and those discussing character, and subdivide each of these two areas into more specific categories. We focus almost exclusively on the *messages* generated by the candidates, rather than on other events (e.g., selection of Jack Kemp as Bob Dole's running mate or the resignation of Dick Morris). While this focus on messages means we overlook some factors in the campaign (of course, no treatment can consider everything that could play a role in a presidential election) our purpose is to provide a broad understanding of the rhetoric employed in campaign '96.

Part II

Republican Primaries: Who Shall Lead Us?

Chapter 4

Debates: A Free-for-All

New Hampshire Primary Debate (excerpts)

Forbes: Some say that a flat tax—that is, a tax cut for families—is the main part of my agenda. But it's only part of my agenda. Parents should control education, not the unions. People on Medicare should control their health plans, not the bureaucrats. . . .

Buchanan: Bob Dole . . . says in that ad that Pat Buchanan wants to give away— or wanted to give away—nuclear weapons to our Asian allies. Bob, that's not true.

Dole: That's what you said. I didn't say that.

Buchanan: It's not true, and your folks . . .

Dole: That's in writing.

Buchanan: . . . know it's not true. . . .

Dole: I'm very proud of the Republican Congress . . . The one thing that stands in our way, there's one barrier named Bill Clinton. President Bill Clinton. He talks left and governs right, or talks right and governs left, whichever it is. He's never the same. One day he's this way and one day he's the next day [*sic*]. We need to remove that obstacle.

I think we've done an outstanding job. We passed the first balanced budget in a generation. We sent it to the president and he vetoed it. We passed welfare reform with an overwhelming vote, and every governor I know of and every ex-governor except Lamar Alexander is for, and he vetoed that. We passed tax cuts for families with children, a $500 tax cut and he vetoed that. We passed farm legislation and he vetoed that. . . .

Forbes: That 1983 rescue of the Social Security system, senator, was very typical of the way Washington solves problems.

Dole: No.

Forbes: They raised taxes—they raised taxes and they cut benefits. We need to do it a new way, turn the problem into an opportunity, which is the core of my campaign. We must keep our promises to those who are in the system and those who are going to go on the system in the next fifteen years in terms of benefits.

Keyes: Listening to Senator Dole talk about how he's going to stand forthrightly and toughly negotiate our trade agreement.... You had your opportunity to be tough and you blew it and now you're telling us, "I wasn't tough in the Senate but I will be tough in the White House." Why on earth should we believe you?

Alexander: The reason I did so well in Iowa was because I kept on the high road. My television ads were positive, about what I'm for, the future. And people got sick of Senator Dole and Mr. Forbes slamming each other. And they pretty well persuaded a lot of Iowans that they were right in what they were saying about each other, and a lot of them voted for me.

As far as Mr. Forbes goes, he knows what a capital gain is. I was proud of that. The reason everyone knows about that is I have disclosed my tax returns since 1978, even when I'm in private life. Steve, why don't you disclose your tax returns as well? If your tax-cutting agenda is our agenda, then we need to know what taxes you pay. And if we're not careful . . .

Forbes: Governor, that's a diversion.

Alexander: . . . we're going to spend all of our time talking about each other.

Forbes: You, as governor, have invested $20 million . . .

Alexander: Steve . . .

Forbes: . . . in various scams that you have gotten $1.9 million return for—1.9 million. . . .

Buchanan: This campaign is on fire because we don't care about doing television attack ads. We've got a vision and an agenda. You know, and a slew of attack ads and negative ads is no substitute for an agenda for America, for ideas dealing with immigration, dealing with tax reform, dealing with bringing the jobs back to America. That's what we've got. And I think that really that a vision of America is what is missing in many of these campaigns. When they use attack ads, there's a hollowness at the core of the campaign. There's no thought, there's no heart. . . .

Dornan: I used the battle cry I've used since 1984 in a political comeback: faith, family, and freedom. I add to that fidelity. Fidelity to some faith. Fidelity to freedom. Fidelity to your family. Clinton broke his oath to the people of Arkansas. It's called Whitewater and it's multilevel corruption. He broke his faith with his wife. He broke his faith with his country three times, he dodged the draft. What will he do to us in a second term? Gentlemen, keep your eye on the ball. The target is Clinton.

Little research has been conducted into primary debates. Kane (1987) argued for longer speeches and no questions by journalists, illustrating his argument with analysis of the 1948 Dewey-Stassen primary debate.

Pfau (1984) conducted an experimental study of contrasting debate formats. He also showed that three 1984 Democratic debates created issue learning (1988). Hickman (1984/85) used public opinion poll data to analyze effects of the 1984 Democratic primary debate in New Hampshire. Murphy (1992b) analyzed the arguments in the 1968 California primary debate between Robert Kennedy and Eugene McCarthy. Finally, Blankenship, Fine, and Davis (1983) analyzed six Republican primary debates from 1980 to show that Reagan emerged as the comparison point for evaluating the other candidates. Research has not attempted to analyze the functions of primary debates (more research has been conducted on general election debates, which will be reviewed in Chapter 12).

1996 REPUBLICAN PRIMARY DEBATES

We decided to analyze the three 1996 Republican primary debates that included the eventual Republican nominee (in point of fact, the first debate, from Orlando, occurred in late 1995): Orlando, New Hampshire, and South Carolina. Debates also were staged in Georgia (Alexander, Buchanan, and Forbes) and Texas (Buchanan, Forbes, and Keyes). Four candidates appeared in all three of the debates we chose to analyze (Lamar Alexander, Pat Buchanan, Bob Dole, and Steve Forbes), three candidates participated twice (Bob Dornan, Alan Keyes, and Dick Lugar), and three entered one debate each (Phil Gramm, Arlen Specter, and Morry Taylor).

THE FUNCTIONS OF REPUBLICAN PRIMARY DEBATES

We found that all of these candidates engaged in acclaiming, attacking, and defending (the lone exception was Taylor, who acclaimed and attacked but did not defend). Overall, the candidates spent more of their utterances acclaiming (54%) than attacking (38%), and devoted the smallest number of utterances to defending (9%). A chi-square conducted on the data for candidate and acclaims versus attacks (the number of defenses was too small to include) was significant ($X^2[df = 9] = 36.6$, p < .001). These data are displayed in Table 4.1.

Acclaiming was a frequent component of the debates. For example, in New Hampshire Forbes described his goals: "Parents should control education, not the unions. People on Medicare should control their health plans, not the bureaucrats." These sound like initiatives that most viewers would agree are desirable. In the passage from the New Hampshire clash, Dole praised his past accomplishments with the Republican Congress while attacking Clinton (and Alexander):

Table 4.1
Acclaims, Attacks, and Defenses: Primary Debates

	Acclaims	Attacks	Defenses
Alexander	89 (55%)	66 (41%)	7 (4%)
Buchanan	95 (58%)	60 (37%)	8 (5%)
Dole	133 (57%)	52 (22%)	48 (21%)
Dornan	43 (56%)	31 (41%)	3 (4%)
Forbes	72 (45%)	82 (52%)	5 (3%)
Gramm	26 (74%)	8 (23%)	1 (3%)
Keyes	31 (47%)	34 (52%)	1 (2%)
Lugar	43 (64%)	22 (33%)	2 (3%)
Specter	21 (75%)	6 (21%)	1 (4%)
Taylor	31 (53%)	28 (47%)	0 --
Total	584 (54%)	389 (38%)	76 (9%)

We passed the first balanced budget in a generation. We sent it to the president and he vetoed it. We passed welfare reform with an overwhelming vote, and every governor I know of and every ex-governor except Lamar Alexander is for, and he vetoed that. We passed tax cuts for families with children, a $500 tax cut and he vetoed that. We passed farm legislation and he vetoed that.

In addition to the acclaims, this passage also enacted a strategy of defense—defeasibility—suggesting that the reason the Republican-controlled Congress failed to enact some reforms was an obstacle beyond their control: the president and his veto power.

In New Hampshire, Alexander also combined praise of his own openness while questioning Forbes: "I have disclosed my tax returns since 1978, even when I'm in private life. Steve, why don't you disclose your tax returns as well? If your tax-cutting agenda is our agenda, then we need to know what taxes you pay." This not only suggests that Forbes is secretive, but that his flat-tax might be intended in part to increase his personal wealth.

Defense occurred in the debates as well as acclaims and attacks. For instance, Buchanan took the opportunity accorded by the New Hampshire debate to respond to a charge in a television advertisement run by Dole's campaign: "Bob Dole . . . says in that ad that Pat Buchanan wants to give away—or wanted to give away—nuclear weapons to our Asian allies. Bob, that's not true." This is clearly an instance of simple denial. Similarly, when accused by an Alexander television spot of opposing term limits, Dole responded in the South Carolina debate: "I've said I support term limits. In fact, there's an Ad Watch analysis of that ad today that showed that it was completely wrong." This statement clearly denies Alexander's accusation.

There were some differences between the candidates in their use of the functions of political campaigns that are worth noting. Gramm (74%) and Lugar (64%) tended to acclaim more than the average, while Forbes (52%) and Keyes (52%) were the only candidates to attack more than they acclaimed (Taylor, at 47%, was a close third). Dole engaged in the largest amount of defense (21%) of any of the candidates. Most of the other candidates hovered around 3–5% defense. Taylor was the only candidate who did not defend at all in his debate.

DEFENSE

As just mentioned, every candidate but Taylor engaged in persuasive defense. Most defenses by far were produced by Dole (48), who was the front-runner. Alexander, Forbes, and Buchanan also offered several defenses. The most common defensive strategy by a large margin was denial (50 instances). For example, when questioned about statements a Dole ad had made about Buchanan in South Carolina, Dole responded: "He said it. I didn't say it. I don't run around making these things up." Another common defensive strategy was defeasibility (15). During the Orlando debate, Buchanan asked why the Congress (i.e., Gramm and Dole) hadn't eliminated the Department of Education. Dole responded that "It takes a while to do it, Pat. Give us a little time. . . . It takes more than one year or two years to make these fundamental changes." The implication is that there are obstacles to taking swift action that are not under Dole's control. Transcendence was used eleven times. When it was pointed out in South Carolina that taxes had increased in Tennessee when Alexander was governor, he replied that "we had reduced the debt, fewer employees, and the fifth-lowest taxes of any state," suggesting that these other factors justified the tax rate. Differentiation occurred seven times. During the altercation over whether Dole called Buchanan an extremist in South Carolina, Dole denied calling him an *extremist*: "I didn't use the word 'extremist.' " However, Dole also used differentiation: "I said his views are too extreme. You've got to listen carefully." In Orlando, Dole also differentiated "loophole closers" from "rate increases." Shifting the blame was used almost as often. After Buchanan noted that Dole had voted for tax hikes in 1982 and 1983, Dole shifted the blame: "That was sent up by Ronald Reagan." Provocation (2), mortification (2), and good intentions (1) were infrequently used. See Table 4.2.

TARGET OF ACCLAIMS

In general the candidates were much more prone to acclaim themselves (97%) than their party (3%). For instance, in South Carolina, Forbes declared that "I've concentrated simply on getting my message of growth, hope, and opportunity across to the American people." Similarly, Dole stated in that debate: "If we can eliminate much of the IRS we can save a lot of money, and we can make it easier for taxpayers to comply with the law." Forbes almost entirely acclaimed himself (99%), while Keyes devoted the largest percentage of acclaims to his party (13%). In New Hampshire, for example, Keyes explained that "It was that contrast between Republicans and Democrats that elected an overwhelmingly pro-life moral conservative freshman class for the Republicans." These descriptors—"pro-life," "moral," "conservative"—are all favorable. See Table 4.3 for a summary of these findings.

TARGET OF ATTACKS

The candidates frequently attacked each other. Other Republicans accounted for 58% of the targets of attacks in these primary debates. For example, Keyes criticized fellow-Republican Dole when he observed during the New Hampshire contest that he had been "listening to Senator Dole talk about how he's going to stand forthrightly and toughly negotiate our trade agreement. . . . You had your opportunity to be tough and you blew it and now you're telling us 'I wasn't tough in the Senate but I will be tough in the White House.' Why on earth should we believe you?" Here, Keyes attacked Dole, reasoning from past failures that Dole was unlikely to perform well if elected. So fierce was the in-fighting that Dornan felt compelled to remind his colleagues in that debate, "Gentlemen, keep your eye on the ball. The target is Clinton." Despite this admonition other Republicans were the principal target in these primary debates.

Second, the establishment was the recipient of 25% of the attacks. For instance, when asked in New Hampshire about the anticipated future problems of funding the Social Security system, Taylor proposed that we "take all the congressmen, take the president, take the senators, and take all the federal government workers and stick them on Social Security, knock off their pensions." He attacked members of the establishment indiscriminately, suggesting their pensions were too costly.

Finally, Clinton (and the Democratic Party) was the target 17% of the

Table 4.2
Defense Strategies: Primary Debates

	Deny	Defeas	Trans	Diff	Sblame	Prov	Mort	GoodInt	Total
Alexander	10	1	7	2	0	2	0	0	22
Buchanan	7	0	0	1	0	0	0	0	8
Dole	24	11	3	4	5	0	0	1	48
Dornan	2	1	0	0	0	0	0	0	3
Forbes	5	1	0	0	1	0	2	0	9
Gramm	1	0	0	0	0	0	0	0	1
Keyes	0	0	0	0	0	0	0	0	0
Lugar	1	1	1	0	0	0	0	0	2
Specter	0	0	0	0	0	0	0	0	1
Taylor	0	0	0	0	0	0	0	0	0
Total	50 (54%)	15 (16%)	11 (12%)	7 (7%)	6 (6%)	2 (2%)	2 (2%)	1 (1%)	94

Table 4.3
Target of Acclaims: Primary Debates

	Candidate	Party	Total
Alexander	88 (99%)	1 (1%)	89
Buchanan	90 (95%)	5 (5%)	95
Dole	130 (98%)	3 (2%)	133
Dornan	39 (91%)	4 (9%)	43
Forbes	80 (99%)	1 (1%)	81
Gramm	25 (96%)	1 (4%)	26
Keyes	27 (87%)	4 (13%)	31
Lugar	42 (98%)	1 (2%)	43
Specter	21 (100%)	0 --	21
Taylor	31 (100%)	0 --	31
Total	573 (97%)	20 (3%)	593

time. In New Hampshire Dole leveled this attack at Bill Clinton: "He talks left and governs right, or talks right and governs left, whichever it is. He's never the same. One day he's this way and one day he's the next day [sic]." Surely we want our president to be consistent in word and deed. Thus, the attacks of these candidates had three different targets: other Republicans, the establishment, and Bill Clinton. These data are displayed in Table 4.4.

There were some differences between these debaters in their choice of targets. Taylor (43%), Buchanan (40%), Forbes (38%), Keyes (32%) and Lugar (32%) all tended to attack the establishment more than the average, while Alexander (11%), Dole (4%), Dornan (6%), and Gramm (13%) attacked the establishment less than the average. Specter (50%), Dornan (48%), Gramm (38%) and Dole (37%) led the chorus of criticism against Clinton. Buchanan never attacked Clinton directly in these debates.

We conducted a secondary analysis to determine which of the Republicans were the targets of their attacks on each other. The attacks did not seem to be distributed randomly. Dole was the target of 39% of the attacks. Gramm (16%), Alexander (14%), Forbes (12%), and Lugar (12%) clustered roughly together. Buchanan received 7% of the attacks. Others were never (Keyes, Specter, Taylor) or rarely (Dornan) attacked.[1] See Table 4.5.

Table 4.4
Target of Attacks: Primary Debates

	Other Republicans	Establishment	Clinton	Total
Alexander	55 (83%)	7 (11%)	4 (6%)	66
Buchanan	36 (60%)	24 (40%)	0 --	60
Dole	31 (60%)	2 (4%)	19 (37%)	52
Dornan	14 (45%)	2 (6%)	15 (48%)	31
Forbes	43 (54%)	30 (38%)	7 (9%)	80
Gramm	4 (50%)	1 (13%)	3 (38%)	8
Keyes	23 (46%)	16 (32%)	11 (22%)	50
Lugar	8 (36%)	7 (32%)	7 (32%)	22
Specter	3 (50%)	0 --	3 (50%)	6
Taylor	15 (54%)	12 (43%)	1 (4%)	28
Total	232 (58%)	101 (25%)	70 (17%)	403

POLICY VERSUS CHARACTER

Throughout these three debates, the candidates discussed policy in 58% of their comments and character in 42% of their remarks. A chi-square indicated that these differences were significant ($X^2[df = 9] = 57.7$, $p < .001$). During the South Carolina debate, the question of U.S. policy toward Cuba arose (two private planes had been shot down by the Cubans). Buchanan described his future plans if he won the election: "I would have American airplanes patrolling the Florida Straits, and I would shoot down any Cuban aircraft which tried to shoot at a civilian plane in the Florida Straits. I would not recommend an invasion of Cuba." This statement describes Buchanan's policy toward Cuba. In Orlando, Gramm took up the question of welfare reform: "I want to make people riding in the wagon get out of the wagon and help the rest of us pull. I want to stop inviting people to America with their hands out to go on welfare. And I want to stop giving people more and more money to have more and more children on welfare." Thus, these candidates frequently addressed policy in their utterances.

However, character was discussed in these debates as well. In New Hampshire, Forbes criticized Alexander for business dealings Forbes characterized as "scams":

Table 4.5
Target of Attacks on Republicans: Primary Debates

	Number of Attacks
Alexander	38 (14%)
Buchanan	19 (7%)
Dole	103 (39%)
Dornan	1 (0.4%)
Forbes	31 (12%)
Gramm	42 (16%)
Keyes	0 --
Lugar	31 (12%)
Specter	0 --
Taylor	0 --

Forbes: You, as governor, have invested $20 million . . .

Alexander: Steve . . .

Forbes: . . . in various scams that you have gotten $1.9 million return for—1.9 million.

This attack is a slur on Alexander's character, not on his governmental policies. See Table 4.6.

Some candidates devoted even more of their time to policy than the group norm: Gramm (74%), Forbes (71%), Dole (63%), and Taylor (63%). Buchanan, Dornan, and Lugar (all at 52%) split their remarks about evenly between policy and character. Keyes spent the smallest amount of time on policy (36%).

POLICY

Most contenders spent more time attacking the past deeds of others than praising their own accomplishments. In South Carolina, Alexander pointed to "the $320 billion in taxes you [Dole] raised between 1982 and 1990." Forbes chimed in, adding that "Senator Dole has voted for 16 tax increases totaling almost one trillion dollars." Both candidates attacked Dole's past deeds. Similarly, Forbes argued in South Carolina that "Governor Alexander, when he headed up the Education Department, in-

Table 4.6
Policy versus Character: Primary Debates

	Policy				Character			
	Deeds	Plans	Goals	Total	PQual	Leader	Ideals	Total
Alexander	25/11*	4/15	3/31	32/57 (57%)	24/11	6/8	4/14	34/33 (43%)
Buchanan	45/5	0/15	0/14	45/34 (52%)	11/13	1/3	3/41	15/57 (48%)
Dole	29/27	0/11	4/45	33/83 (63%)	12/14	3/15	4/21	19/50 (37%)
Dorman	14/9	2/7	1/5	17/21 (52%)	12/10	1/4	1/7	14/21 (48%)
Forbes	54/3	1/19	2/36	57/58 (71%)	16/4	2/1	5/18	23/23 (29%)
Gramm	4/5	2/2	1/11	7/18 (74%)	1/3	0/1	0/4	1/8 (26%)
Keyes	18/1	0/4	1/5	19/10 (36%)	11/1	3/0	17/20	31/21 (64%)
Lugar	12/3	1/6	0/12	13/21 (52%)	7/7	0/7	2/8	9/22 (48%)
Specter	4/0	0/8	0/4	4/12 (59%)	1/4	1/0	0/5	2/9 (41%)
Taylor	14/2	1/5	1/14	16/21 (63%)	9/3	2/6	1/1	12/10 (37%)
Total	219/66	11/92	13/177	243/335 (58%)	104/70	19/45	37/139	160/254 (42%)

*left number = attacks, right number = acclaims.

creased it by several billion dollars—so much for downsizing." Here Forbes also attacked Alexander's past deeds.

Specifically, Alexander was over twice as likely to attack on past deeds (25) than to acclaim them (11). Buchanan had almost ten times as many attacks (45) as acclaims (5) on past deeds; Forbes had over ten times as many (54 attacks, 3 acclaims). Dole (29 attacks, 27 acclaims) and Gramm (4 attacks, 5 acclaims) were exceptions, balancing their acclaims and attacks on this topic. In the Orlando debate, Dole pointed out that "Tonight, I just left the Senate floor thirty minutes ago, and by a vote of 52–47, we are going to cut taxes $245 billion for the American people. That's the Bob Dole record and I am proud of it." Here, Dole praised his past deeds.

On the other hand, virtually every speaker had more acclaims than attacks on future plans (Gramm had 2 of each). Specter acclaimed his tax reform plan in Orlando: "Now my colleagues here talk about wanting to reduce the capital gains tax. I want to eliminate the capital gains tax entirely." One of his future plans is to abolish the capital gains tax. In the debate in South Carolina, Buchanan explained that "We're going to build a security fence along the Mexican border, whence most of those drugs now come." Thus, Buchanan praised his future plans for reducing illegal drug trafficking.

Every candidate was more likely in these encounters to praise than attack general goals. In Orlando, Forbes declared that "The whole purpose of this campaign is to remove the obstacles to growth, hope, and opportunity." These are noble sentiments, but they are not specific. Lugar is no less general when he stated that "I think we ought to be talking about the environment, about the cities, about a good number of situations that verge on economics but that clearly stay away from it." Thus, these candidates' goals were more often praised than attacked.

CHARACTER

As with general goals, every candidate praised his own ideals more frequently than he attacked his opponents' ideals. This was true in almost every case for leadership ability (Keyes had three attacks and no acclaims; Forbes attacked twice and acclaimed once on those grounds). Most of these candidates (Alexander, Dornan, Forbes, Keyes, and Taylor), though, were more likely to attack on personal qualities than to acclaim on those grounds. One of Dole's ads was discussed during the South Carolina debate, a spot that seemed to suggest that Buchanan's views were extreme. Buchanan chided Dole for running television spots "about an old friend that you know are not true." Forbes jumped in, suggesting that Dole's ad clearly characterized Buchanan as an "extremist," and "only a lawyer would think that you'd come away from that ad without calling him an extremist." Dole retorted that "only a newspaper—only a magazine publisher" would think so. Personal qualities were more often a source of attacks than acclaims.

STRATEGIES FOR ELABORATING ACCLAIMS AND ATTACKS

Every candidate but Specter, who only participated in one debate, elaborated some of their utterances. The most common strategy for developing their utterances was to stress extent. This is followed by discussions of the effects on the audience and consistency. Forbes' statement in South Carolina that under his flat-tax proposal "a typical South Carolina family will save up to $1,000 a year" uses both extent ($1,000) and effects on the audience ("typical South Carolina family") to elaborate this acclaim. Alexander, in the South Carolina clash, accused Dole of inconsistency in raising taxes but attacking others for raising taxes: "While I was keeping taxes low, you raised taxes. Why don't you say that, if you want to talk about records?" Persistence and vulnerability were strategies for elaborating utterances that were less commonly used. These data are displayed in Table 4.7.

ISSUES ADDRESSED

Forbes (17), Alexander (16) and Lugar (14) led the participants in references to jobs and the economy. Alexander had most references to education (8), followed by Forbes (6) and Dole (5). Dole had over three times as many utterances on the budget deficit as any other candidate (15). On Medicare and health, Forbes had over twice as many comments as any other contender (13). Most candidates (Buchanan, Dornan, Gramm, Keyes, Lugar, Specter and Taylor) did not acclaim, attack, or defend on welfare; Alexander (6), Dole (6), and Forbes (4) did discuss it. Forbes referred to taxes most frequently (35 times), followed closely by Dole (33). Crime was discussed more than once by Dole (6), Alexander (5), Buchanan (4), and Forbes (3). Many other topics, including the choice of a vice president, immigration, and foreign policy were "other" topics. These data are shown in Table 4.8.

This summary suggests that Alexander was one of the leaders on the two topics most important to voters, jobs and the economy and education. Dole was one of the leaders on two topics (deficit, third most important, and taxes, sixth). Forbes was a leader on jobs and the economy (the most important topic to voters), Medicare and health (fourth most important topic) and taxes (sixth). Lugar, who only debated once, fre-

Table 4.7
Strategies for Elaborating Acclaims and Attacks: Primary Debates

	Extent	Effects	Consistency	Persist	Vulnerable
Alexander	3/ 4*	0/ 4	1/1	1/0	0/0
Buchanan	16/ 1	3/ 7	3/3	1/0	1/0
Dole	7/ 3	2/ 5	5/0	3/3	0/0
Dornan	8/ 1	0/ 0	0/0	0/1	0/0
Forbes	13/ 2	4/ 6	7/0	1/0	0/0
Gramm	1/ 0	1/ 0	0/0	0/0	0/0
Keyes	0/ 0	0/ 0	2/0	0/0	2/0
Lugar	3/ 2	1/ 2	0/0	0/0	1/0
Specter	0/ 0	0/ 0	0/0	0/0	0/0
Taylor	5/ 0	2/ 0	0/0	0/0	0/0
Total	56/13	13/24	18/4	6/4	4/0

*left number = attacks, right number = acclaims.

quently addressed the most important topic, jobs and the economy. Buchanan, Dornan, Gramm, Keyes, Taylor, and Spector did not direct the most utterances to any of the most important topics (but, of course, of these only Buchanan participated in all three of the debates we analyzed).

IMPLICATIONS

These candidates were inclined to use more acclaims than attacks. This makes sense, because each candidate must appear desirable to voters. Stressing one's desirable policy positions and character traits can encourage voters to choose that candidate. Pointing out an opponent's shortcomings can make them appear less appealing to voters. However, given voters' negative feelings about mudslinging, these candidates tended to acclaim more than they attacked. Alexander even observed that "People got sick of Senator Dole and Mr. Forbes slamming each other." Only two candidates devoted as much as half of their time to attacks (Forbes and Keyes). Neither led in the polls.

Defense was present, but the candidates spent less time defending than

Table 4.8
Issues Addressed: Primary Debates

	Rank	Alexander	Buchanan	Dole	Dornan	Forbes	Gramm	Keyes	Lugar	Specter	Taylor
Jobs and Economy	1	16	9	9	0	17	1	0	14	1	10
Education	2	8	2	5	0	6	0	1	1	0	0
Budget Deficit	3	3	1	15	4	1	4	1	0	4	4
Medicare/ Health	4	3	1	7	2	13	1	2	3	0	4
Welfare	5	6	0	6	0	4	0	0	0	0	0
Taxes	6	19	19	33	4	35	4	2	4	6	4
Crime/ Drugs	7	5	4	6	0	3	1	0	0	1	0
Other	---	20	43	35	28	35	14	23	12	4	15

acclaiming or attacking. They may not have wished to appear to be on the defensive; they may not have wanted to spend too much time on topics of their opponents' choosing. So, we are not surprised to find that while there are several instances of defense in these debates, defense is less common than either acclaiming or attacking.

We conducted a secondary analysis to determine who was the target of attacks on other Republicans. Again, two authors reached agreement on the target of each attack against other Republicans. Some attacks had no identifiable target; others had multiple targets (for example, the three Senators—Dole, Gramm, and Lugar—were frequently attacked together in the Orlando debate). Dole, who performed the most defense, was the target of over twice as many attacks (103) as any other candidate in these debates. It is reasonable for the person who is attacked the most to defend the most, and Benoit and Wells (1996) found that Bush, like Dole in these debates, was attacked the most and defended the most.

This analysis reveals that there is a relationship between attack and defense. However, attacks do not automatically provoke defenses. Gramm was the target of the second highest number of attacks (42), but he produced only a single defense. The third largest number of defenses came from Buchanan, despite the fact that five candidates received more attacks than he did. So, attacks have a tendency to provoke defenses, but other factors besides sheer number of attacks must influence use of defense (e.g., a candidate far ahead in the polls may not wish to appear defensive; some charges are easier to refute than others; some attacks may be less damaging than others and thus easier to ignore).

The candidates spent the most time acclaiming themselves (97%) rather than their party. Although the candidates surely wanted to appear to be solid Republicans to voters, praising the party doesn't particularly distinguish an individual candidate in the same way that praising oneself does. Thus, it is reasonable to find that the candidates lavished most of their praise on themselves (individually; of course they did not heap praise on each other).

Similarly, most attacks were aimed at each other (58%) and many other attacks (25%) were directed toward the establishment—several of these primary candidates being prominent members of the establishment. Although Clinton was the presumed Democratic nominee and the eventual target, the immediate targets were the other contenders for the Republican nomination. It also makes sense that candidates who were outsiders—Taylor and Forbes (both in business), Buchanan and Keyes (a commentator and an ambassador, who never held national elective offices), and Lugar (a senator, but not one with the same national reputation as other contenders)—tended to attack the establishment the most. Thus, it makes perfect sense for these candidates to have directed most of their attacks to one another (either directly or as part of the establishment). These contenders had to appear preferable to each other to win the Republican nomination; they needed to appear preferable to Clinton only if they became the nominee (and, presumably, they would all agree that any Republican was preferable to Clinton).

These candidates, as a whole, devoted more time to policy than character. Even Keyes—who stressed the importance of the moral crisis over the economy—spent about one-third of his remarks on policy. Although they may not have gone into great depth or detail in their policy discussions, they did not concentrate their utterances on character, or image.

These candidates were more likely to attack than acclaim on past deeds. Several contenders, like Buchanan, Forbes, and Taylor, did not have a record in elective office as a resource to use for acclaiming. On the other hand, everyone had plans for the future, which seem easier to acclaim than attack. General, abstract positions (goals and ideals) also seem easier to praise than to criticize.

Candidates were most likely to elaborate their acclaims and attacks using the strategies of extent and effects on the audience. In their defenses, denial was the most common strategy. These strategies are all relatively easy to use and relatively direct.

Alexander was in the group of candidates who devoted the most utterances to jobs and the economy, education, and welfare. Dole was in the highest group on education, on the deficit (in fact, he made almost four times as many comments as any other candidate in this category), on welfare, and on taxes. Forbes devoted many of his comments to jobs and the economy, education, Medicare and health (his medical savings accounts were frequently mentioned, and he had almost twice as many comments as the next candidate in this category), welfare, and taxes. Lugar was in the top group on jobs and the economy. Buchanan, Dornan, Gramm, Keyes, Specter, and Taylor failed to dominate any of these topics. Alexander, Dole, and Forbes participated in all three of these debates, which explains why they had so many comments in these categories— they had more turns at talking than most of the candidates.

However, Buchanan also participated in all three debates, which means that he was not taking advantage of his opportunities as much. He frequently, but not exclusively, discussed NAFTA and illegal immigration, which are conceptually related to jobs and the economy—although he often did not make that connection explicit.

CONCLUSION

Thus, these Republican primary debates relied heavily on acclaiming, frequently on attacking, and occasionally on defending. The candidates tended to target themselves (not their party) for acclaims, and they were prone to target one another (and the establishment to which many of them belonged) in their attacks (rather than Clinton). They devoted more of their utterances to policy than character. They revealed a tendency to attack on past deeds and personal qualities and to acclaim on future plans, general goals, and ideals.

NOTE

1. The numbers of attacks on other Republicans in Table 4.5 may vary somewhat from the number of attacks on other Republicans in Table 4.4. It was possible for a candidate to name more than one person in a single utterance (e.g., "Senators Dole, Dornan, Gramm, and Lugar all voted for a tax hike"). This would be considered a single attack on other Republicans in Table 4.5, but would appear as (separate) attacks on each of the other candidates in Table 4.4.

Chapter 5

Television Advertisements:
I'm More Conservative Than You

Dole, *"Conservative Agenda"*

[Bob Dole:] "The American people want change." And Bob Dole's conservative agenda will change America.

The first balanced budget plan in a generation. A pro-family, middle-class tax cut. [Bob Dole:] "We can cut taxes and balance the budget." Less government, lower taxes.

Bob Dole's conservative convictions and character will lead an American renewal.

[Bob Dole:] "Let's begin today, let us do it together. God Bless the United States of America."

Dole, *"Untested"*

Have you heard about Steve Forbes' risky ideas?

Forbes opposes mandatory life sentences for criminals convicted of three violent felonies.

Forbes' economic plan will add $186 billion a year to the deficit.

No wonder Forbes opposes the constitutional amendment to balance the budget.

The more you learn about Steve Forbes, the more questions you have.

Steve Forbes: Untested leadership. Risky ideas.

Buchanan, "Generations"

[Pat Buchanan:] "The future of America belongs to our children. We owe them the right to life.

A tax code that rewards work, marriage, and family.

A fair trade policy that keeps American jobs on American soil.

Safe streets.

Secure borders.

Schools that work.

A culture that promotes faith, family, and freedom.

That's the kind of America I want: for your family and mine."

Buchanan, "That Ain't Conservative"

Phil Gramm says, "I was conservative before conservative was cool." Wait a minute Phil. You voted for two of the biggest tax increases in history [$270 billion in 1982; $58 billion in 1983].

Phil Gramm says, "I was conservative before conservative was cool." But Phil, you voted to put two pro-abortion judges on the Supreme Court.

"I said, I was conservative before conservative was cool." But Phil, you voted to force racial quotas on American businesses. That ain't conservative. That ain't cool.

Forbes, "Deceptive"

Bob Dole, slipping in the polls, is desperate. Running negative ads claiming conservative Steve Forbes opposes three strikes and you're out for criminals.

Dole deceptively left out part of Forbes' statement. Here's what Steve Forbes really said: "I don't believe in three strikes and you're out. I believe in one strike and you're out."

Bob Dole: Deceiving voters. A Washington politician. It's time for a change.

Forbes, "Blue"

The last time Bob Dole ran for president he promised not to raise taxes. [Bob Dole:] "We don't need to raise tax rates." But after the election, Bob Dole voted to raise taxes $137 billion.

Again, Bob Dole promised voters, [Bob Dole:] "First, I'm opposed to increased tax rates." But then Bob Dole voted to raise tax rates.

Bob Dole: A Washington politician. It's time for a change.

Previous research on television spots focuses much more heavily on advertisements from the general election than from primaries (we review the literature on general election spots in Chapter 10). However, some studies have examined political spots during the primaries. This research investigates the proportion of acclaiming (positive) versus attacking (attacking) ads, as well as the consideration of policy (issue) and character (image) in primary spots.

Payne, Marlier, and Barkus (1989) found that 11% of the 1988 primary ads were negative. Kaid (1994) found that about 17% of the Republican and Democratic primary ads in 1992 were negative. Kaid and Ballotti (1991) found that 18% of the ads from 1968–1988 were negative. West (1993) reported that primary spots were more negative (55%) than general election ads (52%) between 1952–1992. Here, most studies report that negative ads account for between 10 and 20% of primary ads—the exception being West, who found about half of the ads were negative.[1]

Kaid and Ballotti (1991) analyzed 1089 presidential primary ads from 1968–1988, finding that 48% concerned issues and 32% images. West (1993) analyzed 150 presidential spots from 1972 to 1992. He reported that policy appeals were over twice as prominent in primaries (65%) than character (30% of ads; the remainder of the ads concerned the campaign and parties). Kaid (1994) found roughly similar results for the 1992 Republican and Democratic primaries: 59% of the television advertisements concerned image and 24% addressed issues. These studies are unanimous in reporting that primary spots focus more attention on policy (issues) than on character (image).

1996 REPUBLICAN PRIMARY SPOTS

We analyzed 96 television spots from the 1996 Republican primaries sponsored by five of the leading candidates (Dole: 19; Buchanan: 14; Forbes: 34; Alexander: 18; Gramm: 11). We discuss each conclusion derived from our analysis using illustrations from the advertisements we analyzed.

FUNCTIONS OF POLITICAL DISCOURSE

These television advertisements devoted more utterances to acclaiming (58%) than attacking (40%) or defending (2%). The contrast between acclaims and attacks (there were too few defenses to include that function) was significant ($X^2[df = 4] = 22.1$, $p < .001$). Alexander had the largest percent of acclaiming in his ads (78%); figures for the other candidates were clustered between 50% and 62%. For example, Alexander's advertisement "NH Aim" lists several of his accomplishments, revealing that he is "a conservative governor who balanced eight budgets, kept taxes

Table 5.1
Acclaims, Attacks, and Defenses: Primary TV Spots

	Acclaims	Attacks	Defenses
Alexander	83 (78%)	23 (21%)	1 (1%)
Buchanan	51 (53%)	45 (47%)	0 -
Dole	74 (50%)	70 (47%)	4 (3%)
Forbes	127 (54%)	100 (43%)	7 (3%)
Gramm	31 (62%)	19 (38%)	0 -
Total	366 (58%)	257 (40%)	12 (2%)

the fifth lowest of any state, reformed education, brought in the auto industry with Saturn, and later helped found a new business that now has 1200 employees." Similarly, Dole's spot "Conservative Agenda" acclaimed his goals: "Less government, lower taxes." Acclaims have the potential to attract supporters by increasing a candidate's apparent desirability. See Table 5.1.

Buchanan and Dole had the highest percentage of attacking remarks in their advertisements: 47%. For instance, in "That Ain't Conservative" Buchanan's ad attacked Gramm: "Phil Gramm says, 'I was conservative before conservative was cool'. But Phil, you voted to put two pro-abortion judges on the Supreme Court." Not only does this suggest that Gramm is pro-abortion—and many Republicans oppose that position—it also suggests that Gramm may not be truthful when he stresses his conservative ideology. For example, Dole's "Untested" spot reports that "Forbes opposes the constitutional amendment to balance the budget." Forbes was relatively close in percentage of attacking remarks (43%). Alexander, not surprisingly given his heavy emphasis on acclaiming, had the smallest percentage of attacks by a wide margin (21%). Attacking their competitors may incline some voters to view the targets less favorably, thereby improving the relative position of the sponsors of these attacks.

DEFENSE

These advertisements were not directly confrontational, as a political debate would be, so it is not surprising to find that defense is relatively uncommon. Still, some of these advertisements did engage in defensive discourse. Dole and Forbes (who were prime targets of attack during the primaries) were tied with the largest percentage of defense: 3% (as Table

Table 5.2
Defense Strategies: Primary TV Spots

	Denial
Alexander	1
Buchanan	0
Dole	4
Forbes	7
Gramm	0
Total	12

5.4 reveals below, they were also the primary targets in these advertisements). The only strategy used in these spots was denial. To illustrate, Dole's "Untested" spot attacked Forbes, claiming that Forbes opposed the "three strikes and you're out" approach to recidivism. Forbes responded in his ad "Deceptive," explaining that Dole was

running negative ads claiming conservative Steve Forbes opposes three strikes and you're out for criminals. Dole deceptively left out part of Forbes' statement. Here's what Steve Forbes really said: "I don't believe in three strikes and you're out. I believe in one strike and you're out."

This spot clearly denies Dole's accusation (it also counterattacks by charging that Dole is deceptive). Buchanan and Gramm did not make any defensive remarks in these spots. When a candidate is the target of a political attack, his or her apparent desirability to voters may suffer. Accordingly, some candidates choose to respond to such attacks with defense, in an attempt to restore their apparent desirability. See Table 5.2.

TARGET OF PERSUASIVE ATTACK

Overall, 71% of the attacking utterances in these commercials were directed toward other Republicans. For example, Forbes, in "Blue," declared that "The last time Bob Dole ran for president he promised not to raise taxes. [Bob Dole:] 'We don't need to raise tax rates.' But after the election, Bob Dole voted to raise taxes $137 billion." Here, Forbes attacks Dole for raising taxes and for breaking a pledge not to do so. Similarly, in "Untested" Dole attacked Forbes' future plans: "Forbes' economic plan will add $186 billion a year to the deficit." Dole (88%), Alexander

Table 5.3
Target of Attacks: Primary TV Spots

	Other Republicans	Establishment	Clinton
Alexander	19 (83%)	4 (17%)	0
Buchanan	22 (49%)	23 (51%)	0
Dole	62 (88%)	1 (1%)	7 (10%)
Forbes	69 (69%)	29 (29%)	2 (2%)
Gramm	10 (53%)	8 (42%)	1 (5%)
Total	182 (71%)	65 (25%)	10 (4%)

(83%), and Forbes (69%) were the candidates who attacked other Republicans the most. Attacking one's competitors may increase one's relative position. These data are displayed in Table 5.3.

We conducted a secondary analysis to determine which of these candidates were the most frequent target of attacks in televised primary advertisements. In these spots, Dole received the brunt of the attacks (40%), with Forbes (29%) and Alexander (23%) also receiving a fair share of the jibes. For example, in "Untested" Dole singled Forbes out for criticism when he charged that "Forbes opposes the Constitutional Amendment to balance the budget." In "Blue" Forbes went after Dole: "The last time Bob Dole ran for president he promised not to raise taxes [Bob Dole]: 'We don't need to raise tax rates.' But after the election, Bob Dole voted to raise taxes $137 billion." Dole's spot "The Great Pretender" attacked Lamar Alexander: "Just how liberal is Lamar Alexander? As Governor of Tennessee, he raised taxes and fees more than 50 times. He increased the sales tax 85%. And he doubled state spending." Neither Gramm (5%) nor Buchanan (3%) was singled out for attack as often as the other candidates. See Table 5.4.

The establishment was the second most frequent target in these spots, accounting for 25% of the attacks. In "No New Taxes" Buchanan derides the election year conversions of career politicians: "Friends, have you noticed all the career politicians are suddenly taking the no new taxes pledge?" This spot is clearly aimed at members of the current establishment ("career politicians"). Buchanan, an outsider who has held appointive but not elective office, aimed about half of his attacks (51%) at the establishment. Dole, with a long tenure in the Senate, attacked the establishment the least in these advertisements (1%). See Table 5.3.

Clinton (and the Democratic Party) was by far the least frequent target of attack in these Republican primary spots, receiving only 4% of the

Table 5.4
Target of Attacks on Republicans: Primary TV Spots

	Number of Attacks
Alexander	39 (23%)
Buchanan	5 (3%)
Dole	68 (40%)
Forbes	49 (29%)
Gramm	9 (5%)

negative remarks. For example, Dole's advertisement "Balanced Budget" asks viewers whether they "Remember how Bill Clinton promised New Hampshire a balanced budget plan, a middle-class tax cut? He never delivered." Dole devoted the largest proportion of attacks to Clinton (10%). On the other hand, neither Alexander nor Buchanan attacked Clinton once in these spots. See Table 5.3.

Although the candidates are competing against each other in these primaries, and not Clinton (yet), it seemed odd that only 4% of their attacks were directed toward the presumptive Democratic nominee. An attack against Clinton may make the sponsor look better to a Republican voter (if the voter agrees with the sentiments expressed in the attack). However, an attack against a Republican competitor can not only help the sponsor, but it may also reduce the relative favorability of a competitor. This can be especially important if the candidate being attacked is currently ahead in the public opinion polls. See Table 5.3.

POLICY VERSUS CHARACTER

As a group, these candidates spent virtually the same amount of time on policy (48%) as on character (52%). However, Buchanan (60%), Dole (59%), and Gramm (54%) all devoted more of their utterances in these ads to policy matters than character. A chi-square revealed that differences in topic by candidate were significant ($X^2[df = 4] = 20.7, p < .001$). For example, the spot "Alaska" from Buchanan promised that "We'll give the land of Alaska back to the people of Alaska." Similarly, "Conservative Agenda" by Dole pointed out that he had produced "the first balanced budget plan in a generation." Gramm's spot "Look Inside" boasted that "He wrote the Gramm-Rudman law to reduce the deficit." These three remarks all address policy matters. These data are displayed in Table 5.5.

Table 5.5
Policy versus Character: Primary TV Spots

| | Policy | | | | Character | | | |
	Deeds	Plans	Goals	Total	PQual	Leader	Ideals	Total
Alexander	2/15*	0/ 9	0/15	2/39 (39%)	14/17	2/ 6	5/21	21/44 (61%)
Buchanan	32/ 1	1/14	0/10	33/25 (60%)	6/17	1/ 3	5/ 6	12/26 (40%)
Dole	28/ 3	17/17	0/21	45/41 (59%)	7/ 3	6/11	12/19	25/33 (41%)
Forbes	34/ 8	1/27	1/18	36/52 (39%)	40/21	1/ 9	23/44	64/74 (61%)
Gramm	12/ 9	0/ 1	1/ 4	13/14 (54%)	5/ 7	1/ 2	0/ 8	6/17 (46%)
Total	108/36	19/68	2/68	129/172 (48%)	72/65	11/31	45/98	128/194 (52%)

*left number = attacks, right number = acclaims.

On the other hand, Forbes (61%) and Alexander (61%) devoted more attention to character than policy. In Forbes' ad "Voice" viewers were told of his positive personal qualities: "A true vision. An honest voice." Alexander's wife, in "Honey," explained to voters that "Lamar is very optimistic" and that "He listens well," two desirable personal traits.

The candidates were, with the sole exception of Alexander, far more likely to attack (108 times) than to acclaim (36 times) on the basis of past deeds. Forbes' spot "Conservative" attacked both Dole and Gramm for past votes in Congress: "Bob Dole and Phil Gramm both voted for a $366 billion tax increase in 1982. And they both voted for more tax increases in 1983, '85, '86, '89, '91 and 1992. $547 billion in tax increases." Pat Buchanan railed against NAFTA, arguing in "Trade" that "We've lost 300,000 jobs. We now have a record trade deficit. And wages have fallen." The relatively small number of acclaims based on past deeds could be related in part to the fact that two of the candidates, Buchanan and Forbes, had no record in elective office to brag about. While they could boast of other matters, one of the most important resources for a candidate's acclaims was not available to them.

On the other hand, the candidates were more likely to acclaim (68) than attack (19) on future plans (Dole's remarks were split evenly: 17 attacks and 17 acclaims on future plans). For instance, Alexander's ad "Future" promised to "establish a branch of the military to protect our borders from drugs and illegal immigration." In "Serious Business" Dole asked viewers to "take a look at our tax cut. Eighty-five percent of it goes to working families with children." These utterances promise to enact plans in the future if elected. It is surely easier to promise attractive future actions than to undermine the plans of others.

Similarly, only twice did goals serve as the basis for an attack (Forbes, Gramm), but goals frequently served as the basis for acclaims (68 times). Forbes repeatedly advocated that we "Scrap the tax code. Put in a flat tax" ("Power"). In Alexander's "Mudballs" spot he told voters that "I'd cut taxes and unleash free enterprise to create good new jobs." Without details about how these ends are to be accomplished, these utterances declare goals but do not provide specific future plans.

The five contenders were twice as likely (98 times) to acclaim their own ideals than they were to attack their opponents' ideals (45 times). Forbes managed to both attack and acclaim in "Pensions," announcing this contrast: "Bob Dole: Washington values. Steve Forbes: Conservative values." They were about three times as likely to praise their own leadership qualities than to attack their opponents on those grounds.

When they discussed their personal qualities, they were about as likely to attack (72 times) as to acclaim (65 times). For instance, in "Courage" Gramm's narrator told viewers that he possessed "Common sense. Uncommon courage." Clearly these are desirable personal characteristics.

Table 5.6
Strategies for Elaborating Acclaims and Attacks: Primary TV Spots

	Extent	Effects	Persistence	Consistency
Alexander	4/ 8*	0/ 0	3/2	0/0
Buchanan	9/ 0	4/ 2	2/1	3/0
Dole	8/ 4	3/12	3/0	5/0
Forbes	14/ 9	5/14	3/1	4/0
Gramm	3/ 0	1/ 0	0/1	1/0
Total	38/21	13/28	11/5	13/0

*left number = attacks, right number = acclaims.

He also attacked one of his opponents in "Allowance," complaining about his negative ads: "Forbes' money talks, but it's not telling the truth." Personal qualities are one potential point of comparison in candidates' attempts to appear preferable.

STRATEGIES FOR ELABORATING ACCLAIMS AND ATTACKS

These candidates' instances of acclaiming and attacking are most frequently elaborated with extent. In "Balanced Budget" Dole claimed that he was "saving New Hampshire tax payers $100 million a year." When he attacked Alexander in "Great Pretender," Dole declared that "As governor of Tennessee, he raised taxes and fees more than 50 times. He increased the sales tax 85%. And he doubled state spending." All of these utterances are intensified by describing extent. See Table 5.6.

The second most common form of development was to stress effects on the audience. In the "Conservative Agenda" spot, Dole described his "pro-family, middle-class tax cut." On the screen, a graphic stressed that this meant "$330 million for Iowa families." These politicians also elaborated with persistence and—when attacking—inconsistency. It is not surprising to see that consistency is rarely the basis of an acclaim. We tend to assume that people are consistent. Thus, violations of this expectation (inconsistency) are noteworthy for attacks, while consistent behavior is relatively unremarkable for acclaiming.

ISSUES ADDRESSED

Buchanan's spots devoted far more comments than any other candidate to jobs and the economy (mostly jobs allegedly lost to NAFTA). On education, Forbes (8) and Alexander (5) spent more time than the other candidates. Dole addressed the budget deficit in his commercials more than his competitors (17). Forbes' ads spent the most time on Medicare and health (8). Dole (7) and Gramm (5) talked most about welfare. Finally, Forbes (49) spent more than twice as much time as any other candidate on taxes, mostly presenting his flat tax as an alternative to the current system. Finally, Dole discussed crime and drugs more than the other four candidates (11). In sum, Buchanan led on the most important topic (jobs and the economy), Dole led on three topics (deficit, welfare, with Gramm, and crime and drugs), and Forbes led on three topics (education, with Alexander, Medicare and health, and taxes). Gramm and Alexander did not fair well on this analysis. These data are reported in Table 5.7.

IMPLICATIONS

These 1996 Republican primary spots used acclaiming (58%) more than attacking (40%). The figure we obtained for attacking (negative) ads is notably higher than the figures obtained in previous studies. Payne, Marlier, and Barkus (1989) reported that 11% of the spots in 1988 were negative. Kaid's (1994) study indicated that 17% of the Republican and Democratic spots from 1992 were negative. Kaid and Ballotti's (1991) analysis of television advertisements from 1968–1988 arrived at a figure of 18% negative ads. Only West's study (1993) varied from this norm, indicating that 55% of the spots from 1952 to 1992 he examined were negative. Why did our study reach a figure of 40%?

There are three obvious possible explanations for these discrepancies. First, it is possible that the 1996 Republican primary was much more negative than earlier campaigns. Second, our procedures were different, because we analyzed each utterance as acclaiming or attacking (or defending, although there were few defenses in these spots), while previous research classifies an entire advertisement as *either* positive *or* negative. However, many spots contain a combination of acclaims and attacks (or are partly positive and partly negative). If every ad were, say, 60% acclaims and 40% attacks, classifying entire ads would conclude that the ads were 100% positive. Third, it is possible that the definitions of acclaiming/positive and attacking/negative varied by study. Only research that applies our method to spots from earlier primaries can resolve this question with certainty, but we favor the second possible

Table 5.7
Issues Addressed: Primary TV Spots

Issue	Rank	Alexander	Buchanan	Dole	Forbes	Gramm
Jobs and the Economy	1	5	23	0	2	0
Education	2	5	0	0	8	0
Budget Deficit	3	2	3	17	0	2
Medicare and Health	4	0	0	0	8	2
Welfare Reform	5	1	0	7	0	5
Taxes	6	13	8	20	49	2
Crime and Drugs	6	0	1	11	0	0
Other	---	15	23	31	22	16

explanation. We acknowledge that it is possible that candidates have become a bit more brazen in their attacks over time. It is also possible that the definitions varied some from study to study, which could account for West's divergent results (furthermore, West used two samples, "typical" and "prominent" ads, and his sample of "prominent" ads may have been more negative than his sample of "typical" ads). Nevertheless, we believe our procedure is preferable because it allows for a more precise description of the amount of acclaiming and attacking.

Alexander had the largest percentage of self-praise, while Buchanan and Dole had the highest percentage of attacking remarks. Dole and Forbes did most of the defense, which was relatively infrequent (2% of all remarks). The ads targeted other Republicans (each another) the most, the establishment second, and the presumed Democratic nominee, Clinton, the least. Buchanan (who has never held elective office) attacked the establishment the most, and Dole (Senate majority leader) attacked it the least. Although it makes perfect sense that Republicans have to make themselves appear preferable to their opponents—other Republicans (and Democrats in a Democratic primary would want to appear preferable to other Democrats)—we were surprised that Republicans (targets of 71% of attacks) and the establishment (which included several prominent Republican candidates, targets of 25% of the attacks) were attacked so much more than Clinton and the Democratic Party.

These spots were split about evenly between policy and character. Kaid and Ballotti (1991) reported that primary ads from 1968–1988 dealt with policy 50% more than with character. West (1993) found that twice as many spots concerned policy than character. Kaid (1994) reported that 1992 spots from Republicans and Democrats were about twice as likely to stress image (character) than policy (issues). Again, this discrepancy could stem from the fact that we classified each theme as devoted to policy or character, rather than labeling entire ads as either policy-oriented or character-based. A study of televised political spots from earlier primaries would shed more light on these differences.

Gramm, Dole, and Buchanan were more likely to address policy, while Forbes and Alexander focused more on character. Acclaims and attacks were developed most often with extent and effects. Finally, Buchanan's ads devoted more remarks to the most important topic, while Dole and Forbes each led on three of the remaining topics.

NOTE

1. West actually conducted two analyses: one of "typical" ads selected at random and one of "prominent" spots as defined by Jamieson (1996; actually, he used an earlier edition of her book). West's findings on image versus issue were

taken from his typical advertisement study; we were unable to find a figure for positive versus negative primary ads from his typical advertisement study; the figures of 52% and 55% are taken from his prominent advertisement analysis. The prominent ads may well have been more negative than the average ads.

Chapter 6

Talk Radio: What Are the Candidates Saying about Each Other?

Lamar Alexander: My agenda is job growth, more freedom from Washington, personal responsibility. . . .

You know, the shirt [his red and black plaid] for a long time was better known than I am, but now I am ahead of it, and that means I'm probably doing pretty well. . . .

I think Mr. Forbes' idea [of a flat tax] is flaky. . . .

The problem with Mr. Forbes, and I think it comes because of his relative inexperience, is that he took those principles and took them all the way out to the edge, to the Jerry Brown idea. . . .

Pat Buchanan: Our trade surplus is now a $15-billion trade deficit with Mexico; 300,000 lost American jobs [because of NAFTA]. . . .

Look, if we Republicans don't look out for the economic interests, and the preservation of jobs of working people and middle-class people who support us on right to life, they're going to leave us. . . .

Some of these treaties, which are done, . . . they're not done for the benefit of workers or America's middle class; they're done for the benefit of the corporations, whose interests no longer coincide with America. . . .

There's one conservative who believes in right to life, who believes in an America first trade policy, an America first defense policy, who can win. And that's Pat Buchanan. Steve Forbes is a social liberal on the social issues. Bob Dole is Bob Dole. He's a man of pragmatism of the center, of compromise. . . .

Bob Dole: The first thing I would do would be to send a constitutional amendment for a balanced budget to Congress. . . .

Remember President Clinton said he was going to end welfare as he knew it. Well, he hasn't ended anything. Welfare is the same as it was when he came in. . . .

So I would say to Mr. Forbes, you know, understand this program [ethanol] before you knock it and before you try to phase it out. . . .

I'm honest, I listen, I'm a person of integrity. . . .

Steve Forbes: The principal source of power in Washington for decades has been politicians trading favors and loopholes for contributions and political support. That's why the tax code is a form of legalized corruption. . . .

The flat tax with a tax cut will help home ownership, it will reduce interest rates, it will help you keep more of what you earn. . . .

I've always been personally opposed to abortions. I've felt it was a great wrong. My whole family life is a refutation. . . .

We need term limits. It forces politicians—they can't entrench themselves in office. . . .

Phil Gramm: If you want to destroy the family, what you would do is take control of local schools away from parents, give it to government; have them teach that any life style is equivalent to the traditional family. I want to eliminate the Department of Education. . . .

I have a proven record in supporting right to life, in supporting pro-family measures. . . .

His [Buchanan's] protectionist views not only threaten Iowa; building a wall around America and going hiding under a rock somewhere would turn Iowa into a dustbowl. . . .

Steve Forbes . . . is not a social conservative. He . . . has every day of his life until he got into politics been pro-abortion. . . .

This chapter examines the Republican candidates' use of political talk radio to enhance their candidacies in the Iowa Republican caucuses. We begin with a brief review of the most relevant literature concerning talk radio and politics. After that, we apply our method of analyzing acclaiming, attacking and defending themes to discourse on talk station WHO-AM Des Moines on the morning of the Iowa Republican Party caucus (which is of obvious importance because it was the first legitimate contest for convention delegates, Louisiana's primary being boycotted by the party establishment).

POLITICS AND TALK RADIO

The talk radio format has proliferated in the airwaves. Consider that from 1989 to 1994, the number of news/talk stations nationwide has increased from 308 to 1,028 (Petrozello, 1994). Moreover, 18% of American adults report listening to political talk shows at least twice a week (Cappella, Turow, & Jamieson, 1996). A variety of anecdotal evidence suggests that talk radio can be highly influential in the electoral process (Zerbinos, 1995/1996).

Crittendon's (1971) early study of talk radio found that the format is responsible for inciting people to political activity such as voting and town meeting attendance. More recent studies reiterate this finding, with a few caveats. Hofstetter et al. (1993) found an association between talk radio listening and increased political involvement. Furthermore, such listening was not associated with cynicism and political isolation. Hollander (1995/1996; 1996) also found a strong association between regular talk radio listening and political activity. Owen (1996) attributed the 1994 Republican takeover of Congress to conservative candidates' abilities to tap talk radio's influence.

Clearly, talk radio is a political force that deserves more attention. Furthermore, because talk radio is a haven for conservative points of view (Times-Mirror Center, 1993), we believe it is appropriate to examine how the Republican candidates used it to their advantage during the 1996 primaries.

WHO-AM DES MOINES

The first major test of political viability among the Republican candidates was the Iowa Republican caucus on February 12, 1996 (earlier contests in Alaska and Louisiana were shunned by most contenders). A rhetorical event held that day provides an opportunity to find out how the Republican primary candidates used talk radio in Iowa.

All eight of the candidates with political organizations in Iowa (Bob Dole, Pat Buchanan, Steve Forbes, Lamar Alexander, Phil Gramm, Dick Lugar, Alan Keyes, and Morry Taylor) appeared on WHO-AM's Jan Mickelson show the morning of the caucus. One by one, they each came in for a half-hour discussion with Mr. Mickelson and the callers to the program. The conversations dealt with a variety of topics, not the least of which was their opponents' policies and character.

We analyzed the half-hour segments of the five leading candidates: Dole, Forbes, Buchanan, Gramm, and Alexander (Roper Center, 1996). Here, we discuss the conclusions derived from our analysis of their collective talk radio themes of acclaiming, attacking, and defending. In order, we will describe the candidates' use of acclaiming, attacking, and defending; discuss the targets of the attacks; illustrate the tendencies to discuss policy or character; demonstrate the strategies used for elaborating acclaims and attacks; discuss the defense strategies used; and finally, enumerate the issues on which the candidates focused.

FUNCTIONS OF TALK RADIO APPEARANCES

As a group, the candidates' statements functioned most often as acclaiming (66%), followed by attacking (28%) and defending (6%). For example, Dole declared that "The first thing I would do would be to

Table 6.1
Acclaims, Attacks, and Defenses: Talk Radio

Candidate	Acclaims	Attacks	Defenses
Alexander	48 (72%)	17 (25%)	2 (3%)
Buchanan	51 (60%)	31 (36%)	3 (4%)
Dole	79 (76%)	16 (15%)	9 (9%)
Forbes	50 (59%)	27 (32%)	8 (9%)
Gramm	42 (61%)	25 (36%)	2 (3%)
Total	270 (66%)	116 (28%)	24 (6%)

send a constitutional amendment for a balanced budget to Congress," a clear policy acclaim. Gramm attacked Buchanan during his segment: "His protectionist views not only threaten Iowa; building a wall around America and going hiding under a rock somewhere would turn Iowa into a dustbowl." Statistical analysis showed that the difference in distribution of acclaiming and attacking is significant (X^2[df = 4] = 14.4, p < .01). See Table 6.1. Because defenses were so rare, they are not included in the chi-square.

ACCLAIMS

With 79 acclaims, Dole far exceeded the other candidates, whose instances of acclaiming ranged from 51 to 42. For example, Dole spoke of why high-profile Iowa Republicans had endorsed him: "I've been elected and reelected [majority leader] six times by the Chuck Grassleys and others in the Senate because I'm honest, I listen, I'm a person of integrity, and I want to move the country forward." Most voters would surely agree that honesty, integrity, and the desire for progress are desirable qualities for a nominee to possess. Dole clearly presented the greatest volume of praise.

With 51 acclaims, Buchanan was second in amount of praise. For example, he touted his strong following in other states: "The crawfish farmers down there [in Louisiana] support me, just as the tomato farmers in Florida do." Being supported by a major constituent group is important because it indicates that a candidate is politically viable, which is a positive quality. Moreover, one might surmise that demonstrating the support of other farmers might help attract the many farmers in Iowa. Just behind Buchanan was Forbes, who made 50 acclaims, including his thoughts on the virtues of his flat tax proposal: "The flat tax with a tax cut will help home ownership, it will reduce interest rates, it will help you keep more of what you earn." Owning a home, having lower interest rates, and keeping more of what you earn are all desirable goals.

Not too far behind Buchanan and Forbes was Alexander with 48 acclaims. For instance, he praised his priorities: "My agenda is job growth, more freedom from Washington, personal responsibility." The ability to bring more jobs, freedom, and responsibility is something voters would find desirable in a president. Finally, the candidate with the fewest acclaims, Gramm, still used this strategy 42 times. As an example, he discussed his potential to create party unity when he claimed, "I think I'm the one candidate who can put both halves of the party together." Being a source of unity is something of obvious importance to any party, including the Republicans at the time of the Iowa caucus. So, all of the candidates were prolific in their acclaims during their talk radio appearances.

ATTACKS

With 31 total attacks, Buchanan led the field. For instance, he criticized the economic establishment: "The standard of living of working Americans is falling, while the stock market soars." The inconsistency between prosperity for investors and decline for workers is described here as a negative, unjust trend. Just behind Buchanan was Forbes with 27 attacks. He verbally took on the tax code when he stated, "The principal source of power in Washington for decades has been politicians trading favors and loopholes for contributions and political support. That's why the tax code today is a form of legalized corruption." By almost any moral standard, corruption is a negative quality that is highly undesirable in a politician. Both of these statements illustrate attacks in this talk radio discourse.

Also relatively close behind Buchanan was Gramm with his 25 such statements. Referring to his opponent Steve Forbes, Gramm charged, "He has every day of his life until he got into politics been pro-abortion." Calling an opponent "pro-abortion" can only be intended as an attack on the day of a conservative caucus in a midwestern state. Thus, we see how another candidate incorporated attacks into this occasion.

Dole (with 16) and Alexander (with 17) engaged in markedly less attacking than the others. Examples of these attacks include Dole taking on the IRS: "They spend ten billion dollars a year, got 100,000 employees, spend more—twice as much as the CIA, five times as much as the FBI." Where frugality is a conservative value, spending "five times as much as the FBI" is definitely a vice, and therefore this utterance functions as an attack on the establishment and on members of the establishment.

Likewise, Alexander provided an example of his attacks when he said, "I think Mr. Forbes' idea [of a flat tax] is flaky." Since a president should be intelligent and sharp, calling an opponent "flaky" serves as an attack. Both of these verbal incidents show how Dole and Alexander also made attacks, regardless of their less frequent deployment. Thus, all candidates attacked, although Buchanan, Forbes, and Gramm did so more frequently than Alexander or Dole.

DEFENSES

Like the television spots (but unlike the debates), this forum did not provide for direct confrontation. For this reason, we are not surprised that defense utterances are relatively infrequent. Even the candidate with the most defense utterances (Dole, with nine such statements) only devoted 9% of his persuasive remarks to defense. Nonetheless, defense strategies were occasionally employed on Iowa talk radio. For instance, Dole countered assertions that he was ineffective as Senate Majority Leader by asserting, "The problem is some people fail to understand in the Senate you have to have 60 votes to shut off debate." Forbes used defense eight times to deflect criticism, including remarks denying the accusation that he was pro-abortion: [I've] "always been personally opposed to abortions. I've felt it was a great wrong." Dole and Forbes engaged in defense more than twice as much as the other candidates.

However, Buchanan, Gramm, and Alexander used such strategies as well. For example, consider Buchanan's defense against the charge that he was anti–free trade: "Look—let's take a look. We've got a $200 billion dollar trade deficit. That means that we Americans are buying $200 billion more from abroad than we sell abroad." Gramm struck a defensive pose as well when he countered host Mickelson's assertion Gramm was seriously behind in the polls: "I don't think the polls show that anybody's taken off. I think basically, as of today, Senator Dole has a slight lead." Likewise, Alexander also defended himself when Mickelson said he had "gone after" the National Education Association while governor of Tennessee: "Well, they went after me. I thought I was just going forward with a great idea of paying teachers . . . who are really good more for being good. And they [NEA] don't want that." Each of these instances shows that even though defense themes were not used widely, certain charges required persuasive defense measures.

When candidates are under attack, they may choose to engage in defense strategies. These utterances allow them to repair their desirability as potential nominees, the charges against them notwithstanding. Still, acclaims and attacks are the predominant discourse strategies here.

Table 6.2
Target of Attacks: Talk Radio

Candidate	Other Republicans	Establishment	Clinton/Democrats
Alexander	10 (59%)	5 (29%)	2 (12%)
Buchanan	19 (61%)	10 (32%)	2 (6%)
Dole	6 (38%)	4 (25%)	6 (38%)
Forbes	8* (32%)	16 (64%)	1 (4%)
Gramm	18 (86%)	3 (14%)	0
Total	61 (55%)	38 (35%)	11 (10%)

*Forbes also attacked Richard Lugar's consumption tax proposal twice. These two attacks are not included above.

TARGET OF CANDIDATE ATTACKS

The majority of candidates' attacks (55%) are directed at each other. For example, Buchanan chided Forbes for being a "social liberal on the social issues." Another 35% of the attacks were directed at the establishment. Lamar Alexander typified such attacks: "I believe a part-time citizen Congress would be a better Congress." This is clearly an attack on the Washington establishment or career politicians. Notably, only 10% of the attacks were targeted at President Clinton, the opposing party's presumed nominee. Referring to his Republican opponents, Buchanan said, "They'd all be better presidents than Bill Clinton." Attacks on Clinton were less frequent than attacks on each other. See Table 6.2.

As the leading attacker, Buchanan saved the majority (61%) of his attacks for other Republicans, 32% for the establishment, and only 6% for Clinton. The rest of the field, save for Forbes, also attacked their fellow party members the most. Forbes' attacks tended to rebuke the establishment most often. Dole attacked Clinton as much as he attacked his fellow Republicans. Gramm also attacked the establishment least among the candidates, quite possibly because he was a veteran of an important part of the establishment, the Congress.

Attacking one's competitors may influence voters to see one's opponents more negatively. Thus, the voter is less likely to vote for the target of the attack. This helps the attacker indirectly if those voters who are influenced are potential converts to support his/her campaign. Table 6.3 documents the number of attacks each candidate endured.

Table 6.3
Number of Attacks on Republicans: Talk Radio

Candidate	Number of Attacks
Alexander	10 (10%)
Buchanan	21 (22%)
Dole	17 (17%)
Forbes	29 (30%)
Gramm	20 (21%)
Total	97 (100%)

POLICY VERSUS CHARACTER

Collectively, the Republican candidates appearing on WHO-AM that morning addressed policy issues (57%) more than character (43%). Statistical analysis found the difference in distribution of remarks between policy and character among these candidates to be significant (X^2[df = 4] = 47.2, p < .001). These data are displayed in Table 6.4.

Dole, Forbes, and Alexander all used more policy statements than character statements. Gramm used 36 of each. Only Buchanan chose to emphasize character (52) over policy (35). Dole used more than twice as many policy utterances (71) as character statements (33). An example of a policy statement is his acclaim of a past deed: "Last Wednesday we passed the Freedom to Farm Act." Here, Dole hopes to score political points by pointing to his past accomplishments that benefit people in Iowa particularly.

Forbes' discussion of policy centered on his flat-tax proposal: "It's going to help agriculture, it's going to help businesses, it's going to help, most importantly, the American people and the American family." His constant repetition of "it's going to . . ." stresses his future plans for economic policy.

Lamar Alexander also discussed policy more than character. He spoke of his general goal to "eliminate most deductions to pay for the savings [of a capital gains tax cut] and have a simpler internal revenue code." In this excerpt, Alexander's statement focuses on a general type of initiative he would like to implement as president.

Buchanan alone stressed character over policy, including his self-praise for leadership qualities. For example, he asserted, "I believe I can be the leader with the vision to take this country into the twenty-first century."

Table 6.4
Policy versus Character: Talk Radio

| | Policy | | | | Character | | | |
	Deeds	Plans	Goals	Total	PQual	Leader	Ideals	Total
Alexander	8	20	8	36 (54%)	8	7	16	31 (46%)
Buchanan	25	3	7	35 (40%)	20	5	27	52 (60%)
Dole	29	14	28	71 (68%)	19	5	9	33 (32%)
Forbes	22	30	6	58 (68%)	13	0	14	27 (32%)
Gramm	11	11	14	36 (50%)	9	2	25	36 (50%)
Total	95	78	63	236 (57%)	69	19	91	179 (43%)

Here, he hopes to favorably compare his vision with that of the other candidates.

Buchanan also stressed personal qualities more than any other candidate. A prime example of such praise comes when he relates the story that prominent political columnist David Broder had commented that "your [Buchanan's] voice is becoming Reaganesque." In this instance, Buchanan compares his personal qualities with those of the revered Republican Ronald Reagan.

Finally, Buchanan and Gramm almost tied in praising their ideals most. For instance, Gramm stated his beliefs about families: "I think the American people understand that we've got to have strong families to have a strong America." In this statement, Gramm points to his support of the traditional family in order to attract voters.

Summarizing, one should note again that the five Republican candidates spent significantly more time discussing policy issues over character issues. Notably, only Buchanan chose to focus on character over policy.

STRATEGIES FOR ELABORATING ACCLAIMS AND ATTACKS

This field of candidates elaborated their acclaims and attacks largely by pointing to extent and effects (see Table 6.5). When elaborating acclaims, Forbes made the most claims of positive effects on the audience. Referring to social security, Forbes said that "Younger people, I think, are going to be very excited as they learn more and more about how we can save Social Security for them." In other words, younger voters should be excited about what a Forbes presidency could do for them. On the other hand, Dole led in elaborating acclaims by appealing to the extent of benefits on the audience, as exemplified by his earlier reference to the "biggest tax cut in history" for which he took credit.

Elaborating acclaims and attacks has a twofold benefit. Elaborating on acclaims of oneself allows a candidate to demonstrate in a detailed, concrete way how he/she is attractive to the voter. Likewise, elaborating attacks on one's opponents allows a candidate to underscore the undesirability of supporting his/her opponent.

STRATEGIES FOR DEFENSE

As mentioned earlier, there was relatively little defense offered by the candidates in this talk radio forum. In fact, there was a mere total of 24 such utterances out of the total of 410 utterances. These data can be found in Table 6.6.

Table 6.5
Strategies for Elaborating Acclaims and Attacks: Talk Radio

Candidate	Extent	Effects	Persistence	Consistency	Vulnerable
Alexander	0/0*	0/1	1/0	0/0	0/0
Buchanan	7/0	6/0	0/0	0/0	0/0
Dole	4/5	1/0	0/0	2/0	0/0
Forbes	0/2	3/7	0/0	1/0	1/0
Gramm	5/1	4/0	3/0	1/0	0/0
Total	16/8	14/8	4/0	4/0	1/0

*left number = attacks, right number = acclaims.

Of these, the majority consisted of simple denial of guilt. For instance, when asked to respond to Buchanan's charges that he was pro-abortion, Forbes replied, "On the subject of abortion, I do want abortions to disappear in America. They are a tragedy." As such, he flatly denied the charge of being pro-abortion.

Dole shifted the blame when sincerity about changing the way Washington conducts its affairs was questioned. Dole responded: "Well, let me explain—first of all, of course, that's been controlled by a Democratic Congress." In other words, Dole shifted the blame for the way business has been done to the opposing party.

The differentiation strategy is illustrated by Forbes fending off accusations that he is pro-abortion. When confronted with a letter he signed supporting a group favoring abortion rights, Forbes begged to differ: "That [referring to the letter] was a dinner which I was a part of to help raise funds for Republican candidates. Obviously I don't agree with everything that every organization that I helped out that helps Republicans on, but—so that was just a fund raiser." In other words, Forbes explained the difference between the letter in question (a dinner fund raiser) and the accusatory interpretation that the letter was an abortion rights manifesto.

Finally, the single instance of defeasibility comes from Dole's *apologia* for not bringing more legislation to a vote. He asserted, "In the Senate you have to have 60 votes to shut off debate. You can't shut off debate. You can't pass a bill. We only have 53 Republicans." In other words, Dole says he should not be blamed since such legislative failings were beyond his control.

To summarize defense elaborations, it is notable that so little (6%) defense occurred. As described earlier, since these appearances were not

Table 6.6
Defense Strategies: Talk Radio

Candidate	Denial	Differentiation	Shift Blame	Defeasibility	Total
Alexander	1	0	0	1	2
Buchanan	2	1	0	0	3
Dole	5	1	3	0	9
Forbes	6	2	0	0	8
Gramm	1	1	0	0	2
Total	15 (63%)	5 (21%)	3 (13%)	1 (4%)	24

direct confrontations, immediate defensive responses to attacks might not have been necessary or appropriate. The candidates relied heavily on the simple denial strategy.

ISSUES ADDRESSED

The fact that there were more statements related to policy lends importance to examining what issues the candidates were talking about. Taxes (73) was the most frequent issue category, followed by jobs and the economy (25), education (17), the budget deficit (16), and welfare (10). See Table 6.7.

Buchanan talked the most about jobs (10), which was the most important issue to voters. The second most important issue was education, and Alexander spoke the most about education (12). Dole had the most to say about the budget deficit (7), the third most important issue. Dole (5) and Gramm (4) discussed the fifth issue, welfare, about the same amount. Finally, Forbes (29) and Dole (24) devoted the largest number of remarks to taxes. No one mentioned Medicare and health or crime and drugs in these discourses.

IMPLICATIONS

In these talk radio appearances at the dawn of the Republican primary season there were more than twice as many acclaims as attacks, and relatively few defenses. Dole praised the most while Buchanan attacked the most. Forbes was attacked frequently, so it is not surprising that he offered so many defenses. Because the Republican primary is a contest among members of the same party, it is not surprising that most of the attacks were directed at fellow partisans.

Table 6.7
Issues Addressed: Talk Radio

Issue	Rank	Alexander	Buchanan	Dole	Forbes	Gramm
Jobs and the Economy	1	4	10	1	4	6
Education	2	12	0	3	1	2
Budget Deficit	3	4	0	7	0	5
Medicare and Health	4	0	0	0	0	0
Welfare Reform	5	1	0	5	0	4
Taxes	6	10	1	24	29	9
Crime and Drugs	6	0	0	0	0	0
Other	---	6	22	31	21	10

When acclaiming, attacking, and defending, the candidates collectively discussed policy more than character. Buchanan was alone in addressing character more than policy. Finally, these acclaims and attacks were developed most frequently with extensiveness and effects on the audience, Iowans in this case.

Part III

Nominating Conventions: Anointing the Chosen

Chapter 7

Keynote Speeches: It's Great to Be a Republican/Democrat!

Susan Molinari's 8/13/96 Republican Keynote (excerpts)

Tonight, I, too, want to talk to you about the American dream because it seems to be slipping out of reach for too many of us. And I want to tell America how Bob Dole and Jack Kemp and the Republican Party can make that dream easier to achieve again. . . .

You know, people are having trouble just staying afloat, and it's easy to see why. Bill Clinton passed the largest tax increase in history, and now Americans pay almost 40 cents of every dollar they earn in taxes—the most ever. Every year Bill Clinton has been in office, taxes have been higher, and family incomes have been lower.

Bob Dole and Jack Kemp have a better idea—an economic plan for every American who is working harder and taking home less. The Dole-Kemp plan will give every man and woman in this country a 15%, across the board tax cut! It is good news. It's good news because it's a plan for all of us.

It's a plan for the single mother with two kids in Detroit who's trying to pay her bills and pay for child care, too. She'll get $1000 from the Republican's child tax credit. It's a plan for a grandmother in St. Louis who was hit hard by Bill Clinton's tax increase on Social Security benefits. She's gonna get to keep all the benefits she's earned and deserves. And it's a plan for a young couple in Pittsburgh desperately trying to buy their first home. For them, it will mean lower interest rates and mortgage payments they can afford. . . .

And we've got to stop the explosion in drug use by our kids that we've seen over the last three years. . . .

Now, think about Bill Clinton. He promises one thing and does another. He hopes we will forget his broken promises. But I ask you:

Have you forgotten that Bill Clinton promised a middle-class tax cut then passed the largest tax increase in American history? I didn't think so.

Have you forgotten that Bill Clinton promised commonsense health care reform, only to impose a huge Washington-run bureaucracy health care system on all of us?

And have you forgotten that Bill Clinton promised to balance the budget first in five years, then ten, then seven, then nine, then seven, then eight, and went on to veto the first balanced budget in 25 years?

[NO] Americans know that Bill Clinton's promises have the lifespan of a Big Mac on Air Force One. . . .

We must choose the better man, for a better America: and that man, we know, is Bob Dole.

Evan Bayh's 8/27/96 Democratic Keynote (excerpts)

After 12 years of skyrocketing deficits and quadrupling debt, President Clinton is meeting the challenge of balancing our budget. He's brought the deficit down by 60 percent in just the last four years. He and Vice President Gore are cutting the federal work force by 250,000 for the smallest federal government since President Kennedy. And when his opponents threatened our values with deep cuts in Medicare, Medicaid, education and the environment, President Clinton said no and our party stood with him. And when his opponents shut the government down, President Clinton said no again and we stood with him again and the American people won.

Bill Clinton is balancing the budget while keeping our pledge to the elderly, the young and our future, not because it is easy, yes, but because it is right. And he's meeting our economic challenges.

And President Clinton's protecting our traditional value of making hard work pay. He fought for an increase in the minimum wage and 10 million Americans got a pay raise. He cut taxes for 15 million families who get up every morning and work hard all day long, only to get a paycheck on Friday that still leaves them in poverty. But now, anyone who works 40 hours a week in America will not live in poverty. . . .

His agenda balances the budget to keep interest rates down and the economy strong. It protects against wholesale cuts for the elderly, the sick, the young, the environment and the fight against crime and drugs. And it provides for tax cuts, not an election-year gimmick but targeted tax cuts aimed at families trying to care for and educate our kids. A $500 credit for every child, $1,500 to help pay for the first two years of college, a $10,000 deduction for education and training after high school. We create real opportunity with these tax cuts and what's more, we can pay for them. Now that's something our opponents just can't say. They know their plan is too expensive. It will explode the deficit, raise interest rates, slow the economy and still require deeper cuts in the things for which we care. . . .

Today more than a million fewer Americans are on welfare than four years ago. And child support collections are up 40 percent. We're helping families back on their feet and into jobs. . . .

Let us elect the men who are leading the challenges for our country, Bill Clinton and Al Gore, president and vice president of the United States of America!

The keynote speech is supposed to be a highlight of the convention, a key speech. The purpose is to set the tone (note) of the convention. This speech is an opportunity for the party to celebrate its values and policies—and its candidate. It is an opportunity to celebrate unity if the party is unified and appeal for unity if it is divided. The keynote speaker also attacks the opposing party and its nominee (or presumptive nominee). Blankenship, Robson, and Williams (1997) note four functions:

(a) reaffirming the general commitment this country has to the electoral process and to the "rightness of the American way or dream" (reenacting the vision of America, celebrating the party's history and tradition, what we stand for, who we are); (b) formally anointing and legitimating the parties' nominees despite the battle that preceded the convention; (c) identifying the enemy and rallying the troops for the general election ahead; and (d) demonstrating party unity (or creating the impression of unity) while providing public introduction to the candidates' rhetorical agendas for the general election. (p. 1021)

In this chapter, we focus more on the last two of these functions: "identifying the enemy" (attacking the opposition candidate and/or party) and "rallying the troops" (acclaiming candidate and/or party) as well as "providing public introduction to the candidates' rhetorical agendas" (again, acclaiming and attacking).

In previous years, the party nominating conventions were the time and place for selecting the party's nominee. However, contentious conventions (especially the 1968 Democratic convention) are believed to have hurt the parties and their nominees' chances to win the presidency. As a result, both parties moved to select and commit more delegates prior to the nominating conventions, and to do so earlier than before (see, e.g., Felknor, 1992). This process of "front-loading" means that the nominee is known well before the convention, depriving the event of its drama (and much of its divisiveness).

PAST RESEARCH ON KEYNOTE SPEECHES

Considerable research has investigated nominating convention keynotes (see, e.g., Barefield, 1970; Bradley, 1960; Dow & Tonn, 1993; Frye & Krohn, 1977; Henry, 1988; Newell & King, 1974; Pitt, 1968; Smith, 1975; Smith, 1962; Thompson, 1979a, 1979b; for a review, see Benoit, Blaney, & Pier, 1996). While none of these studies adopted the functional theory of campaign discourse as their method, there were hints of the appropriateness of this analysis in some research on keynotes: Benoit and Gustainis (1986) found evidence of praise and attack; Miles (1960) reported praise and ridicule; and Claussen (1965, 1966) reported praise.

Benoit, Blaney, and Pier (1996) analyzed Democratic and Republican keynote speeches from 1960–1996. Keynotes were replete with praise (473 instances) and attack (439 times); defense was found, but not often (12 times). Republicans acclaimed (282) more than they attacked (222), while Democrats attacked (217) more than they acclaimed (191). The sharpest contrast came in comparing which party held the White House: incumbents acclaimed much more often (287) than they attacked (186), while challengers attacked considerably more (253) than they acclaimed (186). As a group, keynotes from 1960–1996 directed more comments to the party than the candidates, although in recent years—as candidates became more central to the process and parties somewhat less important—this trend reversed. These speeches focused on policy (549) more often than they addressed character (347).

THE 1996 KEYNOTES

In 1996, the Republican nominating convention occurred first. Susan Molinari's keynote was given on August 15 in San Diego. Evan Bayh's Democratic keynote was presented two weeks later, on August 27 in Chicago (see Sabato, 1997a). While focusing primarily on how the conventions were for and about women, Blankenship, Robson, and Williams (1997) spend some time on Molinari's keynote. They observe that she "amused . . . abused . . . [a]nd she enthused" (p. 1038), and that she was more successful than Bayh at drawing the crowd's attention. Notably for our purposes, they observe that she attacked and acclaimed: "She did take some swipes at Clinton's economic policy and she did reassure her audience that Dole could do better" (p. 1039). Of course, their goal was not to provide a comprehensive view of our functions of campaign discourse.

FUNCTIONS OF KEYNOTE SPEECHES

Together, the 1996 keynote speeches devoted more utterances to acclaiming (58) than to attacking (31). Bayh engaged in more praise of his party and candidate (33) than attack of his opponent (10), and more praise than Molinari (who had 25 acclaims). A chi-square calculated on Molinari's and Bayh's acclaims and attacks was significant ($X^2[df = 1] = 5.2$, $p < .05$). For instance, Bayh declared that President Clinton has "brought the deficit down by 60 percent in just the last four years. He and Vice President Gore are cutting the federal work force by 250,000 for the smallest federal government since President Kennedy." Similarly,

Table 7.1
Acclaims, Attacks, and Defenses: Keynotes

	Acclaims	Attacks	Defenses
Molinari	25 (54%)	21 (46%)	0
Bayh	33 (77%)	10 (23%)	0
Total	58 (65%)	31 (35%)	0

in the passage from Molinari's keynote quoted above, she praised the Republican nominee's tax cut plan: "The Dole-Kemp plan will give every man and woman in this country a 15%, across the board tax cut!" So, both keynote speakers offered frequent praise in their speeches.[1]

While Molinari did present more praise (25) than attack (21), she engaged in slightly more than twice as much attack as Bayh (10 attacks). For instance, in the excerpt at the beginning of this chapter, Molinari criticized Clinton's tax increase: "Bill Clinton passed the largest tax increase in history, and now Americans pay almost 40 cents of every dollar they earn in taxes—the most ever. Every year Bill Clinton has been in office, taxes have been higher, and family incomes have been lower." Bayh's address also contained several attacks. For example, he discussed the Dole/Kemp tax cut proposal: "They know their plan is too expensive. It will explode the deficit, raise interest rates, slow the economy and still require deeper cuts in the things for which we care." So, both candidates repeatedly used acclaims and attacks. However, neither candidate used persuasive defense in these keynotes. These data are displayed in Table 7.1.

TARGET OF ACCLAIMS AND ATTACKS

Both Molinari and Bayh directed more of their remarks to their party's nominee than to the party itself (or than to both candidate and party together). Eight times as many instances of praise were directed toward the two candidates (40) as to the parties (5) and about five times as many attacks were aimed at the two candidates (26) than at their parties (5). See Table 7.2.

POLICY VERSUS CHARACTER

Over twice as many utterances addressed policy (64) as character (25). Molinari devoted 65% of her utterances to policy, while Bayh directed 79% of his comments to policy (a chi-square did not find a significant

Table 7.2
Target of Acclaims and Attacks: Keynotes

| | Acclaim | | | | Attack | | | |
	Party	Candidate	Both	Total	Party	Candidate	Both	Total
Molinari	4	18	3	25	0	21	0	21
Bayh	1	22	10	33	5	5	0	10
Total	5	40	13	58	5	26	0	31

difference between Molinari's and Bayh's use of policy versus character—$X^2[df = 1] = 5.2$, $p < .05$). For example, Molinari complained about Clinton's health care policies: "Now under Bill Clinton, Medicare will be bankrupt in less than five years." However, she also accused Clinton of inconsistency and broken promises: "Now, think about Bill Clinton. He promises one thing and does another. He hopes we will forget his broken promises." Clearly this is not a desirable personal quality. Molinari explains that Dole, on the other hand, is a man who "still dreams, despite adversity," clearly praising Dole's character. See Table 7.3 for these results.

In the following excerpt, Bayh discusses Clinton's efforts on behalf of working families: "He fought for an increase in the minimum wage and 10 million Americans got a pay raise. He cut taxes for 15 million families who get up every morning and work hard all day long." Occasionally Bayh also addressed character. In the following passage, Bayh discussed Clinton's feelings toward Robert Kennedy:

President Clinton came [to Indianapolis] to consecrate Robert Kennedy's courage and heart with a similar prayer. The memorial that remains is simple—two hands reaching toward one another, fashioned from melted down guns. President Clinton reaches back to that compassionate message of that fateful night, a message he will carry forward into this campaign and into his new term, a message that we and our children must carry with us into the next century.

Thus, like Molinari, Bayh addressed policy as well as character in his keynote.

POLICY

Both speakers were more likely to acclaim their own nominee's future plans than to attack their opponent on those grounds. Similarly, they were both more likely to boast of their nominee's goals than to attack their opponent's goals. However, the majority of policy remarks concerned past deeds. Here, a distinct pattern emerged: Molinari was more likely to attack Clinton's past deeds (15) than to praise Dole's past deeds (2); Bayh, on the other hand, was inclined to praise Clinton's past deeds (17) more than he attacked Dole's past deeds (5). To illustrate, Molinari attacked Clinton's apparently failed drug policies when she lamented "the explosion in drug use by our kids that we've seen over the last three years." Bayh praised Clinton's successes: "Since President Clinton took office, over 10 million new jobs have been created, four times the number during the previous four years. Over a million new jobs in construction and manufacturing alone. And for the first time since the 1970s, America leads the world in making cars, ahead of Japan." Thus, both

Table 7.3
Policy versus Character: Keynotes

	Policy				Character			
	Deeds	Plans	Goals	Total	Ideals	Leader	PQual	Total
Molinari	15/ 2*	1/6	0/ 6	16/14 (65%)	0/2	1/ 2	4/7	5/11 (35%)
Bayh	5/17	1/3	1/ 7	7/27 (79%)	0/5	1/1	2/0	3/ 6 (21%)
Total	20/19	2/9	1/13	23/41 (72%)	0/7	2/3	6/7	8/17 (28%)

*left number = attacks, right number = acclaims.

speakers relied on the President's record in office, but used this resource for sharply different purposes.

At times the speakers discussed more general goals. For example, Bayh observed that "Bill Clinton is balancing the budget while keeping our pledge to the elderly, the young and our future." Similarly, Molinari explained that the Republican ticket would help renew the American dream: "Bob Dole and Jack Kemp and the Republican Party can make that dream easier to achieve again." While not a major component of these speeches, both referred to their candidates' goals.

The speakers at times discussed future plans. In her keynote, Molinari promised that Republicans "can help you spend more time at home with your family." Bayh noted that Clinton supports "Tougher truancy laws, more drug prevention, school uniforms, [and] higher standards so a diploma will mean something." Both indicated that their nominee would improve America.

CHARACTER

Relatively little time was spent by either candidate on ideals (7 utterances) or leadership (5 remarks). Bayh, for instance, noted these Democratic values: "Opportunity for all Americans, responsibility from all Americans, and a renewed sense of community among all Americans." Molinari discussed personal qualities 11 times, more often praising Dole (7 times) than attacking Clinton (4).

STRATEGIES FOR ELABORATING ACCLAIMS AND ATTACKS

The most common form of elaborating an utterance was to stress extent (19 times). For instance, Bayh quantified the gains made on welfare: "Today more than a million fewer Americans are on welfare than four years ago. And child support collections are up 40 percent." The second most common strategy of elaboration is to note effects on the audience (14 times). Molinari's speech had an extensive passage in which she illustrated the benefits of the Dole/Kemp tax cut proposal on voters:

It's a plan for the single mother with two kids in Detroit who's trying to pay her bills and pay for child care, too. She'll get $1000 from the Republican's child tax credit. It's a plan for a grandmother in St. Louis who was hit hard by Bill Clinton's tax increase on Social Security benefits. She's gonna get to keep all the benefits she's earned and deserves. And it's a plan for a young couple in Pittsburgh desperately trying to buy their first home. For them, it will mean lower interest rates and mortgage payments they can afford.

Table 7.4
Strategies for Elaborating Acclaims and Attacks: Keynotes

	Extent	Effects	Consistency	Vulnerable	Persistence
Molinari	4/ 2*	1/ 5	5/0	3/1	1/0
Bayh	2/11	0/ 8	0/0	0/0	1/0
Total	6/13	1/13	5/0	3/1	2/0

*left number = attacks, right number = acclaims.

These examples help viewers visualize the importance of the Republican nominee's plan. Molinari also used consistency and vulnerability, and both keynotes used persistence once. See Table 7.4.

ISSUES ADDRESSED

Bayh devoted more of his remarks to three of the issues analyzed: jobs and the economy (11 to 1), education (3 to 0), and the budget deficit (7 to 1). These three issues are also the ones voters said were most important to their voting decision. On three issues the two speakers spent about the same amount of time (Medicare and health: Molinari 3, Bayh 2; welfare: Bayh 3, Molinari 2; crime and drugs: Bayh 5, Molinari 4). On only one topic, taxes (next to last in importance to voters of the issues analyzed), did Molinari have a decisive advantage (10 to 1). Thus, Bayh directed more of his comments to issues that the voters thought were important. These data are displayed in Table 7.5.

IMPLICATIONS

The 1996 keynotes devoted more time to praise (of own candidate and party) than to attacks (of the opposing candidate and party), which is consistent with previous keynotes.[2] This suggests that similar pressures incline keynote speakers to make some similar choices over time.

Molinari, the Republican keynoter from the challenging party, gave more praise than attack, which is consistent with earlier Republicans, but not with earlier challengers. She did attack more than Bayh, though. Bayh, the Democratic speaker from the incumbent party, engaged in more praise, which is consistent with other challengers, although not with other Democratic speakers. These results may suggest that the party's situation (incumbent or challenger) may be more important in this regard than the party's ideology (Republican or Democratic).

More remarks were directed toward the candidates than the party in

Table 7.5
Issues Addressed: Keynotes

Issue	Rank	Molinari	Bayh
Jobs and the Economy	1	1	11
Education	2	0	3
Budget Deficit	3	1	7
Medicare and Health	4	3	2
Welfare Reform	5	2	3
Taxes	6	10	1
Crime and Drugs	6	4	5
Other	---	9	2

1996. From 1960–1996, keynoters tended to target the party more than their candidates. However, more recently this trend is reversed, with keynote speakers focusing more on the candidates than the party. The 1996 speeches are in line with this more recent trend, which may relate to the decline in the influence of the political party and the rise of candidate-centered presidential campaigns.

In 1996, more comments were policy related than character related. This result, too, is consistent with previous keynote speeches. Although our analysis is not designed to reveal whether the speakers went into depth on policy matters, they did not emphasize image (character) over issue (policy) in 1996.

NOTES

1. These remarks are not technically "acclaims," because we are not interested in what Molinari said about her*self* or what Bayh said about him*self*, but about what they said about their *nominees* (an acclaim, strictly speaking, is *self*-praise). Given that both speakers are praising their own parties' nominees, we do not feel it is unreasonable to use the term "acclaim" with this caveat.

2. Benoit, Blaney, and Pier (1996) analyzed keynotes from 1960–1996. This means, of course, that their study includes analyses of Molinari's and Bayh's keynotes from 1996. However, we do not believe this renders the comparison between those baseline trends (which include these two speeches) and our analysis (aimed at these two speeches alone) invalid. The 1996 keynotes are but one pair of ten, accounting for a bit less than 10% of the utterances analyzed. The past trends we compare with the 1996 speeches might be slightly less consistent with the two 1996 speeches we are studying here if the historic data only in-

cluded keynotes from 1960–1992, but we do not think this is a serious limitation. Given that Benoit, Blaney, and Pier (1996) offer the only systematic baseline data on acclaiming, attacking, and defending in keynote speeches, we are comfortable making these comparisons.

Chapter 8

Acceptance Addresses:
I Will Lead Us to Victory

Bob Dole's August 15 Republican Acceptance Address
(excerpts)

And make no mistake about it, my economic program is the right policy for America.

Here's what it will mean to you. It means you will have a president who will urge Congress to pass and to send to the states for ratification a balanced budget amendment to our Constitution. It means you will have a president and a Congress who have the will to balance the budget by the year 2002.

It means you will have a president who will reduce taxes 15% across-the-board for every taxpayer in America—it will include a $500 per child tax credit for lower- and middle-income families. Taxes for a family of four making $35,000 dollars will be reduced by more than half—56% to be exact. . . .

We must also commit ourselves to a trade policy that does not suppress pay and threaten American jobs. By any measure, the trade policy of the Clinton administration has been a disaster; trade deficits are skyrocketing, and middle-income families are paying the price. . . .

It must be said: because of misguided priorities there have been massive cuts in funding for our national security. I believe President Clinton has failed to adequately provide for our future defense. For whatever reason his neglect, it is irresponsible. . . .

I ask for your vote so that I may bring you an administration that is able, honest, and trusts in you.

Bill Clinton's August 29 Democratic Acceptance Address
(excerpts)

Just look at the facts: 4.4 million Americans now living in a home of their own for the first time; hundreds of thousands of women have started their own new businesses; more minorities own businesses than ever before; record numbers of new small businesses and exports. . . . We have the lowest combined rates of unemployment, inflation, and home mortgages in 28 years. . . . Ten million new jobs, over half of them high-wage jobs, 10 million workers getting the raise they deserve with the minimum wage law. Twenty-five million people now having protection in their health insurance because of the Kennedy-Kassebaum Bill. . . . Forty million Americans with more pension security, a tax cut for fifteen million of our hardest pressed Americans and all small businesses. Twelve million Americans . . . taking advantage of the Family and Medical Leave Law so they can be good parents and good workers. Ten million students who saved money on their college loans. . . .

I want to build a bridge to the twenty-first century, in which we expand opportunity through education. Where computers are as much a part of the classroom as black boards. Where highly trained teachers demand peak performance from our students, where every 8-year-old can point to a book and say I can read it myself. . . .

Now, our opponents, our opponents have put forward a very different plan, a risky $550 billion tax scheme that will force them to ask for even bigger cuts in Medicare, Medicaid, education, and the environment than they passed and I vetoed last year.

The presidential nomination acceptance address is intended to be the highpoint of the party convention. The convention is a "party" event in more than one sense of the word. It is meant as a meeting of the political party, the time to formally nominate its candidates for president and vice president. However, it is also a chance for delegates to celebrate their principles, and their inevitable march to victory in November. The acceptance address is traditionally scheduled at the end of the final day of the convention to serve as the climax of the gathering of party faithful. In recent years conventions have become highly scripted media events where nothing is left to chance (in 1996, Buchanan, who continued campaigning against Dole even after Dole had enough delegates to assure nomination, was told he could speak at the convention for only 15 seconds, and on videotape at that; see Bennett, 1996).

In years past, the nominee was selected at the convention. However, this led to contentious and divisive conventions (e.g., the Democratic national convention of 1968) that had at least two undesirable effects. First, network news coverage of the conventions—and nothing attracts media attention like controversy—exposes internal party squabbles to the entire electorate. Second, the end of the convention signals the start of the general election campaign. The nominee needs to have the enthusiastic support of the entire party in the campaign. However, a contested nomination runs the risk that those who supported the nominee's opponents may not be able to immediately put aside differences to support the winner.

These considerations led the two major political parties to increase the importance of primaries (and caucuses) in the selection of the nominee and move the primaries earlier ("front-loading" the primaries). Hopefully, nonpartisans would not pay as much attention to intraparty conflicts during the primaries (and besides reporting the results, many primaries do not attract national press coverage). Furthermore, if the nominee is decided relatively early, divisions in the party could be healed before national media attention is accorded to the convention.

However, this change has made conventions relatively dull (except for the party faithful). There is no suspense concerning who will be the nominee. In 1996, both nominees and running mates were known for both parties before the conventions began. Still, the acceptance address is well worth watching. It provides a public statement of the principles and themes of the nominee's general election campaign (Trent & Friedenberg, 1995). Even with diminished television coverage of the national nominating conventions, the acceptance addresses are among the features given national media coverage.

PAST RESEARCH ON ACCEPTANCE ADDRESSES

Nomination acceptance addresses are popular subjects for political communication research (see, e.g., Gustainis & Benoit, 1988; Norvold, 1970; Ritter, 1980, 1996; Scheele, 1984; Smith, 1971; Trent & Friedenberg, 1995; Valley, 1974, 1988; Weithoff, 1981). None of this research is intended to identify acclaims, attacks, or defenses. However, several studies did find that these speakers engaged in self-praise (e.g., Trent & Friedenberg, 1995; Scheele, 1984; Valley, 1988; Weithoff, 1981), attack (e.g., Gustainis & Benoit, 1988; Valley, 1988; Weithoff, 1981), and defense (Gustainis & Benoit, 1988; Weithoff, 1981).

Wells, Pier, Blaney, and Benoit (1996) examined acceptance addresses from 1960–1996 using the functional approach to campaign discourse. These speakers engaged in more acclaiming (72%) than attacking (27%). Some instances of defense occurred in these acceptance addresses, but it was rare (1%). Republicans engaged in more attacking (30%) than Democrats (23%), while Democrats performed more acclaims (77%) than Republicans (68%). Incumbents engaged in more acclaiming (77%) than challengers (67%), while challengers were more likely to attack (32%) than incumbents (22%). Wells, Pier, Blaney, and Benoit (1996) noted that

Table 8.1
Acclaims, Attacks, and Defenses: Acceptance Addresses

	Acclaims	Attacks	Defenses
Clinton	205 (90%)	23 (10%)	0
Dole	115 (74%)	39 (25%)	2 (1%)
Total	320 (83%)	62 (16%)	2 (0.5%)

the references to the political parties were more common in the first five sets of acceptance addresses than in the last five. Over half (56%) of all utterances concerned policy rather than character. Republicans devoted more than half of their utterances (57%) to policy matters, while Democrats spent less than half of their remarks (43%) on policy concerns.

THE 1996 ACCEPTANCE ADDRESSES

In 1996, Dole's acceptance address was delivered in San Diego on August 15; Clinton's acceptance speech was presented on August 29 in Chicago. We analyzed these speeches, reporting our results under seven headings: functions, target, policy versus character, policy, character, elaboration, and issues addressed.

FUNCTIONS OF ACCEPTANCE ADDRESSES

Clinton engaged in more acclaiming (90%) than Dole (74%) in these 1996 acceptance addresses. This difference was statistically significant ($X^2[df = 1] = 15.6$, $p < .01$). For example, Dole promises that he will "urge Congress to pass and to send to the states for ratification a balanced budget amendment to our Constitution," and that he will work "to balance the budget by the year 2002." Many voters are concerned about the huge federal deficit, and Dole commits himself to address this problem if elected. Similarly, Clinton reports that "We have the lowest combined rates of unemployment, inflation, and home mortgages in 28 years," clearly a desirable state of affairs. See Table 8.1.

Attack was also a feature of these acceptance addresses: Dole's utterances included more attack (25%) than Clinton's remarks (10%). For example, Dole declared that "President Clinton has failed to adequately provide for our future defense." Even though the threat from the Soviet Union may have abated, Americans want an adequate defense. Clinton also attacked, criticizing Dole's tax cut: "Our opponents have put forward a very different plan, a risky $550 billion tax scheme that will force

Table 8.2
Defense Strategies: Acceptance Addresses

	Denial	Transcendence	Total
Dole	1	1	2
Clinton	0	0	0
Total	1	1	2

them to ask for even bigger cuts in Medicare, Medicaid, education, and the environment than they passed and I vetoed last year." In this passage he also manages to attack Dole for possible future budget cuts and to acclaim the fact that he successfully fought against them in his first term.

Of 384 utterances analyzed, only two (both from Dole) were defenses. Given the fact that these speeches were given on separate occasions, the situation is not as confrontational as presidential debates. Defense may also be infrequent because the candidates do not wish to remind voters of their opponent's accusations, and because they may not want to appear defensive. Because defense was so rarely used, it will not be included in the following comparisons. See Table 8.2.

Historically, Republicans and challengers are more likely to attack than Democrats and incumbents. Given that Dole was both a Republican and a challenger, it is not surprising that he engaged in more attack than Clinton. In addition to the attacks mentioned above, Dole also criticized Clinton's drug policies: "We are not the party that, as drug use has soared among the young, hears no evil, sees no evil, and just cannot say, 'Just say no.' " In this passage Dole manages to mention his antidrug stance while criticizing Clinton.

TARGET OF ACCLAIMS AND ATTACKS

These two candidates were much more likely to talk about themselves than their parties (candidates: 94%; party: 6%). However, when they did address party, there was a contrast in the two candidates' selection of target. Clinton was somewhat more likely to attack the opposing party, while Dole praised his own party more. For example, Dole noted that "The Republican Party is broad and inclusive. It represents many streams of opinion and many points of view." These data are displayed in Table 8.3.

POLICY VERSUS CHARACTER

Together, these two candidates spent more time addressing policy considerations (61%) than character concerns (39%). However, there was a

Table 8.3
Target of Attacks and Acclaims: Acceptance Addresses

	Attacks			Acclaims		
	Party	Candidate	Both	Party	Candidate	Both
Clinton	7 (30%)	16 (70%)	0	2 (1%)	203 (99%)	0
Dole	2 (7%)	27 (90%)	1 (3%)	11 (10%)	103 (90%)	1 (1%)
Total	9 (17%)	43 (81%)	1 (2%)	13 (4%)	306 (96%)	1 (.3%)

sharp contrast between the two candidates. Clinton demonstrated a marked proclivity for discussing policy (73%), while Dole emphasized character (58%). A chi-square revealed that this difference was significant ($X^2[df = 1] = 35.0$, $p < .001$). For example, consider this extended passage on the successes of Clinton's first term:

We have the lowest combined rates of unemployment, inflation, and home mortgages in 28 years. Look at what happened. Ten million new jobs, over half of them high-wage jobs, ten million workers getting the raise they deserve with the minimum wage law. Twenty-five million people now having protection in their health insurance because the Kennedy-Kassebaum Bill says you can't lose your insurance anymore when you change jobs, even if somebody in your family has been sick. Forty million Americans with more pension security, a tax cut for fifteen million of our hardest pressed Americans and all small businesses. Twelve million Americans, twelve million of them taking advantage of the Family and Medical Leave Law so they can be good parents and good workers. Ten million students who saved money on their college loans.

Clearly, Clinton was trying to boast of his policy-related accomplishments in his acceptance address.

On the other hand, Dole was prone to talk about character rather than policy. For instance, this passage creates the impression of humility: "There is no height to which I have risen that is high enough to allow me to forget them, to allow me to forget where I came from, where I stand, and how I stand, with my feet on the ground, just a man, at the mercy of God." In the past, Republicans have been somewhat more prone to discuss policy (57%) than Democrats (54%), which was not the case in 1996. These data are derived from Table 8.4.

POLICY

Clinton's speech repeatedly acclaimed his past deeds (56 times). In one passage, he asked viewers to "Just look at the facts: 4.4 million Ameri-

Table 8.4
Policy versus Character: Acceptance Addresses

| | Policy | | | | Character | | | |
	Deeds	Plans	Goals	Total	PQual	Leader	Ideals	Total
Clinton	7/56*	10/36	1/56	18/148 (73%)	1/14	0/1	4/42	5/57 (27%)
Dole	15/ 7	0/11	1/27	16/45 (42%)	2/24	3/3	9/43	14/70 (58%)
Total	22/63	10/47	2/83	34/193 (61%)	3/38	3/4	13/85	19/127 (39%)

*left numbers = attacks, right number = acclaims.

cans now living in a home of their own for the first time; hundreds of thousands of women have started their own new businesses; more minorities own businesses than ever before; record numbers of new small businesses and exports." Clinton also touted his future plans (36 times). In this extended passage, he described several initiatives to improve higher education:

By the year 2000, the single most critical thing we can do is to give every single American who wants it the chance to go to college. We must make two years of college just as universal as four years of a high school education is today, and we can do it. We can do it, and we should cut taxes to do it. I propose a $1,500 a year tuition tax credit a year for Americans, a Hope scholarship for the first two years of college to make the typical community college education available to every American. I believe every working family ought also to be able to deduct up to $10,000 in college tuition costs per year for education after that. I believe the families of this country ought to be able to save money for college in a tax-free IRA, save it year in and year out, withdraw it for college education without penalty.

These proposals seem to be reasonable vehicles for increasing access to a college education, a desirable goal for many voters.

Dole also acclaimed his past deeds and future plans, but he addressed both of these topics less often (past deeds: 7; future plans: 11) than Clinton. One of Dole's future plans concerned dealing with terrorists: "On my first day in office I will also put terrorists on notice: if you harm one American, you harm all Americans. And America will pursue you to the ends of the earth." Note the especially sharp contrast in the extent to which they tout their respective records (Clinton: 56; Dole: 7). Dole has a strong record in the Senate; he rarely used it as a resource for acclaiming in this speech.

Clinton attacked Dole's past deeds (7 times). The following passage does not identify Dole by name, but it seems clear that he is part of the target:

Now, last year, last year when the Republican Congress sent me a budget that violated those values and principles, I vetoed it and I would do it again tomorrow. I could never allow cuts that devastate education for our children, that pollute our environment, that end the guarantee of health care for those who are served under Medicaid, to end our duty or violate our duty to our parents through Medicare. I just couldn't do it.

Clinton characterizes that proposed Republican budget in clearly negative terms: "devastate education for our children," "pollute our environment," "end guarantees of health care," and "violate our duty to parents."

Clinton also attacked Dole's future plans (10 times). For example, he criticized Dole's proposed tax cut:

Now, our opponents, our opponents have put forward a very different plan, a risky $550 billion tax scheme that will force them to ask for even bigger cuts in Medicare, Medicaid, education, and the environment than they passed and I vetoed last year. But even then they will not cover the cost of their scheme. So that even then this plan will explode the deficit, which will increase interest rates by 2 percent, according to their own estimates last year.

Thus, Clinton gives a variety of reasons for reducing Dole's apparent preferability.

On the other hand, Dole attacked Clinton's past deeds (15 times), but never his future plans. For example, Dole criticized Clinton's foreign trade policy: "By any measure, the trade policy of the Clinton administration has been a disaster; trade deficits are skyrocketing, and middle-income families are paying the price." Clinton proposed a variety of new initiatives for his (potential) second term; Dole failed to take advantage of the opportunity to attack them in his acceptance address.

Both candidates praised their own goals (Dole: 27; Clinton: 56) and rarely attacked their opponent's goals (once each). Under the heading of improving democracy, Clinton endorsed one goal, asking for his audience's help: "Will you help me get campaign finance reform in the next four years?" Dole advocated a goal of restoring families in his acceptance address: "I shall, as president, promote measures that keep families whole." The fact that goals are acclaimed more than attacked may be due to the fact that it is easier to adopt lofty goals than to attack them (or, perhaps, to achieve them). See Table 8.4.

CHARACTER

Both Dole and Clinton were more likely to acclaim their ideals than to attack their opponent's ideals (Clinton: 42 acclaims, 4 attacks; Dole: 43 acclaims, 9 attacks). The two speakers presented conflicting metaphors in their acceptance addresses. In both cases, they were acclaiming their visions for the future, their principles, or their ideals. Dole offered to be a bridge to the past:

Age has its advantages. Let me be the bridge to an America that only the unknowing call myth. Let me be the bridge to a time of tranquillity, faith, and confidence in action. To those who say it was never so, that America has not been better, I say, you're wrong, and I know, because I was there. I have seen it. I remember.

Quite possibly there is some nostalgic appeal in this passage. However, Clinton, in sharp contrast, directed this metaphor in a different direction. Clinton wanted to be a bridge to the future, a link to the twenty-first century:

And I am determined to take our best traditions into the future. But with all respect, we do not need to build a bridge to the past. We need to build a bridge to the future, and that is what I commit to you to do. So tonight, tonight let us resolve to build that bridge to the twenty-first century, to meet our challenges, and protect our values. Let us build a bridge to help our parents raise their children, to help young people and adults to get the education and training they need, to make our streets safer, to help Americans succeed at home and at work, to break the cycle of poverty and dependence, to protect our environment for generations to come, and to maintain our world leadership for peace and freedom. Let us resolve to build that bridge.

These two ideas are not inherently incompatible. However, given the choice, most viewers would probably prefer a bridge to the future than one to the past. In a manner similar to their policy goals, ideals are general and easier to acclaim than to attack.

Dole acclaimed his own personal qualities more frequently than did Clinton (Dole: 24; Clinton: 14). Leadership qualities were infrequently discussed. Dole even made a thinly-veiled attack against the First Lady when he declared that "it does not take a village to raise a child. It takes a family." See Table 8.4.

STRATEGIES FOR ELABORATING ACCLAIMS AND ATTACKS

Clinton showed a clear preference for developing his utterances by discussing the extent of his successes (31 times) and of Dole's weaknesses (3 times). For example, Clinton acclaims his record on crime in the following passage: "On crime, we are putting 100,000 police on the streets. We made three strikes and you're out the law of the land, we stopped 60,000 felons, fugitives, and stalkers from getting handguns under the Brady Bill." These acclaims stress the number of police and the number of felons. Clinton occasionally related an acclaim or an attack to the audience (twice each). These data are displayed in Table 8.5.

Dole was about equally likely to elaborate his remarks with extent (9 times) and effects on the audience (10 times). In this passage, Dole described the size of his proposed tax cut: "Taxes for a family of four making $35,000 dollars will be reduced by more than half—56% to be exact." Elsewhere, Dole related the effects of Clinton's foreign trade policy to America's families: "By any measure, the trade policy of the Clin-

Table 8.5
Strategies for Elaborating Acclaims and Attacks: Acceptance Addresses

	Extent	Effects	Persistence
Clinton	3/31*	2/2	0/1
Dole	3/ 6	5/5	0/0
Total	6/37	7/7	0/1

*left number = attacks, right number = acclaims.

ton administration has been a disaster; trade deficits are skyrocketing, and middle-income families are paying the price." Thus, extent and effects on the audience are the most common forms of elaboration in these acceptance addresses.

ISSUES ADDRESSED

Our analysis reveals that of the seven policy issues considered, Clinton devoted more remarks than Dole in these acceptance addresses to education, jobs and the economy, the budget deficit, Medicare and health, welfare, and crime and drugs (as well as "other"). On the other hand, Dole talked about taxes more often than Clinton. It may seem odd that Clinton leads in so many categories. However, recall that Clinton allocated 73% of his comments to policy matters, while Dole directed only 42% of his remarks to policy. Hence, Clinton spent more time on most of the issues of importance to most voters than Dole. See Table 8.6.

IMPLICATIONS

Both speakers focused more on acclaims than attacks in their acceptance addresses. This is consistent with previous acceptance addresses, although Clinton and Dole acclaimed somewhat more than past nominees. Furthermore, the Democratic incumbent praised more than the Republican challenger (and the Republican challenger attacked more than the Democratic challenger), as has been the case in previous years. Although defense did occur, it was quite rare. These nominees were prone to discuss themselves more than their parties, a pattern found in more recent acceptance addresses.

Clinton spent about three-quarters of his time on policy matters, while Dole devoted about 60% of his remarks to character. Past speeches also concentrated more on policy than character, although the emphasis was stronger in 1996. Both nominees praised their past deeds and future

Table 8.6
Issues Addressed: Acceptance Addresses

Issue	Rank	Clinton	Dole
Jobs and the Economy	1	18	6
Education	2	21	5
Budget Deficit	3	11	2
Medicare and Health	4	8	0
Welfare Reform	5	13	0
Taxes	6	7	13
Crime and Drugs	6	21	10
Other	---	67	25

plans. Clinton attacked Dole's past deeds and future plans, and Dole attacked Clinton's past deeds but not his future plans. Both speakers praised their ideals more than they attacked their opponent's ideals. Dole made more comments about personal qualities than Clinton, and leadership qualities were rarely mentioned. They elaborated their acclaims and attacks most frequently with extent and effects on the audience. Clinton allocated more of his comments than Dole to the issues that mattered most to voters; in fact, because he spent more time on character, Dole spoke more on only one such topic, taxes.

Chapter 9

Stand by Your Man: Elizabeth Dole's and Hillary Rodham Clinton's Convention Speeches

Elizabeth Dole's 8/14/96 Convention Address (excerpts)

Now for the last several days, a number of men and women have been painting a remarkable portrait of a remarkable man, a man who is the strongest and the most compassionate, most tender person that I've ever known—the man who, quite simply, is my own personal Rock of Gibraltar. . . .

Bob Dole, as you know, was born in a small town in Kansas. His parents were poor. In fact, at one point when Bob was a boy, they had to move their family—parents and four children—into the basement and rent out their small home, the upstairs, just to make ends meet . . .

And certainly Bob has known the struggle to make ends meet. In fact, he couldn't have had a college education if it were not for the GI Bill. And so, he's going to protect and preserve and strengthen that safety net for those who need it.

Also, he's dedicated his life to making a difference—a positive difference—for others because of his own experiences. Whether it's on the battlefield, on the Senate floor, or whether it's in his personal life, he's going to be making that difference for others. . . .

He wants to make a difference—a positive difference—for others because he cares, because that's who he is. And I certainly will never forget his last day as majority leader of the United States Senate. I was seated up in the balcony, you know, and I was watching as senator after senator, Democrats and Republicans, stood and paid tribute to my husband on the Senate floor. They talked about his countless legislative achievements, how he had led the United States Senate to successfully pass the largest tax cut in the history of the United States of America. . . .

They also talked about how Bob had led the Senate just last year to save Medicare, increasing spending 62 percent, only to have the White House veto

the legislation, provide no other alternative for saving the system except a mul-
timillion dollar ad campaign to scare our senior citizens. . . .

But above all, these senators, Democrats and Republicans, talked about Bob's
character, his honesty, his integrity. And I remember Senator Pete Domenici, that
beautiful speech that you gave, and when you concluded your speech, you said,
"The next majority leader of the United States Senate better know that he better
be honest. He better tell the Senate the truth because Bob Dole knew no other
way. . . ."

And that's why, ladies and gentlemen, that's why Bob Dole's fellow senators
elected him six times to be their leader—because they know he's honest, trustworthy, a man of his word. His word is his bond, and they know he has exceptional leadership skills. And isn't that exactly what we want in the president of
the United States?

Hillary Rodham Clinton's 8/27/96 Convention address
(excerpts)

I wish we could be sitting around a kitchen table, just us, talking about our
hopes and fears about our children's futures. For Bill and me, family has been
the center of our lives, but we also know that our family, like your family, is
part of a larger community that can help or hurt our best efforts to raise our
child. . . .

You know, Bill and I are fortunate that our jobs have allowed us to take breaks
from work, not only when Chelsea was born, but to attend her school events
and take her to the doctor. But millions of other parents can't get time off. That's
why my husband wants to expand the Family and Medical Leave Law, so that
parents can take time off for children's doctors' appointments and parent-teacher
conferences at school. . . .

We all know that raising kids is a full-time job. And since most parents work,
they are, we are, stretched thin. Just think about what many parents are responsible for on any given day. Packing lunches, dropping the kids off at school,
going to work, checking to make sure that the kids get home from school safely,
shopping for groceries, making dinner, doing the laundry, helping with home
work, paying the bills, and I didn't even mention taking the dog to the vet. That's
why my husband wants to pass a new time law that will give parents the option
to take overtime pay either in extra income or in extra time off, depending upon
whichever is best for your family. . . .

Our family has been lucky to have been blessed with a child with good health.
Chelsea has spent only one night in the hospital after she had her tonsils out,
but Bill and I couldn't sleep at all that night. But our experience was nothing
like the emotional strain on parents when their children are seriously ill. That is
why my husband has always felt that all American families should have affordable health insurance. . . .

Just last week, the president signed a bill sponsored by Senators Kennedy and
Kassebaum, a Democrat and a Republican, that will enable 25 million Americans

to keep their health insurance, even when they switch jobs or lose a job or have a family member who has been sick. . . .

The president also hasn't forgotten that there are thousands of children languishing in foster care who can't be returned home. That's why he signed legislation last week that provides a $5,000 tax credit for parents who adopt a child. . . .

It takes a president who believes not only in the potential of his own child, but of all children. Who believes not only in the strength of his own family, but of the American family, who believes not only in the promise of each of us as individuals, but in our promise together as a nation. It takes a president who not only holds these beliefs, but acts on them. It takes Bill Clinton.

The electorate is exposed to seemingly endless political messages from the time a candidate announces his or her intention to run until the general election is held. One notable event during an election cycle is the party's national convention, at which both the candidate and surrogate speakers espouse the praises of the candidate and the shortcomings of the opposing party (Trent & Friedenberg, 1995).

In recent years one type of surrogate has become invaluable to the hopeful candidate: the family member (Niedowski, 1996). Family members can be an extension of the candidate's ideals, values and goals. In 1996 it became apparent that spouses in particular were utilized by both major candidates for the presidency. Furthermore, the parties' national conventions set a precedent for spousal involvement in 1996: in no other national campaign have marital partners been so prominent (Crawford, 1996). Blankenship, Robson, and Williams (1997) noted that "Two of the most eagerly anticipated events of the two conventions were the dueling speeches of the two presidential candidates' wives in prime time" (p. 1021). Thus, these discourses merit scholarly attention.

On August 14, 16.7 million viewers tuned in to watch Elizabeth Dole's address (Duin, 1996). Hillary Clinton's speech on August 27 drew 20 million viewers ("Democratic Convention," 1996). Blankenship, Robson, and Williams (1997) noted that Elizabeth Dole's speech was to "finish the portrait of her husband, the caring, the compassionate" (p. 1038), which would be character acclaims in our terms. In contrast, Hillary Rodham Clinton's address concerned her husband's social agenda, including stopping "drive-by deliveries" of babies, the Family and Medical Leave Act, and his proposal for flex time. We would characterize these kinds of remarks as policy acclaims. However, Blankenship, Robson, and Williams' purpose was to discuss the role of gender at the nominating conventions (and the "gender gap" in presidential politics), not to employ our functional approach to analyzing these speeches. We analyze their national nominating convention speeches in this chapter.

FUNCTIONS OF SPOUSES' SPEECHES

Both Hillary Clinton and Elizabeth Dole engaged in acclaiming and attacking discourse: 95% of their utterances were praises, 5% were attacks, and none were defenses (a chi-square was not significant [$X^2\{df = 1\} = 0.02$, ns]).[1] For example, Elizabeth Dole praised her husband for his sensitivity toward those who are needy or special:

About 10 years ago, Bob and I were about to celebrate our birthdays . . . and Bob suggested a reverse birthday. He said, "Elizabeth, let's go to Sarah's Circle," which is a very special place in inner city Washington that houses and ministers to elderly poor. And he said, "Let's find out what the 35 or 40 residents most need and want and we'll give them the gifts, give them the party." And so that's what we did.

In the above utterance we see how Mrs. Dole engaged in acclaiming discourse. She painted her husband as a philanthropist by revealing that he purchased gifts for the needy and portrayed him as a spiritual being by indicating that he helped minister to the elderly. Both characterizations of Bob Dole spoke to his moral fiber and sought to elevate him in the eyes of the audience. Similarly, Hillary Clinton's address extolled the virtues of the president's latest reading program for children: "The president announced today an important initiative called America Reads. This initiative is aimed at making sure all children can read well by the third grade. It will require volunteers but I know there are thousands and thousands of Americans who will volunteer to help every child read well." Mrs. Clinton illuminated the president's efforts to make sure that all children can read by the third grade. She linked the positive nature of literacy with her husband's efforts to ensure it, thereby acclaiming his positive qualities.

Ninety-five percent of all utterances in these speeches focused on acclaiming the candidate while five percent of the remarks were attacks. Furthermore, both spouses aimed their praise at their husbands specifically, rather than at the their respective parties. However, neither woman offered any defenses on behalf of their husbands. See Table 9.1.

POLICY VERSUS CHARACTER

Mrs. Clinton and Mrs. Dole each spoke of both policy (33%) and character (67%) when discussing their spouses. For example, Mrs. Clinton noted that "my husband wants to expand the Family and Medical Leave Law, so that parents can take time off for children's doctors' appointments and parent-teacher conferences at school." This is a clear instance of a policy acclaim (specifically, praise of future plans). However, other

Table 9.1
Acclaims, Attacks, and Defenses: Spousal Speeches

	Acclaims	Atttacks	Defenses
Elizabeth Dole	37 (95%)	2 (5%)	0
Hillary Rodham Clinton	21 (95%)	1 (5%)	0
Total	58 (95%)	3 (5%)	0

utterances concerned character. For instance, Elizabeth Dole praised her husband's character when she stated:

Bob called up and he said, "You know, Elizabeth," he said, "I'd like to do something a little different this Thanksgiving." And he sounded kind of sheepish because you see he'd already put the plans in motion. And I said, "Bob, what would you like to do?" And he said, "Well, I've invited 35 young people from some pretty tough parts of Washington and their church sponsors to have Thanksgiving dinner with us." Well, he had already reserved some places for us at a restaurant. He'd had them put in some televisions so the kids could watch the Redskins game . . . Ladies and gentlemen, you didn't read about that Thanksgiving dinner in the newspaper or hear about it in the media because Bob Dole never told anybody about it. He did it from his heart.

Here, Mrs. Dole focused on personal events in the past that speak to the personal qualities of her husband in order to praise his character to her audience. See Table 9.2.

POLICY

Twenty-two percent of Mrs. Dole's acclaiming utterances addressed policy considerations, while 52% of Mrs. Clinton's acclaims concerned policy (X^2[df = 1] = 7.1, p < .01). Of these, six focused on past accomplishments while two were concerned with his general goals. An excellent example of how Mrs. Dole incorporated past accomplishments into her acclaiming utterances can be seen in the following:

They talked about how he had saved Social Security and I just want to quote from a letter—this is from Claude Pepper. As you know he was the champion of seniors. And he wrote to Bob May 11, 1983. He thanked Bob for his extraordinary contributions saying, and I quote, "You never lost hope and faith in our accomplishing the immeasurable task of saving Social Security. We could never have produced this result without your skill and sincerest desire to make a meaningful contribution."

Table 9.2
Policy versus Character: Spousal Speeches

| | Policy | | | | Character | | | | |
	Deeds	Plans	Goals	Total	PQual	Leader	Ideals	Total
Elizabeth Dole	1/6*	0/0	0/2	1/8 (22%)	1/27	0/4	0/0	1/31 (78%)
Hillary Rodham Clinton	1/5	0/5	0/1	1/11 (52%)	0/5	0/1	0/5	0/11 (48%)
Total	2/11	0/5	0/3	2/19 (33%)	1/32	0/5	0/5	1/42 (67%)

*left number = attacks, right number = acclaims.

In this passage Elizabeth Dole praised her husband by elaborating the work that Bob Dole did on a committee to save Social Security. By praising Bob Dole for his past deeds and accomplishments, it makes it easier for Mrs. Dole to claim that Bob Dole's future as president will be successful as well.

Not only did Mrs. Dole concentrate on Bob Dole's past contributions, she also focused somewhat on his general goals for the future. Two of the eight acclaims dealing with policy considerations contained discourse about Bob Dole's general goals. For example, Mrs. Dole suggests that her husband will preserve the GI Bill when he is elected president, "In fact, he couldn't have had a college education if it were not for the GI Bill. And so, he's going to protect and preserve and strengthen that safety net for those who need it." By discussing general goals, Elizabeth Dole offered a glimpse of the future Bob Dole for the audience to consider in their decision.

As noted above, 52% of Hillary Rodham Clinton's acclaims contained references to policy considerations. Five of the eleven utterances dealing with policy focused on past accomplishments of President Clinton. An example of Mrs. Clinton's praise of President Clinton's past accomplishments can be found in her discussion of the Kennedy-Kassebaum Bill:

Just last week, the president signed a bill sponsored by Senators Kennedy and Kassebaum, a Democrat and a Republican, that will enable 25 million Americans to keep their health insurance, even when they switch jobs or lose a job or have a family member who has been sick. This bill contains some of the key provisions from the president's proposal for health care reform.

Mrs. Clinton chose to focus on a past accomplishment that was fairly new and fresh in the mind of the audience. By stating that Bill Clinton's latest accomplishment helped 25 million American people, Hillary Clinton was able to quantify the praise due President Clinton on the audience's behalf.

In addition to mentioning President Clinton's past accomplishments, Mrs. Clinton introduced his future plans for the country through her acclamations. Five of the eleven policy acclaims concentrated on his future plans. For example, Mrs. Clinton introduced the president's idea of family leave and flex time when she stated: "That's why my husband wants to pass a flex time law that will give parents the option to take overtime pay either in extra income or in extra time off, depending upon whichever is best for your family." In this speech segment, Mrs. Clinton praised the legislation that her husband will pursue when elected.

Although Mrs. Clinton spent most of her time dealing with past accomplishments and future plans, she also mentioned President Clinton's general goals once: "That is why my husband has always felt that all

American families should have affordable health care." Thus, both spouses included policy remarks in their speeches.

CHARACTER

Sixty-seven percent of all acclaiming utterances focused on character considerations. A typical example of character utterances spoken on behalf of a candidate can be seen in Elizabeth Dole's discourse: "Pat's told me that when Bob was totally paralyzed and people thought he wouldn't walk again, he literally willed himself to walk. He was a person of great perseverance and determination and drive. And he recovered fully except for the use of his right arm in the three years over at the hospital." Here, she praises her husband's perseverance, determination, and drive, three elements of strong character.

Although the majority of Dole's character considerations focus on personal qualities, several were directed toward Bob Dole's leadership ability. Elizabeth Dole discussed Bob's past leadership in the Senate when she stated: "And that's why, ladies and gentlemen, that's why Bob Dole's fellow senators elected him six times to be their leader—because they know he's honest, trustworthy, a man of his word. His word is his bond, and they know he has exceptional leadership skills. And isn't that exactly what we want in the president of the United States!" Mrs. Dole specifically addressed Bob Dole's past leadership positions in order to convince the listeners that he had ample experience to be the next president of the United States.

Forty-eight percent of Mrs. Clinton's utterances focused on character considerations. Half of the character considerations dealt with personal qualities of President Clinton. An example of personal qualities attached to the president by Mrs. Clinton can be found when she praises him as both a husband and a father: "Issues affecting children and families are some of the hardest we face as parents, as citizens, as a nation. In October, Bill and I will celebrate our 21st wedding anniversary. Bill was with me when Chelsea was born in the delivery room, in my hospital room, and when we brought our baby daughter home." In this speech segment we see Hillary Clinton trying to equate President Clinton's presence at the birth of their daughter and their impending anniversary with strong character.

Not only did Mrs. Clinton highlight President Clinton's personal qualities, she also focused on the ideals that he held: "It takes a president who believes not only in the potential of his own child, but of all children. Who believes not only in the strength of his own family, but of the American family, who believes not only in the promise of each of us as individuals, but in our promise together as a nation." In this utterance

Mrs. Clinton attempted to expand President Clinton's paternal instinct to the nation as a whole in an effort to showcase his ideals that will come into play if he were to be reelected.

ATTACKS

Although both spouses primarily engaged in acclaiming, there were a few attacks present in their speeches. Five percent of the utterances were attacks aimed at the candidates. Mrs. Dole engaged in two of the three attacks. One of her attacks was aimed at the past accomplishments of Bill Clinton and his treatment of Medicare: ". . . only to have the White House veto the legislation, provide no other alternative for saving the system." Mrs. Clinton provided one of the spouses' attacks when she criticized Bob Dole for his role in impeding the Family and Medical Leave Law: "The very first piece of legislation that my husband signed into law had been vetoed twice, the Family and Medical Leave Law." Although Dole is not specifically named, the attack clearly concerns Bob Dole.

STRATEGIES FOR ELABORATING ACCLAIMS

Three different elaboration strategies (extensiveness, effects on the audience, and vulnerability) were employed in sixteen instances. For example, Mrs. Clinton indicated the magnitude of good that the Family and Medical Leave Law had done for 12 million people when she said, "That law allows parents time off for the birth or adoption of a child, or for family emergencies without fear of losing their jobs. Already it has helped 12 million families and it hasn't hurt the economy one bit." Mrs. Clinton also elaborated on her acclaim utterances by indicating that her husband's plans and policies would affect the audience directly. An example of elaborating an acclaim by focusing on the audience effects can be seen when Mrs. Clinton discussed how flex time is a matter of choice for the individual family, "That's why my husband wants to pass a flex time law that will give parents the option to take overtime pay either in extra income or in extra time off, depending upon whichever is best for your family." At the end of this utterance there is a sense that audience members are being directly addressed and have a personal stake in this policy. Finally, Mrs. Clinton indicated that the president cares for those who are vulnerable in society. An example of how Mrs. Clinton suggests that President Clinton watches out for those who are vulnerable can be found in her utterance dealing with mothers and their newborns: "But today, too many new mothers are asked to get up and get out after 24 hours, and that is just not enough time for many new mothers and ba-

Table 9.3

Strategies for Elaborating Acclaims and Attacks: Spousal Speeches

	Extent	Vulnerable	Effects
Elizabeth Dole	0/2*	1/1	0/1
Hillary Rodham Clinton	0/7	0/2	0/2
Total	0/9	1/3	0/3

*left number = attacks, right number = acclaims.

bies. That's why the president is right to support a bill that would prohibit the practice of forcing mothers and babies to leave the hospital in less than 48 hours." Mrs. Clinton suggested in this instance that mothers and newborns need special protection and her husband was ensuring that they received that protection through public policy. See Table 9.3.

Mrs. Dole also used elaborating strategies when acclaiming her husband (4 of 16). Two of her five elaborating strategies focused on the extensiveness of Bob Dole's actions and achievements. For example, Mrs. Dole elaborated on the extensiveness of Bob Dole's past achievements with regard to tax cuts when she stated, "They talked about his countless legislative achievements, how he had lead the United States Senate to successfully pass the largest tax cut in the history of the United States of America." In this utterance Mrs. Dole emphasized the degree of tax relief Bob Dole had ensured for the American public. Elizabeth Dole also indicated that Bob Dole's actions directly affected the audience. An example of this strategy can be seen when Mrs. Dole discussed Bob Dole's involvement in Medicare, "They also talked about how Bob had led the Senate just last year to save Medicare." The assumption here is that Medicare is an issue that directly affects the listening audience and Bob Dole had made strides to preserve an institution that is important to all Americans. Finally, Mrs. Dole elaborated on how her husband was concerned and cared about those individuals who were vulnerable and needed protection. Most specifically, those who were on Medicare need the protection of the government, according to Mrs. Dole.

ISSUES ADDRESSED

Three distinct policy topics were covered in the speeches of Mrs. Clinton and Mrs. Dole: taxes, education, and health care issues. Mrs. Clinton was responsible for nine of the eleven comments on health care. Both Mrs. Clinton and Mrs. Dole discussed education. Mrs. Dole was the only

Table 9.4
Issues Addressed: Spousal Speeches

Issue	Rank	Elizabeth Dole	Hillary Rodham Clinton
Education	2	1	1
Medicare/Health	4	2	9
Taxes	6	1	0
Other	---	4	2

speaker who specifically brought up the issue of taxes; however, she only mentioned it once. See Table 9.4.

IMPLICATIONS

The fact that both attacks and acclaims were uttered by both spouses lends support to our theory that political discourse within the parameters of an election helps to reinforce positive aspects of the candidate as well as to point to perceived deficiencies of the oppositional candidate. Like the majority of the utterances in acceptance addresses (Wells, Pier, Blaney & Benoit, 1996) and keynotes (Benoit, Blaney & Pier, 1996), acclaiming and attack messages are targeted toward the candidate.

Unlike keynote and acceptance speeches, very little attacking took place in the nominating convention speeches given by Mrs. Clinton and Mrs. Dole. Trent and Friedenberg (1995) explain that women are generally perceived as nurturing individuals and accordingly attacking discourse is not expected from them. If this is the case, it makes perfect sense that Mrs. Clinton and Mrs. Dole rarely attacked in these prime time speeches in order to preserve not only a positive view of their husbands but also to avoid appearing unfeminine themselves.

No defenses were offered by either the First Lady or Mrs. Dole. This is not surprising considering that defenses are rare in other conventions speeches as well (keynote and acceptance). Neither one of the spouses were challenged prior to their speeches; that is, there were no direct attacks immediately prior to their addresses. Therefore there was no need to engage in defensive communication. Furthermore, it could be argued that a defense utterance given without a prior attack could be detrimental to the candidate because it draws attention to potential flaws rather than to strengths. Finally, we assume that a defensive utterance made by a spouse may not have the same effect as if the defense were given by the individual attacked. There may be a perception of guilt if the accused offered a defense via a third party.

Historically, keynote and acceptance speeches have focused primarily on the policies of the candidate. However, the focus of the spousal speeches (and especially of Mrs. Dole's speech) was on character (as suggested by Blankenship, Robson, & Williams, 1997). As stated before, the nature of the surrogate (the spouse) may incline the speaker to focus on the personal aspects of the candidate's life to which the audience may not be privy. For example, both Mrs. Clinton and Mrs. Dole spoke of their husbands' dedication to family and to community service and provided personal anecdotes or testimony in order to illustrate that dedication. Perhaps spouses are special kinds of surrogate speakers in the fact that they are experts on their husbands' character, whereas other surrogates (such as keynote speakers) may have special knowledge of the policies associated with the candidate. It should be noted that Mrs. Clinton did spend about half of her time talking about policies (again, Blankenship, Robson, & Williams, 1997, confirm this analysis). However, we still maintain that our claim—that spouses of political candidates will very likely be assumed by the audience to possess extraordinarily intimate knowledge of the character of the candidate—is generally true. In this particular instance, the fact that Hillary Rodham Clinton has been an active part of her husband's presidency (not to mention the fact that he was an incumbent during the 1996 campaign) may serve to explain why Mrs. Clinton appeared especially well acquainted with her husband's policies.

NOTE

1. Like keynote speeches, the utterances which we classify as "acclaims" are not, strictly speaking, acclaims; they are praise of spouse, not self-praise.

Part IV

General Election Campaign: The Final Showdown

Chapter 10

Television Advertisements:
Dole/Gingrich versus the Liberal

Bill Clinton, "Tell"

Dole's risky economic scheme. He still won't tell us how he'll pay for it all. *Business Week* says it could "balloon deficits." Deficits, higher interest rates, slower growth. We've seen that before. Dole's campaign co-chair, Senator D'Amato, says he'd look at raising Medicare premiums to help pay for Dole's promises. Imagine what Newt Gingrich will go after.

President Clinton: $100 billion targeted tax cut while balancing the budget, 10 million new jobs, a better future.

Bill Clinton, "Economic Record"

Ten million new jobs. Family income up $1,600 (since 1993). President Clinton cut the deficit 60%. Signed welfare reform—requiring work, time limits. Taxes cut for 15 million families. Balancing the budget. America's moving forward with an economic plan that works.

Bob Dole: $900 billion in higher taxes. Republicans call him tax collector for the welfare state. His risky tax scheme would raise taxes on nine million families.

Bob Dole. Wrong in the past. Wrong for our future.

Bob Dole, "Do Better"

Today, taxes are the highest in American history . . . Bill Clinton says we have the healthiest economy in "three decades." Believe that? America can do better.

Bob Dole. Jack Kemp. Cutting income taxes on every family 15 percent. A $500 per child tax credit. Higher take-home pay.

Bob Dole. Cut taxes. Balance the budget. Raise take-home pay. Tell the truth. Bob Dole. The better man for a better America.

Bob Dole, "At Stake"

The stakes of this election? Our children. Under Clinton, cocaine and heroin use among teenagers has doubled. Why? Because Bill Clinton isn't protecting our children from drugs.

He cut the drug czar's office 83 percent, cut 227 drug enforcement agents, and cut $200 million to stop drugs at our borders. Clinton's liberal drug policies have failed.

Our children deserve better.

PREVIOUS RESEARCH ON TELEVISED POLITICAL SPOTS

Televised political campaign commercials are an important component of the modern presidential campaign. Jamieson, for example, acknowledges the importance of political spots:

Political advertising is now the major means by which candidates for the presidency communicate their messages to voters. As a conduit of this advertising, television attracts both more candidate dollars and more audience attention than radio or print. Unsurprisingly, the spot ad is the most used and the most viewed of the available forms of advertising. (1996, p. 517)

Similarly, West (1997) notes that "television ads are the single biggest expenditure in most major campaigns today" (p. 1). Ansolabehere and Iyengar (1995) are more specific, noting that "The amounts of money spent on political advertising are staggering: hundreds of millions of dollars are poured into what has become the main means of political communication in the United States" (p. 3). Clearly, televised spots are an important part of the modern presidential campaign and worthy of scholarly inquiry.

Accordingly, scholars have expended considerable effort into understanding televised political advertising (see, e.g., Louden, 1989; Kaid, Nimmo, & Sanders, 1986). Some research is experimental, and that work indicates that political spots are capable of influencing viewers (see, e.g., Basil, Schooler, & Reeves, 1991; Cundy, 1986; Garramone, 1985; Garramone, Atkin, Pinkleton, & Cole, 1990; Garramone & Smith, 1984; Hill, 1989; Just, Crigler, & Wallach, 1990; Kaid, 1991; Kaid, 1997; Kaid &

Boydston, 1987; Kaid, Leland, & Whitney, 1992; Kaid & Sanders, 1978; Lang, 1991; Meadow & Sigelman, 1982; Newhagen & Reeves, 1991; and Thorson, Christ, & Caywood, 1991). Hence, political spots are well worth studying.

Most research that analyzes the nature of political commercials focuses on two dimensions: positive versus negative ads (which corresponds to our functions of acclaiming and attacking), and issue versus image (which corresponds to our topics of policy and character). We will review this research briefly before reporting the results of our investigation into the television spots of the 1996 campaign.

Positive versus Negative Advertisements

Many scholars divide ads into positive (acclaiming) and negative (attacking) commercials (see Johnson-Cartee & Copeland, 1991, 1997; Gronbeck, 1992). Kaid and Davidson's (1986) analysis of 1982 Senate ads found that incumbents used more positive (90%) than negative ads (10%); challengers used a more balanced approach (positive: 54%; negative: 46%). Kaid and Johnston (1991) found that 71% of the ads from 1960–1988 were positive and 29% negative. However, the number of negative ads varied over time. Negative spots spiked at 40% in 1964, dropped to 22–28% in the 1970s, and increased to 35–37% in the 1980s. Kaid and Johnston (1991) did not find that challengers used more negative ads than incumbents, or that Republicans used significantly more negative ads than Democrats. West (1993) examined 150 "typical" political spots from 1952–1992, reporting that 43% were negative. He also indicated that Republican ads were more negative than those from Democrats. West (1997) also conducted a study of "prominent" spots from 1952–1996, indicating that 54% of all ads and 53% of general election ads are negative. Again, he reported that Republican prominent ads were more negative (60%) than Democratic prominent ads (48%).

Devlin (1989) reported that in 1988 Bush produced 37 ads, 14 of which were negative (38%), while Dukakis had 47 ads, 23 of which were negative (49%). However, he pointed out that Bush devoted over 40% of his budget to "airing about a half-dozen of its best negative ads" (p. 406). In 1992, 63% of Clinton's 30 ads were negative, while 56% of Bush's ads were negative. In both cases, though, their media buying was split 50/50 (Devlin, 1993). Kaid (1994) reported that 17% of the ads in the 1992 Republican and Democratic primaries were negative. In the general election Bush employed 44% positive and 56% negative ads; Clinton 31% positive and 69% negative, and Perot had only positive ads. These studies of 1992 suggest that Clinton, the challenger, used more negative ads than Bush—but still more than half of both Bush's and Clinton's ads were negative.

Devlin (1997) discussed the 1996 campaign. He reported that eighteen of Dole's ads were negative, eight were positive, and two were comparative. Clinton used two positive, four negative, and sixteen comparative spots.[1] As usual, his discussion was filled with quotations from members of the campaign advertising teams.

Benoit, Pier, and Blaney (1997) applied the functional approach to 206 televised presidential general election spots from 1980–1996. Rather than classify entire ads as acclaiming (positive), attacking (negative), or defending, they analyzed each utterance in each ad. They reported that attacking (50%) and acclaiming (49%) are common in these spots, while defense (1%) is relatively rare. Utterances in Democratic ads were more likely to acclaim (54%) than attack (46%), while remarks in Republican ads were more likely to attack (55%) than acclaim (45%). They also found that comments in the ads from incumbents are more likely to acclaim (54%) than attack (46%), while remarks in ads from challengers are more likely to attack (55%) than acclaim (45%).

Johnson-Cartee and Copeland (1989) generated a list of topics found in negative political ads, grouped them into ten categories, and asked respondents to rate them as fair or unfair. The topics clustered into two groups, labeled "Political Issues" (political record, stands on issues, criminal record, and voting record) and "Personal Characteristics" (personal life, marriage, family, religion, medical history, and sex life). At least 83% rated each political issue as a fair topic for an attack; no more than 36% rated any of the personal characteristics as an acceptable topic for political attack. This reveals that there was general, albeit not universal, agreement on which topics are fair for an attack. It also suggests that respondents did not condemn political attacks wholesale, but believed that attacks on some topics were more suitable than others.

Thus, with a few exceptions (e.g., Perot), political ads take both positive and negative approaches. We argue that a limitation of past research is that it tends to classify each advertisement as *either* positive *or* negative, despite the fact that some spots contain both positive and negative remarks (even adding a third category, comparative, only helps somewhat, because all comparative spots may not include equal amounts of positive and negative comments). The functional approach (applied in Benoit, Pier, & Blaney [1997] and in this chapter) provides a more precise estimate by classifying each remark as acclaiming (positive), attacking (negative), or defending.

Issue versus Image Advertisements

Other research on televised political spots has investigated the relative emphasis of these campaign messages on issues and image. Patterson and McClure (1976), studying the 1972 campaign, indicated that 42% of the television advertisements focused on issues, and another 28% included issue information. Hofstetter and Zukin (1979) found that 85% of the commercials for Nixon and McGovern addressed issues. Joslyn (1980) found that while 77% of the ads discussed issues, only 47% focused on images. Kern's study of the 1984 advertising campaign concluded that "issues were mentioned in 84 percent of such [30-second] spots" (1989, p. 51). In the 1992 campaign, Kaid (1994) found that 59% of primary television ads addressed image, 24% issues, and 17% were negative ads. In the general election, Bush's ads were divided evenly between issue and image; Clinton used two-thirds issue and one-third image; while Perot used about 60% issue and 40% image. West (1993) found that 65% of the 150 "typical" ads from 1952–1992 that he analyzed concerned issues, while 23% addressed character (the remainder discussed the campaign or party). His study of "prominent" spots (1997) revealed that 59% addressed issues and 39% personal qualities. Benoit, Pier, and Blaney (1997) found that 67% of the ads they analyzed from 1980 to 1996 concerned policy and 33% character. Republicans devoted somewhat less time to policy (63%) and more to character (37%), while Democrats focused a bit more on policy (71%) and less on character (29%). They also reported little difference between incumbents (66% policy; 34% character) and challengers (69% policy; 31% character) on this dimension.

The most extensive instance of this type of study was conducted by Kaid and Johnston (1991), who examined 830 television spots from 1960–1988. They reported that 67% of the positive ads and 79% of the negative ads provided issue information, and that 65% of the positive spots and 64% of the negative spots included image information. Thus, previous research has found that political spots address both issues (policy) and image (character), and that policy tends to be more prominent than character (the exception is Kaid's [1994] study of the 1992 primary, which found more advertisements focused on image than issue).

Two studies provide more details on the use of issues and image in political advertising. Joslyn's (1986) study of 506 political ads from 1960–1984 reported that 37% of the ads revealed future policy plans, 60% evaluate past governmental policy, 57% mention candidate qualities (compassion, empathy, integrity, strength, activity, and knowledge). Shyles (1986) reported the results of analysis of 140 political ads from 1980. He divided his results into issue and image, reporting mentions of these topics: Carter's record, domestic, economy, energy, federalism, foreign policy, government management, national security, and national well-being (issue); altruism, competence, expertise, honesty, leadership, personal, strength, and other qualities (image). It is clear that political advertising addresses both issues and images (see also Benze & Declercq, 1985).

Several studies suggest that more time is devoted to policy than character (although in a 30–second spot, it is impossible to go into great detail). Again, we believe one limitation of past research is that many studies only report that an ad contained some issue information. Because political spots vary in how much time they devote to policy, this is a crude index. The functional approach (Benoit, Pier, & Blaney [1997] and the analysis of the 1996 campaign reported here) analyzes each utterance in a commercial to provide a more precise indication of the degree to which policy and character are addressed in a political advertisement.

1996 GENERAL ELECTION TELEVISION SPOTS

We obtained 60 television advertisements sponsored by Bill Clinton (or the Democratic National Committee on his behalf)[2] and 35 television spots sponsored by Bob Dole (or the Republican National Committee on his behalf). One of the ads for Dole ran for two minutes and two for one minute, while one of the spots for Clinton was 60 seconds. This means that the total time in these ads was 1,830 seconds for Clinton and 1,200 seconds for Dole (accordingly, we discuss most results in percentages to account for the disparity in number of advertisements obtained). Some of these spots were videotaped from local television; some were obtained from newspaper ad watches; some were downloaded from the Clinton and Dole campaigns' web pages; some were downloaded from independent web sites (AllPolitics, PoliticsNow); and some were obtained from a compilation tape sold by Patrick Devlin (University of Rhode Island).

We address ten findings from our analysis of these 1996 general election presidential television spots. Our conclusions are discussed under seven headings: functions, defense, policy versus character, policy, character, elaboration, and issues addressed.

FUNCTIONS OF TELEVISION SPOTS

First, these advertisements as a whole were replete with acclaims (54%) and attacks (46%). For example, the spot "Drums" acclaims by listing a number of Clinton's policy initiatives: "Clinton-Gore. $500/child tax credit. Clean air and water. Internet access for schools. Economic growth. 10,000,000 new jobs." Dole's advertisement "Future" summarizes some of his key themes, reasons to vote for him: "My plan is to cut waste and taxes, preserve Medicare and Social Security, and strengthen our borders to protect our children from drugs." Thus, both ad campaigns accentuate the positive. See Table 10.1.

However, these ads contain more than just acclaims; they also attack the opposition. For example, Clinton's spot "Gamble" declares that our

Table 10.1
Acclaims, Attacks, and Defenses: General TV Spots

	Acclaims	Attacks	Defenses
Clinton	268 (58%)	190 (41%)	2 (0.4%)
Dole	110 (45%)	135 (55%)	1 (0.4%)
Total	378 (54%)	325 (46%)	3 (0.4%)

recent economic progress is at risk from his opponent: "Now Bob Dole endangers it all with a risky last-minute scheme that would balloon the deficit. Higher interest rates. Hurt families." The Dole commercial "Ondine" depicts a single mother lamenting the state of her finances and Clinton's inactivity: "I don't really feel he [Clinton] has done anything really to pull us out of the economic state that we are in." So, both sets of ads also contain criticism of the opponent.

A second finding contrasts the two candidates' relative use of acclaiming and attacking. Clinton, the Democratic incumbent, spent more time acclaiming (58%) than attacking (41%) in his commercials, while Dole attacked (55%) more than he acclaimed (45%). A chi-square test found this to be significant ($X^2[df = 1] = 11.9$, p < .001). In "Economic Record," reproduced at the beginning of this chapter, Clinton praises his past accomplishments: "Ten million new jobs. Family income up $1,600 (since 1993). President Clinton cut the deficit 60%. Signed welfare reform— requiring work, time limits. Taxes cut for 15 million families. Balancing the budget." On the other hand, in "Tell" Clinton attacks his opponent's 15% tax cut proposal: "Dole's risky economic scheme. He still won't tell us how he'll pay for it all. *Business Week* says it could 'balloon deficits.' Deficits, higher interest rates, slower growth." Thus, Clinton's ads employed both acclaiming and attacking, although acclaiming was somewhat more common.

As noted above, Dole, the Republican challenger, devoted more time in his television spots to attacking (55%) than to acclaiming (45%). In the ad "Do Better" Dole reports that "Today, taxes are the highest in American history. . . . Bill Clinton says we have the healthiest economy in 'three decades.' Believe that?" This ad not only criticizes Clinton for raising taxes, but it also maligns his honesty. In "At Stake" Dole attacks Clinton's record on teenage drug abuse:

The stakes of this election? Our children. Under Clinton, cocaine and heroin use among teenagers has doubled. Why? Because Bill Clinton isn't protecting our children from drugs. He cut the drug czar's office 83 percent, cut 227 drug enforcement agents, arid cut $200 million to stop drugs at our borders. Clinton's liberal drug policies have failed. Our children deserve better.

Clearly, these ads function to attack Bill Clinton's record in office, on the economy and on teen drug abuse.

Dole also engages in acclaiming in his political spots. For example, in "Do Better" Dole outlines several of his economic proposals: "Bob Dole. Jack Kemp. Cutting income taxes on every family 15 percent. A $500 per child tax credit. Higher take-home pay. Bob Dole. Cut taxes. Balance the budget. Raise take-home pay." These are positive proposals for our country's future economic success.

A third finding concerns a recurrent form of attack: guilt by association. Twenty-three of Clinton's ads discussed "Dole/Gingrich," clearly trying to associate Bob Dole, the Republican candidate, with Newt Gingrich, the Republican House majority leader who was experiencing some popularity problems (other spots mention Gingrich unfavorably without referring to the hybrid entity "Dole/Gingrich"). For example, "Safe" declared "That's why it's so wrong that Dole and Gingrich tried to slash Medicare $270 billion." The spot "Counting" asserted that "Bob Dole and Newt Gingrich tried to cut vaccines for children." Viewers of "Sad" heard that "Dole/Gingrich tried to slash 'em [school antidrug programs] 50%." Guilt by association is very strong in these spots.

In a similar fashion, seven of Dole's ads tried to hang the label of "liberal" on Clinton. "The Truth" declared that "The real Bill Clinton" is "a real spend & tax liberal." This was an attempt to associate Clinton with liberal policies (especially "tax and spend" liberalism). The most extensive attempt to label Clinton a liberal occurred in "How to Speak Liberal":

[Clinton]: "I'll tell you this, I will not raise taxes on the middle class to pay for these programs."

[Announcer]: "That's liberal for I raised taxes right on the middle class."

[Clinton]: "People in this room [are] still mad at me at this budget 'cause you think that I raised taxes too much."

[Announcer]: "That's liberal for I raised taxes even on Social Security."

[Clinton]: "It might surprise you to know that I think I raised 'em too much too."

[Announcer]: "That's liberal for I raised your taxes and got caught."

Thus, advertisements from both candidates attempted to use guilt by association to attack their opponent.

Table 10.2
Defense Strategies: General TV Spots

	Denial
Clinton	2
Dole	1
Total	3

DEFENSE

There were only three utterances that enacted defense (0.4%). All were instances of denial (see Table 10.2). For example, in the "Fool" spot the Dole campaign asks viewers about accusations made by the Clinton campaign: "How many times have you seen this? 'Last year Dole/Gingrich tried to cut Medicare $270 billion.' It's wrong." This spot clearly denies one of Clinton's attacks.

We do want to acknowledge that our procedures may tend to underestimate defensive ads. In our opinion, several advertisements in the 1996 campaign (especially for Bill Clinton) appear to have been produced as responses to an opponent's earlier ad. However, we considered an utterance to be a defense only if it explicitly referred to a prior accusation. Notice how our example of a defensive utterance from Dole begins by reminding viewers of Clinton's attack. However, if a Dole ad charged that Clinton had failed to stop illegal immigration and Clinton's campaign responded with a spot that stressed Clinton's actions to reduce illegal immigration, the Clinton ad would not be considered a defense unless it explicitly acknowledged those accusations. Otherwise, it would be considered to be an instance of acclaiming. Even considering the fact that our procedures may have underestimated the number of defensive utterances, defense was comparatively rare in these televised spots.

POLICY VERSUS CHARACTER

A fourth finding is that these presidential spots from 1996 focused more on policy than character. Policy considerations accounted for 74% of the utterances in these ads, while character concerns constituted only 26% of the remarks. To illustrate, Clinton's spot "Responsibility" discussed welfare reform, a policy topic: "He signed tough welfare reform. Work requirements. Time limits. Force teenage mothers to stay in school or lose benefits." On the other hand, Elizabeth Dole, in the spot "Elizabeth," declared that "Bob Dole doesn't make promises he can't keep."

Honesty is an important character trait that Bob Dole possesses (there may be a subtle contrast with Bill Clinton here as well). See Table 10.3.

Once again, we find a difference between the extent to which these candidates addressed policy and character, a fourth finding. Both candidates emphasized policy more than character, but Clinton focused on policy even more often than Dole. This difference was significant (X^2[df = 1] = 29.9, p < .001). For Clinton, the Democratic incumbent, 80% of the utterances in his television spots concerned policy matters, and 20% addressed character. In "Tell" Clinton discusses the economy (tax cuts, balancing the budget, jobs). In "Economic Record" Clinton discusses the economy again and welfare reform. Neither of these ads emphasizes character concerns. In some ads, of course, Clinton did address the topic of character. For example, in "Sad" he suggests that Dole is running a negative campaign: "It's sad. All Bob Dole offers are negative attacks." In "Seconds" James Brady (former press secretary who was permanently injured in the attempt to assassinate President Reagan) praises Clinton's integrity: "President Clinton stood up and helped pass the Brady Bill. It wasn't about politics. The president had the integrity to do what was right." Nevertheless, Clinton's commercials stressed policy more than character.

In contrast, Dole, the Republican challenger, devoted 62% of his advertising remarks to policy and 38% to character. Dole's ad "Do Better" discusses economic issues, and "At Stake" considers teen drug abuse, both policy matters. However, "Do Better" does question Clinton's honesty ("Believe that?"). In "From the Heart" Elizabeth Dole tells viewers that "My husband is a plain-spoken man from the heart of America—Russell, Kansas. In Russell, you say what you're going to do and you do it. The truth first, last—always the truth." Thus, Dole is honest. She also contrasts Dole with Clinton: "He's a workhorse, not a show horse." Like Clinton, more of the remarks in Dole's spots focus on policy than character, but a larger percentage of Dole's than Clinton's remarks in these commercials addresses character.

POLICY

Sixth, Clinton did a better job of making use of the potential policy arguments than Dole. Notice in Table 10.3 that Clinton's ads praise both Clinton's past deeds (117) and his future plans (44). Although past deeds are used more than twice as much as future plans, both are prominent ideas in these advertisements. For example, in "Husband" Clinton's past deeds are praised: "President Clinton had the courage to take on the special interests. He banned cigarette ads that target our children." In "Responsibility" Clinton's future plans for addressing the welfare prob-

Table 10.3
Policy versus Character: General TV Spots

| | Policy | | | | Character | | | |
	Deeds	Plans	Goals	Total	PQual	Leader	Ideals	Total
Clinton	110/117*	34/44	8/52	152/213 (80%)	26/13	6/10	6/32	38/55 (20%)
Dole	96/ 5	3/26	2/21	101/52 (62%)	23/28	3/10	8/20	34/58 (38%)
Total	206/122	37/70	10/73	253/265 (74%)	49/41	9/20	14/52	72/113 (26%)

*left number = attacks, right number = acclaims.

lem are outlined: "The next step: create jobs. Tax incentives for businesses that hire welfare recipients. Job training for all workers." Thus, Clinton's ads acclaimed both his past deeds and his future plans.

The contrast with Dole is sharp. Dole repeatedly praises his future plans (26), but rarely acclaims his past deeds (5). For example, in "Future" Dole explains that "My plan is to cut waste and taxes, preserve Medicare and Social Security, and strengthen our borders to protect our children from drugs." Dole has a record in Congress with many notable accomplishments, but he rarely made use of his past deeds when his spots praised himself.

As with acclaims, Clinton's televised advertisements attack both Dole's past deeds (110) and his future plans (34). While these ideas do not occur with equal frequency, they are both fairly common. In "Preserve" Clinton attacks Dole's past actions concerning Medicare. The spot begins by quoting Dole's own statement: "[Dole:] 'I was there, fighting the fight, voting against Medicare, one of twelve, because we knew it wouldn't work.' Last year, Dole/Gingrich tried to cut Medicare $270 billion." This remark functions to attack Dole's past deeds. Clinton also attacked Dole's future plans. "Economic Record" charges that "His risky tax scheme would raise taxes on nine million families." Thus, Clinton's ads attacked both Dole's past deeds and his future plans.

The numbers for Dole's spots reveal a sharply different story. Dole attacked Clinton's past deeds frequently (96), but hardly ever criticized Clinton's future plans (3). In "Classroom" Dole attacked Clinton's policies on illegal immigration: "Bill Clinton has fought California in court, forcing us to support them. Clinton fought Prop 187, cut border agents, gave citizenship to aliens with criminal records. We pay the taxes, we are the victims. Our children get shortchanged." Thus, Clinton exploited all four of these potential topics for arguments (acclaiming one's own past deeds, acclaiming one's own future plans, attacking the opponent's past deeds, attacking the opponent's future plans), but Dole emphasized only two of these four options.

A seventh finding is that while both candidates praised their goals (Clinton: 52; Dole 21), they rarely attacked their opponent's goals (Clinton: 8; Dole: 2). For instance, Clinton's ad "Opportunity" embraced these general goals: "The president: growth and opportunity." Similarly, Dole's spot "The Plan" outlined two of Dole's goals: "Cut wasteful spending. Balance the budget." We believe it is easy to acclaim by declaring a desirable goal, and both candidates do so frequently. However, it is often more difficult to attack an opponent's general goal, which is likely to be abstract and desirable (balance the budget). In contrast, specific plans (e.g., raise taxes, cut defense spending, reduce entitlements) are easier to attack than general goals (reduce the deficit). Thus, both candidates praise their own goals, but neither one attacks his opponent's goals very often.

CHARACTER

Both candidates were more likely to acclaim on the basis of their ideals (Clinton: 32; Dole: 20) than to attack on these grounds (Clinton: 6; Dole: 8), an eighth conclusion. To illustrate, Clinton's ad "Values" declared that Clinton supports "American values. Do our duty to our parents." Dole's spot "America" expressed this ideal: "I see an America with a government that works for us, not the other way around." The fact that the candidates were more likely to acclaim than attack ideals may be similar to the finding concerning goals: lofty ideals are easier to espouse than to criticize.

Furthermore, Clinton's spots were more likely to attack Dole's qualities than to acclaim his own qualities (attacks: 26; acclaims: 13), while Dole's advertisements were more balanced (acclaims: 28; attacks: 23). The fewest remarks were devoted to leadership qualities (Clinton, 16 remarks; Dole, 13 remarks).

STRATEGIES FOR ELABORATING ACCLAIMS AND ATTACKS

The most common form of elaboration in these spots was extent. "Economic Record" touts the magnitude of Clinton's accomplishments: "Ten million new jobs. Family income up $1,600 (since 1993). President Clinton cut the deficit 60%." These are important and desirable developments. Dole's spot "Riady 2" criticized the president's tax hike, emphasizing its historic size: "He gives us the largest tax increase in American history." This is a huge tax increase laid at Clinton's doorstep. Thus, the ads frequently elaborated their utterances (both acclaims and attacks) by stressing their extent. These data are displayed in Table 10.4.

The second most common way to develop an utterance is to mention effects on the audience. In "Look," Clinton discussed the effects of Dole's past deeds on families: "And look closely at his risky tax scheme—he'd actually raise taxes on nine million working families." In the ad "Sorry—Taxes," Dole refers again to Clinton's tax increase. This time, however, he relates it to middle-class voters: "he gave the middle class the largest tax increase in history." Another way to elaborate utterances is to mention effects on the audience.

Both sets of ads address vulnerable groups, although Clinton was more likely to use this strategy when acclaiming, while Dole tended to use it to attack. In "Husband" Linda Crawford (wife of an ex–tobacco

Table 10.4
Strategies for Elaborating Acclaims and Attacks: General TV Spots

	Extent	Effects	Vulnerable	Consistency	Persist
Clinton	32/54*	13/22	10/17	3/ 0	5/1
Dole	25/21	10/21	6/ 2	11/1	2/1
Total	57/75	23/43	16/19	14/1	7/2

*left number = attacks, right number = acclaims.

lobbyist who died from cancer) declared that "When people attack the president's character I think of my children—and millions of others—his leadership is protecting." Clearly these children are unable to protect themselves, and the president is working on their behalf. "Too Late" attacks Clinton's drug policies, relating the effects on teens: "For the thousands of young Americans who became hooked on drugs under Clinton, his apology is too little, too late." So, both acclaims and attacks were elaborated with reference to those who are vulnerable.

Ads from both candidates attacked the other on grounds of inconsistency, and Dole once claimed consistency was one of his virtues. The spot "Dole's Real Record" begins by reminding voters of Dole's antidrug slogan, "Just Don't Do It." Then it observes, "But look at what he's done: voted to cut the President's school antidrug efforts—by 50 percent. Against creating the drug czar." The ad portrays Dole's actions as inconsistent with his words. Dole's ad "More Talk" uses clips of Clinton discussing a balanced budget, accusing him of double-talk: "I would present a five-year plan to balance the budget. . . . We could do it in seven years. . . . I think we can reach it in nine years. . . . Balance the budget in 10 years. . . . I think we could reach it in eight years. . . . So we're between seven and nine, no?" Finally, both groups of advertisements occasionally elaborated with persistence.

ISSUES ADDRESSED

Clinton directed more of the utterances in his televised spots to six of the seven topics. Dole, on the other hand, devoted more utterances only to taxes (Clinton also led on remarks directed to "other" topics, like the environment). Of course, Clinton had more ads (60 to 35) and devoted a larger number of utterances to policy than Dole (365 to 153), so it is reasonable to expect Clinton would tend to lead in references to these issues. However, this does not account for the size of Clinton's lead. On some topics, Clinton's lead is quite sizable (e.g., on jobs and the econ-

Table 10.5
Issues Addressed: General TV Spots

Issue	Rank	Clinton	Dole
Jobs and the Economy	1	39 (12%)	4 (3%)
Education	2	40 (12%)	3 (2%)
Budget Deficit	3	22 (7%)	9 (6%)
Medicare and Health	4	62 (19%)	11 (8%)
Welfare Reform	5	21 (7%)	8 (6%)
Taxes	6	31 (10%)	58 (41%)
Crime and Drugs	6	57 (18%)	22 (15%)
Other	---	50 (15%)	27 (19%)

omy, 39 to 4; on education, 40 to 3; on Medicare, 62 to 11). The percentages show that—except for taxes—Clinton devoted a larger percentage of his policy utterances to issues considered important by the public than Dole. Thus, even considering the large disparity in the number of ads from these two campaigns and the fact that Clinton addressed policy more than Dole, Clinton still devoted a larger percent of his utterances to topics important to voters on six of seven issues. See Table 10.5.

IMPLICATIONS

Our analysis of television advertisements in the 1996 presidential campaign found that 54% of the statements in these ads acclaimed, while 46% attacked. Previous research has tended to find that positive ads outnumbered negative ones (Benoit, Pier, & Blaney, 1997; Devlin, 1989; Kaid, 1994; Kaid & Davidson, 1986; Kaid & Johnston, 1991; West, 1993). However, we also found that the Republican candidate, Bob Dole, used a higher proportion of attacking remarks than the Democrat, Bill Clinton (Dole: 54%, Clinton: 39%). This is consistent with some previous research (Benoit, Pier, & Blaney, 1997; West, 1993), but not all (Kaid & Johnston, 1991). We also note that Dole was a challenger, and previous research has found that they are more likely to attack than incumbents (Benoit, Pier, & Blaney, 1997).

West (1997) analyzed 55 "prominent" spots from 1996, including 47 Republican, 7 Democratic, and 1 Independent spot (36 from the primary, 19 from the general election). He reported that 60% of these spots attacked the opponent. This figure is much higher than our figure of 46%

attacks. Of course, one difference is that we classify each utterance while he classifies entire spots. However, his procedure for selecting his sample also makes it difficult to compare our results. First, West's approach lumps together advertisements from all three parties and from different parts of the campaign. Second, he defines "prominent" ads (for spots from 1952–1988) as commercials mentioned by Jamieson in the second edition of her book *Packaging the Presidency*, and (for spots from 1992 to 1996) as advertisements that appeared on the CBS Evening News. He noted that studying political advertising "is complicated because not all ads are equally important" (p. 41), which is undeniable. However, to ignore all spots that were aired locally (i.e., not on the *CBS Evening News*), or to assume that the spots which were *selected because they best illustrate particular points throughout a book* constitute a desirable sample is questionable (even if that book is as important as Jamieson's work). In the first edition of his book (1993), West usually contrasted his sample of "prominent" spots with a second sample of "typical" spots, which helped provide a more balanced characterization.

Devlin (1997), classifying entire spots, reported that two-thirds of Dole's ads were negative and two were comparative. Again, we found that 55% of the utterances in Dole's spots were attacking (negative), so classifying entire spots tended to overestimate the amount of attacks in his spots. On the other hand, Devlin reported that Clinton had two positive, four negative, and sixteen comparative ads. We found that 41% of the utterances in Clinton's spots were attacking. Our analysis provides a more precise estimate of the proportion of attacks and acclaims.

Our analysis reveals that the utterances in ads from both campaigns addressed policy more than character (74% to 26%). Again, this is consistent with prior research (Benoit, Pier, & Blaney, 1997[3]; Hofstetter & Zukin, 1979; Joslyn, 1980; Kaid, 1994; Kaid & Johnston, 1991; Kern, 1989; Patterson & McClure, 1976; West, 1993). We also found that the statements in ads by Clinton, who was both a Democrat and an incumbent, focused more on policy (80%) than the remarks in spots by Dole (62%), the Republican challenger. This also is consistent with findings in previous research (Benoit, Pier, & Blaney, 1997). West (1997) found that 59% of the spots concerned policy (domestic and international affairs) and 39% addressed character. These figures are in the same ball park (we both found policy discussed more frequently than character), although our figures indicate substantially more policy utterances that West's data. Again, we attribute these differences to (1) the fact that he classifies entire spots while we deal with utterances, and (2) the fact that he used his sample of "prominent" ads.

We would also like to contrast the results that would be possible with a traditional analysis with the results we obtained here. A traditional analysis that classifies each ad as positive or negative would be misleading, because so many of both Dole's and Clinton's ads included both kinds of statements. Adding a third category, comparative, really only serves to acknowledge the problem, not solve it. Such an approach would report that 18% of Clinton's ads were positive, 12% were negative, and 70% comparative. Similarly, 12% of Dole's spots were positive, 44% were negative, and 44% comparative. However, we cannot tell if comparative ads are mostly negative, mostly positive, or about equally positive and negative. These figures could be taken to imply that the two candidates did not acclaim much and had roughly the same percentage of positive advertisements (18%, 12%) and that the percentage of Dole's negative spots was almost four times as large as for Clinton's negative ads (Dole: 44%, Clinton: 12%). The figures for comparative ads (both positive and negative) are impossible to interpret, because we don't know whether these ads are equally split between positive and negative sentiments or skewed in one direction.

Our analysis, in contrast, reveals that Clinton's spots acclaimed 58% of the time, while Dole's ads attacked 55% of the time. This means that both candidates acclaimed far more than the figures for positive ads (18%, 12%) might suggest. It also means that Clinton's ads were notably more positive than Dole's spots (58% to 45%), and by a wider margin than the simple classification by entire ads would suggest (18%, 12%). We can also see that Clinton was much more negative (41%) than the number of negative ads suggests (12%). Also, Dole's ads were more negative than Clinton's (55% to 41%), but by a much narrower margin than is suggested by entire ads (44% to 12%). We believe our approach provides a more precise understanding of the functions of these advertisements.

Similarly, a traditional analysis (like Patterson & McClure, 1976; Hofstetter & Zukin, 1979; Kern, 1989) would note that every one of Clinton's and every one of Dole's ads included (at least a minimal) mention of policy considerations (issues). But this analysis simply does not tell us how much they discussed policy matters: these ads could have been totally devoted to policy questions, or they could have each made only a brief mention. Nor does it allow us to compare the two candidates on this question.

Our analysis, in contrast, reveals that 74% of the utterances in these spots concerned questions of policy, while 26% addressed character. Furthermore, we can report that 80% of the utterances in Clinton's ads addressed policy, while 62% of the remarks in Dole's ads were policy related. Clinton directed more of his ad's remarks to topics considered important by voters. Again, we believe that our approach provides a much more precise understanding of the extent to which these spots address policy and character matters.

NOTES

1. Devlin also mentions that there were four Clinton testimonial spots and some (unspecified) response ads. It is unclear whether these were considered positive, negative, or comparative.

2. About half of the Clinton/DNC spots ran prior to the Democratic National Convention, so technically there were two sets of television advertisements (primary and general). However, President Clinton's nomination was not contested. He did not have to run against (or attack) other Democrats. His television spots were free to attack Dole even before the general election campaign (and these earlier Clinton/DNC spots did in fact attack Dole specifically, rather than other Republican contenders). Had Clinton been challenged in the primaries or attacked other Republican candidates in his advertisements, we would have separated these ads into primary and general spots (as we did with Dole). However, because the spots for Clinton targeted Dole from the start, we felt it was more accurate to treat these ads here in Chapter 10, as if Clinton had started the general election campaign early.

3. We compare these results with the study of ads from 1980–1996 (Benoit, Pier, & Blaney, 1997). Because that study includes ads from 1996, there is overlap in the messages analyzed. However, because this is the only study to apply the functional theory of campaign discourse to televised political advertisements, and because it does include ads from four other campaigns, we believe this comparison is still useful.

Chapter 11

Radio Addresses: Hear Ye, Hear Ye

Bill Clinton's August 31 Radio Address (excerpts)

Good morning. On this bright Labor Day Weekend I'm speaking to you from America's heartland. . . .

It is clearer to me than ever before we are on the right track to the twenty-first century. Our economy is growing, creating opportunity for people. Just this week we got new news of how our economy is moving forward and creating opportunity. Consumer confidence is the highest in years, and in the most recent statistics, economic growth at 4.8 percent.

In the past couple of weeks we've made real progress for working families. Ten million Americans got an increase in their incomes when we increased the minimum wage law. . . .

We passed a $5,000 tax credit to encourage people to adopt children. We passed the Kennedy-Kassebaum Bill so you don't lose your health insurance if you move from job to job or if a member of your family has been sick. . . .

We should make college available to all young Americans. Now that we've ended welfare as we know it, it must be a national mission to provide jobs for the people who will move off welfare. We must clean up two-thirds of the toxic waste sites in America, so our children live near parks, not poison. . . .

Our administration has put in place a comprehensive strategy to increase home ownership, including dramatically bringing down mortgage rates. In the last four years, 4.4 million more Americans became homeowners; that's the highest level in 15 years. Home sales are rising over twice as fast this year as in each of the past three years. . . .

For working families, their home is the most important asset, their biggest financial investment. Our tax cut means that working families will never have to pay taxes when they sell their homes. . . .

This tax cut, like every one I've proposed, is fully paid for in my balanced budget plan. We won't bust the budget to pay for tax cuts. We'll cut spending and close corporate loopholes. . . .

Happy Labor Day, and thanks for listening.

Bob Dole's August 31 Radio Address (excerpts)

Hello, I'm Bob Dole. It has now been eleven days since the Clinton administration released the results of a national survey on teenage drug use. The news could not have been much worse: Since President Clinton took office, drug use among 12- to 17-year-olds has more than doubled—skyrocketing by 105%. Marijuana use has increased by 141%. LSD use has increased by 183%. And monthly use of cocaine by teenagers has increased by an appalling 166% in just the last year alone. . . .

At a time when many businesses were trying to create drug-free workplaces, the Clinton administration hired individuals whose drug use was so extensive or so recent that the United States Secret Service recommended denying them access to the White House. The Clinton administration rejected the Secret Service's recommendations. . . .

And there's more. President Clinton slashed the Office of National Drug Control Policy by 83%. He scaled back spending for interdiction efforts that would have stopped drugs before they reached our shores. He proposed eliminating hundreds of drug enforcement positions. And he appointed a Surgeon General who suggested that drugs ought to be legalized.

Instead of slashing the Office of National Drug Control Policy and other drug control efforts, I will ensure that they have enough staff and funding to get the job done. We cannot win the war on drugs "on the cheap."

Instead of a Justice Department that cuts drug prosecutions by 10%, as this one has done, a Dole Justice Department will aggressively prosecute those who poison our children. . . .

The bottom line is that in a Dole administration, we will return to what works: A policy of zero tolerance for drug smugglers, drug pushers, drugs in the workplace, and drugs in school. Our country and our children deserve nothing less.

Thanks for listening. Elizabeth joins with me in wishing everyone a safe and enjoyable Labor Day weekend.

We selected a pair of radio addresses by Clinton and Dole from each month from June through October to be the basis of this analysis. The texts of Clinton's weekly radio address were readily available from the White House World Wide Web page; texts of some (but not all) of Dole's radio addresses were available on the Dole/Kemp World Wide Web page. A few radio addresses featured the candidates' running mates, and we decided not to include any of those in our sample. We wanted to select speeches given on the same day in order to control for the possible effects of national and international events on these speeches. Given

Table 11.1
Acclaims, Attacks, and Defenses: Radio Addresses

	Acclaims	Attacks	Defense
Clinton	146 (100%)	0	0
Dole	69 (53%)	60 (46%)	2 (2%)
Total	215 (78%)	60 (22%)	2 (1%)

these limitations on comparable texts available to us, we selected pairs of radio addresses from June 29, July 6, August 31, September 28, and October 4/5. The conclusions derived from our analysis will be addressed under four headings: functions, policy versus character, elaboration, and issues addressed.

FUNCTIONS OF RADIO ADDRESSES

First, we found that both candidates were more likely to acclaim than attack in these messages. This effect was most dramatic in Clinton's case: in fact, he *only* performed acclaiming in these speeches (given the fact that Clinton had 0 attacks, we did not calculate a chi-square). For instance, Clinton's August 31 speech reported that "Consumer confidence is the highest in years, and in the most recent statistics, economic growth at 4.8 percent." The fact that Clinton decided not to attack in his radio addresses means that he did not take advantage of the potential for attacks to reduce his opponent's apparent preferability. Perhaps he wanted to "take the high road" in this forum, eschewing all attacks. Dole spent slightly more than half of his time on self-praise (53%). In his August 31 message, Dole acclaimed his future antidrug stance: "The bottom line is that in a Dole administration, we will return to what works: A policy of zero tolerance for drug smugglers, drug pushers, drugs in the workplace, and drugs in school. Our country and our children deserve nothing less." Both candidates engaged in considerable acclaiming in their speeches. See Table 11.1.

Dole's radio addresses devoted 46% of their utterances to attacks. For example, in his August 31 speech, Dole savaged Clinton's drug policies: "Since President Clinton took office, drug use among 12- to 17-year-olds has more than doubled—skyrocketing by 105%. Marijuana use has increased by 141%. LSD use has increased by 183%. And monthly use of cocaine by teenagers has increased by an appalling 166% in just the last year alone." These are alarming problems to be laid at the president's door. So, Dole frequently attacked Clinton in his radio addresses.

The situation for Dole seems to be more complex than it may first appear. Dole did not attack in his June radio address. In July, 37% of his utterances were attacks. In August, that figure increased to 64%, and in September, 67% of Dole's remarks attacked Clinton. In his October radio address, 33% of Dole's utterances were attacks. Although these speeches may not be typical, it appears that Dole's addresses became more negative from June through September, becoming less negative in October.

Defense, on the other hand, was quite rare. As was the case with attacks, Clinton engaged in no defense in these radio addresses, while Dole used defense only twice out of 131 utterances analyzed. For example, in his August speech, Dole used simple denial to respond to attacks from Clinton about Medicare:

The president also won't tell you that ever since a commission that includes two of his own cabinet members told him that Medicare was going bankrupt in five years, he has done absolutely nothing, to ensure its solvency—nothing, that is, except to mislead seniors into thinking that Republicans want to cut Medicare. The president won't tell you that he knows that charge is not true.

This passage acknowledges the accusation (Clinton has tried to scare senior citizens into believing Dole and his fellow Republicans want to cut Medicare) and ends with a clear denial of that accusation.

Given the fact that each pair of speeches was broadcast on the same day (except October, when the speeches occurred on the 4th and 5th), there was no opportunity to respond to the most current message. It would be possible to respond to prior attacks or attacks from other kinds of messages (and Dole did defend twice), but it is reasonable that defense occurred infrequently. A response to a prior attack might function to remind the audience of that attack—or even to inform them of it if they had not heard it. Relying heavily on defense could make the candidates appear to be on the defensive, reacting rather than acting.

POLICY VERSUS CHARACTER

Both Clinton and Dole were more likely to address policy issues than character questions (72% policy, 28% character; a chi-square did not find a difference between the candidates here [$X^2\{df = 1\} = 2.9$, ns]). For instance, in Clinton's June radio address, he boasted that:

We cut the budget deficit in half and proposed a plan to balance the budget. Lower interest rates have helped us to slash unemployment to 5.6 percent and create 9.7 million new jobs. Inflation is near a 30-year low. Interest rates have stayed down. Business investment is up nearly 30 percent. And America is the number one exporter and the most competitive nation on earth.

These are all notable accomplishments that voters can appreciate. These data are displayed in Table 11.2.

Of the two candidates, however, Dole was more likely to address character (33%) than Clinton (23%). To illustrate, Dole impugned the leadership ability of the Clinton administration in his August radio address, charging it with "neglect and ineptitude." This attack clearly impugns Clinton's character.

Clinton devoted most of his remarks (59% overall; 77% of policy-related comments) to acclaiming his past deeds. In his August message, Clinton reported that "In the past couple of weeks we've made real progress for working families. Ten million Americans got an increase in their incomes when we increased the minimum wage law." He also described his goals (20 times) and occasionally discussed his future plans (6 times). For instance, in his June speech, he lamented the attack on U.S. forces stationed in Saudi Arabia, and committed himself to this goal: "I'll do everything in my power to discover who's responsible, to pursue them and to punish them." He does not offer the specifics that would qualify as a future plan.

If we consider Dole's policy-oriented attacks, he primarily attacked Clinton's past deeds (89%). He only attacked Clinton's future plans once and Clinton's goals four times. His policy-related acclaims were mainly divided between his future plans (53%) and his goals (43%); he acclaimed his past deeds only twice.

Most of Clinton's character-related utterances concerned his ideals (53%), as in his August message: "I look forward to taking our argument for opportunity, responsibility, and community to the American people." Like Clinton, Dole's character acclaims were primarily discussions of his ideals (69%). In June, Dole illustrated one of his ideals: "Peace through strength is more than a slogan; it is the blueprint for American survival in a world bristling with danger." Dole's character attacks focused on both Clinton's ideals and his personal qualities.

STRATEGIES FOR ELABORATING ACCLAIMS AND ATTACKS

The most frequently used strategy for developing their utterances was extent. In September, Clinton spoke of the magnitude of his accomplishments in collecting child support payments: "In four years, child support collections in our country have risen from $8 billion to $11.8 billion—a nearly 50 percent increase in child support collections. And nearly 800,000 paternities were identified. That's an increase of 50 percent over 1992." Dole was much more likely to develop his attacks than his acclaims this way (Clinton did not attack in these speeches, so his use of

Table 11.2
Policy versus Character: Radio Addresses

	Policy				Character			
	Deeds	Plans	Goals	Total	PQual	Leader	Ideals	Total
Clinton	0/86*	0/ 6	0/20	0/112 (77%)	0/ 8	0/ 8	0/18	0/34 (23%)
Dole	42/ 2	1/21	4/17	47/ 40 (67%)	6/ 5	1/ 4	6/20	13/29 (33%)
Total	42/88	1/27	4/37	47/152 (72%)	6/13	1/12	6/38	13/63 (28%)

*left number = attacks, right number = acclaims.

Table 11.3
Strategies for Elaborating Acclaims and Attacks: Radio Addresses

	Extent	Effects	Vulnerable	Consistency	Persist
Clinton	0/44*	0/15	0/ 5	0/0	0/4
Dole	26/ 9	8/17	7/ 5	7/0	0/1
Total	26/53	8/32	7/10	7/0	0/5

*left number = attacks, right number = acclaims.

extent, of course, was only in acclaiming). In his September message, Dole asserted that "the very first major economic proposal of his administration was a $16 billion package of pork barrel spending." Extent is a relatively easy way to intensify acclaims and attacks. See Table 11.3.

On the other hand, Dole was more likely to acclaim than to attack on the basis of effects on the audience. In his September radio address, Dole explained what a savings of $1,261—the amount a family of four earning $30,000 would save from his proposed tax cut—could mean to voters:

What does 1,261 more dollars mean to American families? Well, I recently visited a child care center in Ankeny, Iowa. And 1,261 dollars could pay for four months of child care at that center. Or it could pay for one year's tuition at many community colleges. Or it could pay for a month or two of your rent or mortgage. Or it could pay for a personal computer for your children. Or you could take your family on a well-deserved vacation.

This rather lengthy elaboration of the possible effects on the audience of his tax cut helped put his proposal into perspective. Both candidates also discussed vulnerable groups as a way to elaborate their ideas. Earlier passages quoted from Dole, for example, lamented the number of teens who abuse drugs.

Dole charged Clinton with inconsistency, and persistence occurred occasionally. For example, in September Dole tried to establish expectations for the upcoming presidential debate as he attacked Clinton for not delivering on his promised middle-class tax cut:

What the president won't talk about is the fact that when he asked for your vote in 1992, he promised America a middle-class tax cut. And he won't tell you that in 1993, after he was elected, he hit all Americans with a $265 billion tax increase—an increase, which, according to Democrat Senator Daniel Patrick Moynihan of New York was "the largest tax increase in the history of . . . the U.S. and anywhere else in the world."

Table 11.4
Issues Addressed: Radio Addresses

Issue	Rank	Clinton	Dole
Jobs and the Economy	1	26	7
Education	2	1	7
Budget Deficit	3	7	1
Medicare and Health	4	13	4
Welfare Reform	5	31	1
Taxes	6	4	17
Crime and Drugs	6	4	46
Other	---	26	5

This passage not only attacks Clinton for having signed a tax increase; it also portrays him as inconsistent, one who broke a campaign promise.

ISSUES ADDRESSED

Clinton devoted more of his remarks than Dole to the issues of jobs and the economy, the budget deficit, Medicare and health, and welfare. On the other hand, Dole directed more of his comments than Clinton to the topics of education, taxes, and crime. It is also worth noting that the topics on which Clinton led tended to be more important to voters than the topics on which Dole led. See Table 11.4.

Throughout his campaign, Dole attempted to make taxes (acclaiming his proposed tax cut) and crime (attacking the failures of Clinton's drug policies) his issue centerpieces, so it is not surprising to see him devote many comments to these topics. On the other hand, Clinton's most common comment on taxes was to attack Dole's proposed 15% tax cut. Thus, because Clinton decided not to attack in his radio addresses, it is not surprising to find few comments on this topic. It is a little odd to find him not touting some of the reductions in crime. It is especially surprising to see that Clinton did not spend much time on his proposals for improving education (e.g., connecting all classrooms to the Internet, helping all children read, tax cuts targeted to improve access to education). Most of his radio addresses tended to discuss a single theme (e.g., terrorism, or safe and healthy food), and perhaps we would have found more comments from Clinton on education if we had examined other radio addresses.

IMPLICATIONS

These speeches focused more on acclaiming than attacking. In fact, Clinton did not attack at all, and Dole praised 53% of the time. Defense was quite infrequent. Policy was addressed in 72% of the comments. Dole spent about twice as much time on character as Clinton. Dole was more likely to attack past deeds than future plans; he praised future plans and goals more than past deeds. Both speakers discussed ideals. Comments were most often elaborated with extent. Clinton addressed four of the five most important issues more often than Dole, while Dole spent more time on two of the three less important topics.

Chapter 12

Debates: Direct Confrontation

The Hartford Presidential Debate: October 6, 1996

Clinton: I want to begin by saying again how much I respect Senator Dole and his record of public service, and how hard I will try to make this campaign and this debate one of ideas, not insults. . . .

Ten and a half million more jobs, rising incomes, falling crime rates and welfare rolls, a strong America at peace. We are better off than we were four years ago. Let's keep it going. We cut the deficit by 60 percent. Now let's balance the budget and protect Medicare, Medicaid, education, and the environment. We cut taxes for 15 million working Americans. Now let's pass the tax cuts for education and child rearing, help with medical emergencies and buying a home. We passed Family and Medical Leave. Now let's expand it so more people can succeed as parents and in the workforce. We passed the 100,000 police, the assault weapons ban, the Brady Bill. Now let's keep going by finishing the work of putting the police on the street and tackling juvenile gangs. We passed welfare reform. Now let's move a million people from welfare to work. And, most important, let's make education our highest priority so that every eight-year-old will be able to read, every 12-year-old can log on to the Internet, every 18-year-old can go to college. We can build that bridge to the twenty-first century. . . .

We have ten and a half million more jobs, a faster job growth rate than under any Republican administration since the 1920s. Wages are going up for the first time in a decade. We have record numbers of new small businesses. We had the biggest drop in the number of people in poverty in 27 years. All groups of people are growing. We had the biggest drop in income inequality in 27 years in 1995. The average family's income has gone up over $1,600 just since our economic plan passed. . . .

Well, let me say, first of all, I'd be happy to have a commission deal with this, and I appreciate what Senator Dole did on the '83 Social Security commission.

But it won't be possible to do if his tax scheme passes, because even his own campaign co-chair, Senator D'Amato, says he'll have to cut Medicare even more than was cut in the bill that I vetoed. I vetoed that bill because it cut more Medicare and basically ran the risk of breaking up the system. My balanced budget plan puts 10 years onto Medicare. We ought to do that. Then we can have a commission. But Senator Dole's plans are not good for the country.

Dole: I happen to like President Clinton personally. I am addressing him all evening as Mr. President. I said in 1992 he didn't extend that courtesy to President Bush. . . .

I look at the slowest growth in this century. He inherited a growth of 4.7, 4.8 percent; now it's down to about 2.4 percent. We're going to pass a million bankruptcies this year for the first time in history. We've got stagnant wages; in fact, women's wages have dropped 2.2 percent. Men's wages haven't gone up; gone down. So we have stagnation. We have the highest foreign debt in history, and it seems to me if you take a look, are you better off? Well, I guess some may be better off. Saddam Hussein is probably better off than he was four years ago. Rene Preval is probably better off than he was four years ago, but are the American people? They're working harder and paying more taxes. For the first time in history you pay about 40 percent of what you earn—more than you spend for food, clothing, and shelter combined—for taxes under this administration. So some may be better off. . . .

Drug use has doubled the past 44 months all across America. Crime has gone down, but it's because [of] the mayors like Rudy Guiliani where one-third of the drop happened in one city: New York City. . . .

This is not a Wall Street tax cut, this is a family tax cut. This is a Main Street tax cut. Fifteen percent across—let's take a family making $30,000 a year. That's $1,261. Now, maybe to some in this Bushnell Memorial that's not a lot of money, but people watching tonight with a couple of kids, a working family, that's four or five months of day care, maybe a personal computer, it may be three or four months of mortgage payments. This economic package is about families. But it's a six-point package. First of all, it's a balanced budget amendment to the Constitution, which President Clinton defeated. He twisted arms and got six Democrats to vote the other way. We lost by one vote. It's balancing the budget by the year 2002. It's a tax cut, cutting capital gains 50 percent so you can go out and create more jobs and more opportunities. It's estate tax relief. It's a $500 per child tax credit. It's about litigation reform. Now that the president gets millions of dollars from the trial lawyers, he probably doesn't like this provision. In fact, when I fell off that podium in Chico, before I lit the ground—hit the ground, I had a call on my cell phone from a trial lawyer saying "I think we've got a case here." So—and it's also regulatory reform.

IMPORTANCE OF PRESIDENTIAL DEBATES

Presidential debates have become an institutionalized part of contemporary presidential campaigns. Swerdlow noted that "given the present ascendancy of campaign debates, there is every reason to believe that they will continue to flourish" (1987, p. 14). The elections since 1976 have established the expectation that the leading candidates will face off in general election presidential debates (see, e.g., Denton & Woodward, 1990; Friedenberg, 1994). Because the election is a choice between two (or more) candidates, a helpful way for voters to choose between the candidates is to learn each candidate's stance on the issues and to compare their character.

Debates give viewers an opportunity to see the leading candidates, side by side, discussing the same topics (Hellweg, Pfau, & Brydon, 1992; Carlin echoes these remarks in 1994; see also Swerdlow, 1984). Jamieson (1987) explains that "As messages running an hour or longer, debates offer a level of contact with candidates clearly unmatched in spot ads and news segments. . . . The debates offer the most extensive and serious view of the candidates available to the electorate" (p. 28; see also Lamoureaux, Entrekin, & McKinney, 1994, p. 58). Voters can compare the candidates in a relatively extended period of time in a presidential debate.

Voters may obtain a somewhat less contrived impression of the candidates from watching debates than they can get from other kinds of campaign messages, like television spots. While candidates do prepare for the debates, not every question from the panelists, moderators, or audience members can be anticipated; not every remark from an opponent can be anticipated. Furthermore, unlike speeches or television spots with scripts and teleprompters, candidates are not usually allowed to bring prepared notes to debates. Thus, viewers may get a somewhat more spontaneous and accurate view of the candidates in debates.

Finally, other campaign messages do not attract audiences as large as those who watch debates (Jamieson & Birdsell, 1988; Wayne, 1992). In 1964, for example, no message by either Johnson or Goldwater was seen by even a quarter of the audience that watched the first 1960 Kennedy-Nixon debates (Jamieson & Birdsell, p. 122; see also Chaffee, 1979). Carlin advances a detailed argument about the size of the audience for presidential debates:

Nielson (1993) reported that the second presidential debate in 1992 attracted 43.1 million television households or 69.9 million viewers . . . (p. 4). Those numbers contrast sharply to the 4.1 million homes or 20.5 million viewers who tuned in for each of the major party conventions (p. 1). In 1980, nearly 81 million people watched Ronald Reagan and Jimmy Carter in their only debate encounter (p. 4). Miller and MacKuen (1979) noted that 90% of the adult population watched at least one of the Kennedy-Nixon debates, and 83% watched at least one Ford-Carter matchup. These numbers compared favorably to 73 percent who read about the campaigns in the paper, 4 percent who read magazines, and 45 percent who listened to radio reports (p. 328). (1994, pp. 6–7; see also Hellweg, Pfau, & Brydon, 1992; Alexander & Margolis, 1980)

The sheer size of the viewing audience for presidential debates means that potential for influence from these campaign messages is substantial.

EFFECTS OF PRESIDENTIAL DEBATES

The effects of presidential debates on voters is a subject of considerable research (see, e.g., Becker, Sobowale, Cobbey, & Eyal, 1978; Desmond & Donohue, 1981; Hagner & Rieselbach, 1978; Lang & Lang, 1978; Lanoue & Schrott, 1989; McLeod, Bybee, & Durall, 1979; Nimmo, Mansfield, & Curry, 1978; and the essays in part 2 of Kraus, 1979). Several studies demonstrate that presidential debates can increase voter knowledge. Jacoby, Troutman, and Whittler (1986) found that viewers recalled about 80 percent of the 1980 debates. Lemert (1993) found that exposure to the 1988 Bush-Dukakis debates increased voter knowledge (see also Drew & Weaver, 1991). Hellweg, Pfau, and Brydon concluded that "most studies suggest debate viewing contributes to considerable learning about the candidates and their positions" (1992, pp. 106–107). Thus, presidential debates have been found to provide issue information to voters (but see also Bishop, Oldendick, & Tuchfarber, 1978; Graber & Kim, 1978; Jamieson & Birdsell, 1988; McLeod, Durall, Ziemke, & Bybee, 1979; Swerdlow, 1984).

Some research indicates that the debates have limited effects on voting intentions, and hence, on the outcome of campaigns (Abramowitz, 1978; Lang & Lang, 1977; Lanoue, 1991; Lubell, 1977; or Miller & MacKuen, 1979). However, other studies suggest that presidential debates can influence voting behavior. Middleton (1962) indicated that the 1960 Nixon-Kennedy debates were "extremely important" for the voting decision of one out of eight voters. Roper (1960) reported that 4 million viewers changed their voting intention on the basis of the 1960 Kennedy-Nixon debates. Chaffee concluded that some voters have been affected by presidential debates:

Those [voters] who were the most regular viewers changed the most in their voting intentions, were the ones least influenced by dispositional factors, and were the most likely to vote in conformance with policy differences they perceived between themselves and the candidates. (1978, p. 341; see also Davis, 1979)

Debates may also affect the outcome of elections. Wayne asserted that "Kennedy and Carter might not have won without the debates" and that "Reagan probably would not have won by as much in 1980" (1992, p. 229). Davis (1982) found that votes for Reagan in 1980 were influenced by the debate—but not votes for Carter. Kelley (1983) indicated that about one-fifth of voters reported that they had decided how to vote after watching the Carter-Reagan debate. Geer (1988), analyzing the 1976 and 1984 debates, concluded that "a sizable minority of the public altered their preference for president" (p. 498). The co-chair of the Commission on Presidential Debates, Paul Kirk, reported that "focus groups and exit polls told us that more people based their decision in 1992 on the debates than any other single means of information throughout the course of the campaign" (1995). Pfau and Eveland argued that studies of the 1992 debates revealed that:

The regression analysis of the survey data, subsequent paths computed from beta weights, and the focus group responses reveal that the 1992 presidential debates exerted considerable direct impact on voter knowledge and their perceptions of candidates' competence and persona and as a result, the debates played an important, if indirect, role influencing attitudes and voting disposition during the final weeks of the 1992 campaign. (1994, p. 161)

So, considerable research concludes that presidential debates can influence voters and election outcomes.

PREVIOUS RESEARCH ON THE NATURE OF PRESIDENTIAL DEBATES

Benoit and Wells (1996) analyzed attack and defense (but not acclaiming; bolstering and corrective action were considered part of defense in their method) in the 1992 presidential debates. They concluded that Bush, Clinton, and Perot "engaged in copious attack and defense" (p. 110). If we combine the amount of bolstering and corrective action into acclaims (and subtract that figure from defense), we arrive at the following proportions: 56% acclaims, 30% attacks, and 14% defense. Bush, the Republican incumbent, acclaimed in 54% of his utterances, attacked 24% of the time, and spent 21% of his time defending. Clinton, the Democratic challenger, acclaimed about as much as Bush (57%), but attacked more (35%) and defended less (75%). Riley and Hollihan's (1981) study of the Reagan-Anderson debates found both critical statements (attacks) and defenses. Previous research by Ellsworth (1965) suggested that defense was more likely to occur in debates than in other forms of campaign messages.

Although they did not systematically divide utterances into policy and character, Benoit and Wells noted that both topics were present in the debates. They also reported that the number of attacks varied across the debates; in particular, the audience participation debate featured pleas to eschew mud-slinging, which diminished the number of attacks from Bush.

Furthermore, the number of defenses varied with the number of attacks: debates with more attacks elicited more defenses. Similarly, Bush was the target of more attacks than either Clinton or Perot, and Bush produced the most defenses. Tiemens, Hellweg, Kipper, and Phillips (1985) found that Carter attacked more than Reagan, while Reagan refuted more than Carter in 1980. Brydon (1985) reported that in 1984, Mondale criticized Reagan more, while Reagan refuted Mondale more. Thus, research consistently finds that attacks or criticism provoke defense or refutation.

Benoit and Wells (1996) found that many of the attacks concerned Bush's record in his first term; several attacks addressed Clinton's record as governor of Arkansas. As a consequence, Bush and Clinton frequently defended their records in office. Benoit and Wells also report that the discourse focused more on offensiveness than responsibility. They found that most attacks were not elaborated.

Hart and Jarvis (1997) have published part of the results from the Campaign Mapping Project which contrasts presidential debates with stump speeches and televised spots and reports a longitudinal analysis of presidential debates from 1960. Although the 1996 debates are included, the article is not primarily focused on elucidating those debates; the Clinton-Dole encounter seems to serve more as a source of familiar illustrations for their more general results. Their method is DICTION, a computer content analysis program that counts the occurrences of words in several dictionaries (five main ones—certainty, optimism, activity, realism, and commonality—and six custom ones developed for this project—patriotic terms, party references, voter references, U.S. leader references, religious terms, and irreligious terms). They note that this program is "lexically based, not syntactically based" (p. 1099).

Four of their conclusions identify generic features of presidential debates. Debates use "less certainty than stump speeches" and "more ambivalence than political advertising," which means they *"add sobriety to the campaign"* (p. 1100). Second, they *"reduce campaign bombast"* because they are less optimistic (more realistic) and more idealistic than speeches or spots (p. 1102). Third, their "high insistence scores" means they *"bring focus to the campaign"* (pp. 1104–5). Finally, presidential debates *"ensure self-involvement"* as evidence by more self-acknowledgment and less affability than speeches or ads (p. 1106).

Furthermore, Hart and Jarvis investigated several situational features. First, they argue that there are only a few minor differences between incumbents and ascendants (challengers). This is based on the five main variables (activity, certainty, commonality, optimism, and realism). They also report that of the 47 variables studied, political party produced effects on 38 of them in stump speeches, but only on 7 of these variables in debates. Thus, based on analysis of word choice, they argue for generic differences between debates, speeches, and spots. They also argue that differences by party or situation (incumbent versus challenger) are quite minor in debates.

Kendall (1997) contributed to the recent update of Friedenberg's (1994) studies of national political debates. However, her focus was on "the way television news covered the presidential debates of 1996" (p. 1). There is no question that some voters do not watch the debates, and their only exposure is indirect, through media coverage. Even voters who do watch the debates themselves may have their views colored by media coverage. Thus, media coverage of the debates is a valuable topic, but this essay is not intended to help us understand what actually occurred in the debates.

THE 1996 DEBATES

We analyzed the two general election presidential debates between Clinton and Dole (there was also a vice presidential debate between Gore and Kemp that we did not analyze; see Ragsdale, 1997). These encounters were held on October 6 in Hartford, Connecticut, and October 16 in San Diego, California.

FUNCTIONS OF PRESIDENTIAL DEBATES

Clinton and Dole devoted most of their remarks (59%) to acclaiming (much as did Bush and Clinton in 1992, 56% acclaiming), followed by attacks (33%) and defenses (7%). A chi-square revealed that these differences were significant ($X^2[df = 2] = 105.91$, $p < .001$). For example, Clinton boasted of the accomplishments during his first term in office during debate one:

We have ten and a half million more jobs, a faster job growth rate than under any Republican administration since the 1920s. Wages are going up for the first time in a decade. We have record numbers of new small businesses. We had the biggest drop in the number of people in poverty in 27 years. All groups of people are growing. We had the biggest drop in income inequality in 27 years in 1995. The average family's income has gone up over $1,600 just since our economic plan passed.

Clearly, more jobs, higher wages, more small businesses, fewer people in poverty, less income inequality, and higher family income are all desirable outcomes, worth bragging about. In the second debate, Dole stressed his compassion for those who need government assistance:

And I'm standing here as someone who a long time ago, as the county attorney in Russell, Kansas, one of our jobs every month was to go through all the welfare

Table 12.1
Acclaims, Attacks, and Defenses: General Debates

	Acclaims	Attacks	Defenses
Clinton	371 (71%)	98 (19%)	57 (11%)
Dole	250 (48%)	249 (48%)	21 (4%)
Total	621 (59%)	347 (33%)	78 (7%)

checks and sign them. And three of those checks were my grandparents'. So I know what it's like to have to look welfare head on.

His past experiences have given him an important insight into the problems some voters face today. See Table 12.1.

Attacks accounted for about one-third of the utterances in the debates (attacks were 30% in 1992). In the first debate, Dole criticized the failings of the Clinton administration's first term:

We're going to pass a million bankruptcies this year for the first time in history. We've got stagnant wages; in fact, women's wages have dropped 2.2 percent. Men's wages haven't gone up; gone down. So we have stagnation. We have the highest foreign debt in history.

In contrast with Clinton's acclaiming, bankruptcies, stagnant or falling wages, and foreign debt are undesirable economic indicators. In debate two, Clinton criticized Dole's stance on Medicare:

Senator Dole said 30 years ago he was one of twelve people that voted against Medicare and he was proud of it. A year ago he said, "I was right then; I knew it wouldn't work." American seniors have the highest life expectancy in the world. We need to reform it, not wreck it.

In this passage Clinton suggests by past and recent statements that Dole does not support the Medicare program, which is important to the health care of many senior citizens.

Defense was relatively less common, accounting for only about 7% of the comments in the general election debates (half the figure of 14% in 1992). For instance, after Dole had criticized cuts in our national defense in the second debate, Clinton responded by minimizing the differences between his proposed defense budget and Dole's: "I propose to spend $1.6 trillion on defense between now and the year 2002. And there's less than one percent difference between my budget and the Republican budget on defense." This utterance functions to minimize the extent of the cuts Clinton proposes. In the same debate Dole responded to accusations that he was trying to cut Medicare: "So let's stop talking about cutting Medicare. In my economic plan we increase it 39 percent." This denies the charge that Dole plans to cut this government program.

The two candidates were most likely to use simple denial, a relatively straightforward strategy for defense. It accounted for 65% of Clinton's defense and 67% of Dole's defense. For example, when Dole charged in the first debate that he trusts the people while Clinton trusts government, Clinton responded: "I trust the people," a simple and direct negation of Dole's attack. Similarly, when Clinton charged in the first debate that Gingrich and Dole had permitted polluters to "come into the halls of Congress, into the rooms, and rewrite the environmental laws," Dole interrupted to interject: "That's not true," a clear denial of Clinton's attack. See Table 12.2.

Another fairly common defensive strategy was transcendence. When accused of not supporting Medicare, Dole put his lack of support in a broader context in the initial debate: "Well, I must say, I look back at the vote on Medicare in 1965, we had a program called Eldercare that also provided drugs and was means-tested, so people who needed medical attention received it." Thus, he argued that his vote against Medicare should not be interpreted as a lack of support for medical assistance for the elderly, just that he supported a different program to accomplish that goal (and do it better, he implied).

The third most common form of defense was differentiation. Dole accused Clinton of trying to institute a government takeover of health care. In the second debate, Clinton explained that "that's not a government takeover, that's like the Family and Medical Leave Law. It just tries to set out the rules of the game." Thus, Clinton differentiates between government regulation (what he proposed) and a government takeover (what Dole accused him of proposing).

The two candidates also occasionally used mortification (apology), defeasibility, minimization, shifting the blame, and good intentions in the debates. Still, by far the most common defensive strategy was denial.

There were some contrasts between the two candidates. Clinton acclaimed much more frequently (71%) than he attacked (19%), while Dole acclaimed and attacked at identical rates (48%). Neither candidate spent much time defending, but Clinton defended more than twice as frequently (11%) as Dole (4%). Note that Dole (249) attacked more than twice as often as did Clinton (98) and that Clinton (57%) defended more than twice as often as Dole (21%).

POLICY VERSUS CHARACTER

More time (72%) was devoted to policy than to character (28%) in the debates, and Clinton emphasized policy (80%) even more than Dole

Table 12.2
Strategies for Defense: General Debates

	Denial	Trans	Diff	Mort	Defeas	Minim	Shift Blame	Good Intent
Clinton	37	7	2	3	2	3	2	1
Dole	14	2	3	1	1	0	0	0
Total	51	9	5	4	3	3	2	1

(64%). A chi-square calculated on these data reached significance (X^2[df = 2] = 27.6, p < .001). Interestingly enough, in the first debate when Clinton was attacked for not keeping his word—a personal quality—he responded by reciting numerous policy accomplishments:

When I ran for president, I said we'd cut the deficit in half in four years; we cut it by sixty percent. I said that our economic plan would produce eight million jobs; we have ten and a half million new jobs. We're number one in autos again, record numbers of new small businesses. I said we'd pass a crime bill, that we'd put one hundred thousand police on the street, ban assault weapons, and deal with the problems that ought to be dealt with, capital punishment, including capital punishment for drug kingpins. And we did that.

Thus, even in defending his personal character, Clinton discusses policy considerations. In the first debate, Dole pointedly asked: "What about drugs that have increased double in the last forty-four months? Cocaine is up 141 percent—or marijuana. Cocaine up 160 percent." This attacks the Clinton administration's record on illegal drugs. These data are displayed in Table 12.3.

Both candidates also discussed character, although Clinton spent less than half as much time on character as on policy. For instance, in the first debate Dole contrasted Clinton's and his candidacies for the presidency:

President Clinton ran for governor in 1990 and said he was going to fill out his term, but he didn't. He's president, so I guess it's a little better deal. But I wanted the American people to know that I was willing to give up something—it wasn't just getting more power and more power, so I rolled the dice. I put my career on the line because I really believe the future of America is on the line.

The suggestion here is that because Dole was willing to resign from the Senate, he demonstrates more personal commitment to the presidency than did Clinton in 1990. He also declared that "People will tell you who served with Bob Dole that, agree or disagree, he kept his word. That's what this race is all about." Here, Dole acclaimed his trustworthiness, another personal quality.

However, Clinton also talked about his character at times. In the first debate, he explained that "the things I do as president are basically driven by the people whose lives I have seen affected by what does or doesn't happen in this country." However, even when explaining that he cares about the problems of the electorate, he relates this personal quality back to policy. The previous excerpt continues: "The auto worker in Toledo who was unemployed when I was elected and now has a great job because we're number one in auto production again." At the end of

Table 12.3
Policy versus Character: General Debates

| | Policy | | | | Character | | | |
	Deeds	Plans	Goals	Total	PQual	Leader	Ideals	Total
Clinton	60/171*	14/41	5/ 8	80/220 (80%)	10/19	1/4	7/55	18/78 (20%)
Dole	165/51	9/41	9/46	183/138 (64%)	45/55	5/5	16/52	66/112 (36%)
Total	225/222	24/82	14/54	263/358 (72%)	55/74	6/9	23/107	84/190 (28%)

*left number = attacks, right number = acclaims.

the second debate, Clinton contrasted his ideals with those of his opponent:

This election is about two different visions about how we should go into the twenty-first century. Would we be better off—as I believe—working together to give each other the tools we need to make the most of our God-given potential, or are we better off saying you're on your own? Would we be better off building that bridge to the future together so we can all walk across it, or saying you can get across yourself?

Thus, Clinton suggests that his ideals are preferable to those of Dole.

An interesting pattern emerged in the two candidates' use of past deeds as a source for campaign utterances. Both candidates used past deeds as a resource over two hundred times. However, Clinton used past deeds as a basis for acclaiming (praising his own past deeds) almost three times as often (171 to 60) as he used it as a ground for attacking his opponent (criticizing Dole's past deeds). For example, in the second debate, Clinton observed that "We've gained manufacturing jobs since I've been president. We've negotiated over 200 separate trade agreements." The increase in this kind of employment is a desirable accomplishment. In direct contrast, Dole was over three times more likely (165 to 51) to attack Clinton's past deeds than to acclaim his own past deeds. Dole retorted by declaring that "They're setting new records this year. We have the worst economy in a century. We've had the slowest growth, about 2.5 percent." Surely, a president wants to have strong economic growth. Given that Clinton was an incumbent in the office sought by both contenders, his record functioned as a resource for his own self-praise and his opponent's attacks. Dole had a record in the Senate, and both candidates mentioned it. However, a record in the office being sought is more relevant than a record in another office, so it should not be surprising that Clinton's first term was used for acclaiming by the incumbent and attacking by the challenger.

The two candidates engaged in identical amounts of praise of their respective future plans (41). In debate one Clinton declared, for example, that "my balanced-budget plan adds ten years to the life of the Medicare trust fund." No one wants to see Medicare run out of money. In the first debate, Dole declared that his plan "is not a Wall Street tax cut, this is a family tax cut. This is a Main Street tax cut. Fifteen percent across— let's take a family making $30,000 a year. That's $1,261." Dole repeatedly praised his proposed 15% tax cut. However, Clinton was more likely to attack Dole's future plans (15) than Dole was to attack Clinton's future plans (9). As in this passage from the October 6 debate, Clinton repeatedly charged that Dole's tax proposal was not a practical program. It's a $550 billion tax scheme that will cause a big hole in the deficit, which will raise interest rates and slow down the economy and cause people to pay more for home mortgages, car payments, credit card payments, college loans, and small business loans.

Clinton offered many attacks on the key proposal in Dole's platform.

Dole used general goals more than Clinton, primarily as a resource for acclaiming. In the first debate, Dole explained that "we need campaign finance reform," although he didn't provide specific plans for achieving this goal. Later, he noted that "we are increasing defense reasonably—not too much, but we are increasing defense some—because we want to be prepared." Another general goal for Dole.

Turning to character, Dole was over three times as likely (100) as Clinton (29) to discuss personal qualities, and both candidates were more likely to acclaim than attack on those grounds. Near the beginning of the first debate, Dole revealed that "I'm a plain-speaking man, and I learned long ago that your word was your bond." Clarity and trust are important qualities in a person's character. There were only a very few comments about leadership ability (15 out of 968 utterances).

Both candidates discussed their ideals, and were more likely to acclaim their own ideals than to attack their opponent's ideals. In the first debate, Dole explained that "I trust the people. The president trusts the government." This is a basic difference in political ideals. In the same debate, Clinton sketched several of his fundamental beliefs: "I don't believe in discrimination. I believe you can protect the environment and grow the economy. I believe that we have to do these things with a government that's smaller and less bureaucratic, but that we have to do them nonetheless." His vision, or ideals, is laid out in this passage.

STRATEGIES FOR ELABORATING ACCLAIMS AND ATTACKS

In these debates, the candidates used five strategies for elaborating their utterances: extent, effects on the audience, vulnerability, consistency, and persistence. By far the most common form was extent. For instance, in the second debate, Dole mentioned the fact that Clinton promised a middle-class tax cut in 1992, but did not fulfill his promise. In fact, Dole reported, "You got a $265 million tax increase." This is a huge tax hike. In that debate, Clinton bragged that "60,000 felons, fugitives, and stalkers have been denied handguns," obviously a beneficial effect on crime. See Table 12.4.

The candidates also mentioned effects on the audience. Recall how Dole characterized his tax cut proposal as directed toward Main Street, not Wall Street. Vulnerability was also used to elaborate their utterances.

Table 12.4
Strategies for Elaborating Acclaims and Attacks: General Debates

	Extent	Effects	Vulnerable	Consistency	Persist
Clinton	25/84*	5/14	12/12	5/ 8	0/8
Dole	74/27	17/11	7/ 6	11/0	5/4
Total	99/111	22/25	19/18	16/8	5/12

*left number = attacks, right number = acclaims.

For instance, in the final debate, Dole noted that "drug use in 12- to 17-year-olds has doubled in this administration, the last forty-four months. Marijuana use is up 141 percent; cocaine use up 160 percent. They're your kids." Consistency has already been mentioned (Clinton's 1992 promise of a middle-class tax cut). Persistence also occurred. For example, in the first debate, Dole explained that he did not support the Brady Bill because "I've got a better idea. It's something I've worked on for fifteen years. It's called the automated check or the instant check." This is a program on which Dole had been persistently working.

ISSUES ADDRESSED

Two issues were relatively close: jobs (Clinton 41, Dole 44) and welfare (Clinton 17, Dole 14). Of the remaining five topics, Clinton had clear leads on four of them: education (47 to 17), the deficit (22 to 12), health care (60 to 45), and crime (48 to 32). Dole had a substantial lead on only one issue, taxation (46 to 30). Thus, Clinton devoted more utterances to more of the top issues than Dole. See Table 12.5.

IMPLICATIONS

Clinton, the Democratic incumbent, acclaimed more than three times as often as he attacked. Dole, the Republican challenger, acclaimed almost exactly as often as he attacked. In 1992, the two candidates acclaimed about the same amount. Dole attacked Clinton more than Clinton attacked Dole, and Clinton defended more frequently than Dole. In 1992, the Democratic challenger attacked more than the Republican incumbent, and the Republican incumbent defended more than the Democratic challenger. As in previous debates, the candidate who was the recipient of more attacks (the incumbent, who was attacked more by the

Table 12.5
Issues Addressed: General Debates

Issue	Rank	Clinton	Dole
Jobs	1	41	44
Education	2	47	17
Budget Deficit	3	22	12
Medicare/Health	4	60	45
Welfare	5	17	14
Taxes	6	30	46
Crime/Drugs	7	48	32
Other	---	108	111

challenger) produced more defenses. Although only two sets of presidential debates have been examined from this perspective so far, this suggests that incumbency (and/or who is the target of more attacks) is a more important determinant of discourse function (acclaim, attack, defend) in debates than political party.

We found that both candidates focused more on policy than character in these debates. However, Clinton, the Democratic incumbent, discussed policy even more often than Dole, the Republican challenger (and frequently Clinton's discussions of character turned directly to policy).

How do our findings compare with those of Hart and Jarvis (1997)? We looked at quite different things, performing an analysis that is more semantic than lexical, so direct comparisons are simply not possible. Unlike Hart and Jarvis, we found sizable (and, in our opinion, conceptually important) differences between the incumbent and the challenger. We found systematic differences in acclaiming, attacking, and defending. Analysis of the 1992 presidential debates also found differences between attack and defense (Benoit & Wells, 1996). Of course, we do not dispute their findings per se; we found consequential differences on other variables their method is not designed to investigate.

The strategy used most often in defense is simple denial. After bolstering and corrective action (which we consider acclaims), Benoit and Wells found simple denial was the most frequent form of defense in 1992, used over three times as often as other strategies. Denial is simple, forceful, direct, and—assuming the candidate presents an effective denial—effective.

The candidates elaborated their acclaims and attacks most often with extent, followed by effects on the audience (on the voters). Clinton devoted more of his remarks to four of the most important issues for voters, while Dole spent more time on only one issue: taxation (the candidates had roughly the same number of utterances on two topics).

Chapter 13

Free Television Remarks:
Their Unfiltered Utterances

Fox's "Voice of the People," 10/2/96 (Question 6):
What Do You Feel Is the Most Critical Problem Facing Our
Nation Today?

Bill Clinton: America's greatest challenge is giving our people the tools they need to build strong families and successful lives. That means a growing economy. A world-class education system. Safe streets. A clean environment.

It also means helping parents to succeed both at home and at work. That's why we passed the Family Leave Law, over my opponent's filibuster. Families have used it 12 million times now to be with a sick family member or new baby, and we're working to expand it modestly to cover regular parent-teacher conferences and doctor visits. We're fighting to fully fund Safe and Drug-Free Schools, and saying no to tobacco ads that target our children.

We're demanding more responsibility from our young people—taking driver's licenses from those who drink and drive, encouraging curfews and the enforcement of truancy laws.

Giving parents the tools to raise strong families is critical to building a bridge to a twenty-first century where our values are strong, and our families more secure.

Bob Dole: Our biggest economic problem is that American families are working harder and longer just to pay the tax bill. The average American family now pays more in taxes than it does for food, shelter, and clothing combined. And that's wrong.

High taxes also mean low growth for our economy. According to the Joint Congressional Economic Committee, the economies of 66 other nations grew at a faster rate than our economy did last year. I think we can do better than 67th place.

Beyond purely economic problems there is a moral crisis that we must address. We have seen an increase of 105% in teenage drug use during Clinton's administration. An increase in juvenile crime, and the loss of values that made America great. Values like hard work, honesty, and personal responsibility.

When I am president, my economic plan will cut taxes and create more jobs and rising wages and I will use the White House as a bully pulpit to provide strong moral leadership.

The Free TV for Straight Talk Coalition undertook a crusade to compel network television to provide free television time to the major presidential candidates (Bill Clinton and Bob Dole) in 1996. This organization ran newspaper advertisements attempting to secure a forum (or forums) for candidates to speak to voters, unencumbered and uninterpreted by media. Unlike television news coverage, the candidates would not have their statements edited by the news media before they were broadcast. Television anchors would provide no background or context to influence how voters might react. Unlike debates, these statements would not require voters to watch an hour and a half of television to hear and see the candidates' complete statements. Furthermore, there would be no commentary by media pundits afterwards, trying to explain to voters the "real" meaning or significance of the candidates' statements. Unlike television spots, these messages would only feature the candidates themselves (no video footage, music, special effects, or spokespersons).

Fox, PBS, NBC, and CBS agreed to participate in this experiment (see, e.g., Free TV for Straight Talk Coalition, 1996). Fox broadcast ten segments in which the two candidates provided one-minute answers to ten different questions. PBS aired weekday segments beginning October 17, featuring one candidate per day, alternating who received the free television time through November 1 (12 messages, 6 for each candidate). These statements were made available the following day on the PBS world wide web site. CBS devoted two and one-half minutes each to the two leading candidates at the end of each evening newscast during October 21–24. NBC aired segments from the candidates during its "Prime Time Live" show. The segments featured both candidates on the same day and alternated who went first each day.

Fox News graciously provided us with a compilation of their "Voice of the People" series (Bill Clinton's campaign web site posted some, but not all, of Clinton's Fox statements). We videotaped the CBS segments and transcribed them for our analysis. We downloaded the PBS statements from their web site. These three sources provided us with the bulk of the candidates' free television time for our analysis.

We would like to discuss the conclusions that emerge from our analysis of Clinton's and Dole's free television time remarks. Each conclusion will be discussed and, where possible, illustrated from the excerpts at

Table 13.1
Acclaims, Attacks, and Defenses: Free TV Remarks

	Acclaim	Attack	Defense
Clinton	296 (87%)	46 (13%)	1 (.3%)
Dole	161 (65%)	87 (35%)	0
Total	457 (77%)	133 (23%)	1 (.2%)

the beginning of this chapter. These findings are discussed under six headings: functions, policy versus character, policy, character, strategies of elaboration, and issues addressed. Because there is no literature to review on this new form of campaign discourse, we turn immediately to our analysis.

FUNCTIONS OF FREE TELEVISION REMARKS

First, we found that both of these candidates were more likely to acclaim (77%) than to attack (23%) in their free television remarks. A chi-square indicated that there was a significant difference here ($X^2[df = 1]$ = 38.3, p < .001). Only one instance of defense was found in these statements (by Clinton). For example, Bill Clinton's statement at the beginning of this chapter (Fox, 10/2/96) proclaimed that: "We passed the Family Leave Law, over my opponent's filibuster. Families have used it 12 million times now to be with a sick family member or new baby, and we're working to expand it modestly to cover regular parent-teacher conferences and doctor visits." Notice that the one attack of his opponent—that Bob Dole had filibustered to try to kill this bill—is a relatively small portion of this excerpt. Clinton stresses one of his successes, taking partial responsibility ("*We* passed") for this law. He makes it clear why this is a desirable accomplishment (allowing families "to be with a sick family member or new baby"). He notes that this is a significant boon, because "Families have used it 12 million times." Thus, the Family Leave Law is portrayed as an important and praiseworthy past deed. Clinton's work is not finished, though. He notes that "we're working to expand it modestly to cover regular parent-teacher conferences and doctor visits." Thus, Clinton also has future plans to create additional benefits for voters in this area. These findings are presented in Table 13.1.

President Clinton also touches on crime and children, mentioning the Safe and Drug-Free Schools Act, the fight against tobacco advertising aimed at children, drunk driving, curfews and truancy. He ends his statement by mentioning his theme, "building a bridge to a twenty-first cen-

tury where our values are strong, and our families more secure."
Stressing the importance of values praises Clinton's ideals.

Bob Dole rephrases the question to focus on one of his campaign
themes, high taxes under President Clinton: "Our biggest economic
problem is that American families are working harder and longer just to
pay the tax bill. The average American family now pays more in taxes
than it does for food, shelter, and clothing combined. And that's wrong."
Clearly, Dole argues that the high taxes paid by American voters are
undesirable: "that's wrong." He notes that voters pay more in taxes than
for "food, shelter, and clothing combined," making taxes a large portion
of a family's expenditures. Although this statement does not explicitly
blame Clinton for taxes, the fact that Clinton promised a middle-class
tax cut in 1992 but signed a large tax increase after he was elected is a
charge made throughout Dole's campaign. Viewers are likely to assume
that Dole means to indict Clinton as the cause of this problem.

In Dole's next paragraph, he observes that "High taxes also mean low
growth for our economy." He stresses the significance of this problem,
noting that the United States ranks 67th in the world in economic
growth, another attack on President Clinton.

Dole then turns to teenage drug abuse. "We have seen an increase of
105% in teenage drug use during Clinton's administration." Voters are
sure to see an increase in teen drug abuse as a troubling trend, and Dole
clearly blames the President for this state of affairs. An increase of 105%
means the problem has more than doubled—a significant threat to our
youth.

Dole ends his statement by discussing his future plans ("When I am
president, my economic plan will cut taxes and create more jobs and
rising wages"). Not only will Dole's 15% tax cut give voters more after-
tax income, but it will create more jobs and increase wages. Dole also
stressed his character ("I will use the White House as a bully pulpit to
provide strong moral leadership"). Dole's personal virtues have been a
consistent theme in his presidential campaign.

Clearly both candidates acclaimed their own desirable qualities. They
also attacked their opponents. Each candidate made it clear why what
he did (or proposed to do) was desirable and what his opponent did (or
would do in the future) was undesirable. At times, the blame or credit
was implicit, but other times responsibility was an explicit part of this
discourse.

Out of a total of 591 utterances that we analyzed, only one functioned
to defend one of the candidates. The two candidates taped their statements separately; even when both candidates statements were broadcast
together (e.g., on CBS's segments), they were not engaged in the same
kind of confrontation that occurs during a political debate. The format
ensured that the candidates could not respond to their opponent's actual

remarks on that topic. It was possible to respond to prior allegations, but that might remind the audience of accusations they had forgotten. Relying heavily on defense might also seem to make the candidate look reactive rather than active. Thus, we were not surprised to see little defense in these statements. The fact that Clinton did defend himself once again confirms that the candidates do have three options (acclaiming, attacking, and defending). The fact that defense was so rare (1 out of 591 utterances) clearly demonstrates that these candidates preferred to acclaim and attack.

Second, we found that while both candidates acclaimed more than they attacked, Dole was more likely to attack than Clinton: Clinton attacked in 13% of his free television time statements while Dole attacked in 35% of his statements. The excerpts at the beginning of this chapter, in which Dole discussed the heavy tax burden and the increase in teenage drug abuse, clearly illustrate Dole's tendency to attack more than Clinton.

POLICY VERSUS CHARACTER

A third finding is that both Clinton and Dole were more likely to discuss policy (76%) than character (24%). For example, in the opening excerpts, Clinton's initial paragraph mentions the economy, education, crime, and the environment. Dole's first paragraph focuses on taxation. Although neither candidate can go into detail in one minute (and even CBS only permitted two and a half minutes each), both Clinton and Dole emphasized policy more than character. In point of fact, Clinton devoted 85% of his remarks to policy considerations, while Dole directed 64% of his comments to policy matters. See Table 13.2.

Fourth, our results also reveal that, while both rhetors focused on policy over character, Dole's free television time addressed character more than Clinton's remarks. In fact, the percentage of Dole's comments spent on character—36%—is more than double Clinton's remarks—15%. A chi-square confirmed that these differences were significant ($X^2[df = 1] = 33.9$, $p < .001$). In the text at the beginning of this chapter, notice how Dole stresses his "moral leadership."

POLICY

One interesting finding from this analysis concerns how Clinton exploits opportunities for acclaims and attacks more consistently than does Dole, a fifth finding. Clinton's free television remarks devoted more time to acclaiming his past deeds (82%) than to attacking Dole's past deeds

Table 13.2
Policy versus Character: Free TV Remarks

| | Policy | | | | Character | | | | |
	Deeds	Plans	Goal	Total	PQual	Leader	Ideals	Total
Clinton	21/98*	15/67	4/84	40/249 (85%)	0/1	0/1	5/45	5/47 (15%)
Dole	54/15	0/49	3/37	57/101 (64%)	11/18	3/7	16/35	30/60 (36%)
Total	75/113	15/116	7/121	97/350 (76%)	11/19	3/8	21/80	35/107 (24%)

*left number = attacks, right number = acclaims.

(18%). Similarly, Clinton's messages acclaimed his future plans (82%) more than he attacked Dole's future plans (18%).

Dole's free television remarks reveal a different pattern. Although he too acclaimed (65%) more than he attacked (35%), Dole's use of past deeds favored attacks on Clinton (78%) rather than acclaims of Dole's own past accomplishments. Dole never once attacked Clinton's future plans, although he praised his own plans for future policy action.

Consider this excerpt from Clinton's remarks on CBS, October 21: "We've started the job of improving school standards; now math scores, science scores, and SAT scores are up. We've expanded Head Start, and increased scholarships and student loans and lowered the costs of those loans. We're on the right track." In this first segment Clinton talks about his past accomplishments: test scores up, programs enhanced. Then he describes his future plans for our educational system: "Now we should require that our students pass tough tests to move up in school. We should reward teachers who do well, and remove those who don't. We should expand public school choice by opening 3000 charter schools: schools formed by teachers and parents, that survive only if they produce results." Clinton also attacks his opponent. In the following passage, note how he criticizes both Dole's past deeds (voting against creating the Department of Education) and Dole's future plans (proposing to abolish the Department of Education):

My opponent disagrees with this approach. He voted against the creation of the Department of Education, and now he wants to abolish it. Just think about it: as we move into the twenty-first century, at his cabinet meetings there would be no one at the table to fight for our children's education. He also voted against the creation of Head Start and student loans. That's the wrong approach for our children's future.

Thus, Clinton's free television remarks provide striking balance. Clinton acclaims his past deeds and his future plans. He attacks Dole's past deeds as well as his future plans.

The story with Dole's remarks of October 21 on CBS is decidedly different. He begins by attacking the state of education in America (with Bill Clinton as president): "Let's face it: there are parents across America who are forced to send their children to bad or crime-ridden schools." Dole touts his future plans in this passage: "Through my opportunities scholarship program, lower- and low-middle income families will have the same right as the president and vice president of the United States— and that's the right to send your children to the school of your choice." However, in sharp contrast with Clinton, Dole does not acclaim his past deeds in the area of education. Neither does Dole attack Clinton's future plans for education.

Thus, Clinton's remarks are fairly well balanced: Clinton attacked both Dole's past deeds and his future plans; he praised both his own past deeds and his own future plans. Dole, on the other hand, failed to take advantage of all of the potential arguments: Dole attacked Clinton's past deeds but never Clinton's future plans; he praised his own future plans but rarely his past deeds.

Sixth, we would also like to consider the third aspect of policy considerations: general goals. Both candidates devoted a fair number of utterances to acclaiming their goals (Clinton: 84; Dole: 37). However, neither candidate devoted much time to attacking their opponent's goals (Clinton: 4; Dole: 3). We believe it is relatively easy to articulate a desirable goal—and both candidates did so repeatedly. However, it appears that it is more difficult to attack a general goal (e.g., balance the budget) than to attack more specific proposals (e.g., cut Medicare, cut defense spending, raise gasoline taxes)—and neither Clinton nor Dole made much effort to attack the other's goals.

CHARACTER

As indicated earlier, both candidates devoted less time to character than policy. Still, some conclusions do emerge from this analysis. A seventh finding concerns the candidates' ideals. Ideals are, by nature, abstract. Thus, we were not surprised to find that, as was the case with goals, both candidates tended to acclaim their ideals (Clinton: 45; Dole: 35) more than they attacked their opponent's ideals (Clinton: 5; Dole: 16). Furthermore, Clinton rarely addressed personal qualities, while Dole both acclaimed (18 times) and attacked (11 times) on these grounds. Finally, neither candidate discussed leadership qualities frequently in their remarks.

STRATEGIES FOR ELABORATING ACCLAIMS AND ATTACKS

The most frequently used form of elaborating their attacks and acclaims was extent. Dole was slightly more likely to attack (26 times) than to acclaim (21 times) with extent, while Clinton was much more likely to acclaim (74 times) than to attack (13 times) with this strategy. For example, Dole lamented the fact that "The average American family now pays more in taxes than it does for food, shelter, and clothing combined." While Dole does not provide a precise figure for taxes paid, his comparison makes it clear that it is very large. Clinton praised the extent of the benefits from the Family Leave Law: "Families have used it 12 million times now to be with a sick family member or new baby." This law

Table 13.3
Strategies for Elaborating Acclaims and Attacks: Free TV Remarks

	Extent	Effects	Vulnerable	Consistency	Persist
Clinton	13/74*	5/19	6/13	0/1	1/1
Dole	26/21	9/18	8/13	5/7	4/2
Total	39/95	14/37	14/26	5/8	5/3

*left number = attacks, right number = acclaims.

appears to provide help for many citizens. These data are reported in Table 13.3.

The second most common strategy was to mention effects on the audience. Here, both candidates were more likely to acclaim than to attack. Dole explained how his proposed tax cuts would affect families in this elaboration of an acclaim: "If you're a family of four making $30,000, our plan will cut your taxes by $1,261. That's an 86% tax cut." These candidates were also more likely to acclaim than attack with vulnerability. In this example, though, Dole is attacking Clinton's drug policy when he relates it to the nation's youth: "We have seen an increase of 105% in teenage drug use during Clinton's administration." Less commonly used strategies were inconsistency and persistence.

ISSUES ADDRESSED

Clinton devoted more of his remarks than Dole to most of the issue topics we investigated: jobs and the economy (22 to 3), education (66 to 13), Medicare and health (56 to 35), welfare (19 to 0), and crime and drugs (27 to 23). Only on the issue of taxes did Dole offer more comments than Clinton (48 to 22). These data are summarized in Table 13.4.

Clinton discussed jobs and the economy, claiming to have reduced interest rates "so we now have ten and one-half million new jobs, the lowest unemployment in seven years" (CBS, 10/22/96). On education, Clinton proposed an increase in charter schools: "We should expand public school choice by opening 3000 charter schools: schools formed by teachers and parents, that survive only if they produce results" (CBS 10/21/96). After discussing his proposed tax cuts, Clinton addressed the budget deficit, declaring that "These tax cuts are fully paid for, line by line, dime by dime" (Fox, 9/19/96). Clinton declared on Medicare and health that "I will never accept my opponent's devastating cuts in Medicare for the elderly" (Fox, 10/96). Clinton also discussed welfare: "We passed historic welfare reform, and increased child support collection by

Table 13.4
Issues Addressed: Free TV Remarks

Issue	Rank	Clinton	Dole
Jobs and the Economy	1	22	3
Education	2	66	13
Budget Deficit	3	19	15
Medicare and Health	4	56	35
Welfare Reform	5	19	0
Taxes	6	22	48
Crime and Drugs	6	27	23
Other	---	58	11

fifty percent. Now let's move a million more people from welfare to work" (PBS, 10/18/96). Dole discussed his proposed 15% tax cut: "The bottom line: under our plan, your family will save about $1,300 on your federal tax bill" (PBS, 10/17/96). Finally, Clinton talked about crime and drugs: "We fought for the Brady Bill that has stopped 60,000 felons, fugitives, and stalkers from buying guns" (Fox, 9/29/96).

Thus, Clinton devoted more of his remarks to the issues that were most important to voters. It may seem odd that Clinton dominated six of the seven potential issues (and "other" as well). However, recall that Clinton spent more time discussing policy (85%) than Dole (64%); this analysis only considers the topic of policy-related utterances. Because Clinton decided to spend more time on policy than Dole, he has more remarks that can address the issues that were important to voters. However, he could have spent his time on issues the voters did not think were that important (e.g., foreign policy); he not only made more policy-related comments than Dole, but Clinton also directed his policy utterances to topics that were important to voters.

IMPLICATIONS

Thus, our analysis of free television time remarks by Clinton and Dole supports several conclusions. First, both candidates acclaimed more than they attacked. These utterances were more positive than negative. Second, Dole, the Republican challenger, devoted more time to attacks than Clinton, the Democratic incumbent. Third, both candidates devoted more time to policy considerations than to questions of character. However, again, Dole spent more time on character than Clinton. Clinton offered a more balanced approach than Dole. Clinton acclaimed both his past deeds and his future plans, and he attacked both Dole's past deeds and his future plans. Dole, in contrast, acclaimed his future plans much more than his past deeds, and he attacked Clinton's past deeds but never his future plans. It is easier to acclaim one's goals than to attack an opponent's goals. Similarly, it is easy to acclaim one's ideals when discussing character: ideals tend to be general and often sound desirable in the abstract. The candidates used several strategies for elaborating their utterances: extent, effects on audience, vulnerability, inconsistency, and persistence.

Part V

Conclusion and Implications

Chapter 14

Outcomes: Who Won (and by How Much)?

In this chapter we will consider the results of the 1996 presidential campaign as revealed by (1) results of the Republican Party caucuses and primaries, (2) polling details concerning the "bounce" after each party's national convention, and (3) the comprehensive exit polling data for the general election shared by the major news organizations (All politics CNN/*Time*, 1996).[1]

THE REPUBLICAN CONTEST

Although Louisiana held the first primary of the election season, only Buchanan and Gramm actively campaigned there (C-SPAN, 1996). It was largely ignored by the Republican field who saw Louisiana's Republicans as engaging in an influence grab by moving to be the first contest (see Sabato, 1997c). As such, the Iowa Republican caucus on February 12, 1996 was the first genuine test of political viability. Bob Dole, who was from the neighboring agricultural state of Kansas, finished first with 26% of the votes. Patrick Buchanan (23%) was close behind, followed by Lamar Alexander (18%) and Steve Forbes (10%). Phil Gramm, who garnered only 9% of the Iowa votes, and subsequently dropped out of the race (C-SPAN, 1996). See Table 14.1.

New Hampshire provided the Republican contest with some surprises. Buchanan edged out Dole to win this influential primary by a 27% to 26% margin. Alexander (23%) came in third, followed by Forbes (12%) and Lugar (5%) (C-SPAN, 1996). These data are displayed in Table 14.2.

Because the Iowa and New Hampshire events are traditional monitors

Table 14.1
Iowa Caucus Results

Dole	26%
Buchanan	23%
Alexander	18%
Forbes	10%
Gramm	9%
Keyes	7%
Lugar	4%
Taylor	1%
Dornan	0%

Source: ⟨http://www.c-span.org/campaign⟩.

of political viability for prospective nominees, it is understandable that their outcomes are much ballyhooed. However, in this case, New Hampshire did not predict the Republican victor. Gallup (March, 1996) polling data reveals that before and after the New Hampshire primary Dole had tremendous support among Republicans nationwide. In a pre–New Hampshire poll, Dole led the field with support from 47% of registered Republicans, compared to 16% for runner-up Forbes. Similarly, just after the New Hampshire primary Dole enjoyed 41% support, compared to 27% for the next in line, Buchanan.

Eventually, Dole managed to clinch the Republican nomination on Tuesday, March 18, 1996. In a midwestern sweep including the states Illinois, Ohio, Michigan, and Wisconsin, Dole officially obtained 1,002 delegates, surpassing the 996 needed to clinch the nomination. However, eager to mark a symbolic victory in California, a state rich in electoral votes, Dole waited to declare that he had clinched the Republican nomination until after California's primary the following week (Associated Press, March 19, 1996).

THE CONVENTION "BOUNCE"

Both Clinton and Dole benefitted from "bounces," or temporary upward swings in the polls, upon completion of their respective conven-

Table 14.2
New Hampshire Primary Results

Buchanan	27%
Dole	26%
Alexander	23%
Forbes	12%
Lugar	5%
Keyes	3%
Taylor	1%
Dornan	0%

Source: ⟨http://www.c-span.org/campaign⟩.

tions. Because the Republican convention came first, so did Dole's bounce. A Field Poll released the Wednesday after the convention showed that Clinton's lead had been cut in half, from 20 to 10 percentage points (Associated Press, August 21, 1996).

The Democratic convention scored a bounce for Clinton as well. In spite of the well publicized resignation of Clinton strategist Dick Morris during the convention, Clinton's lead surged ahead with a 54% to 34% margin, up from a more modest 9% lead found earlier in the tracking poll (Associated Press, August 30, 1996). All of the polls indicated bounces benefitting each party as they concluded their convention.

THE GENERAL ELECTION

In this section we will describe the electoral outcome of the 1996 presidential campaign (see also Sabato, 1997b). After that, we discuss exit polls and the top policy issues affecting votes. This will be followed by exit polling data about preferences concerning personal factors. Finally, we will provide a brief examination of the various demographic tendencies in the election.

The Outcome

The conclusion derived from the tracking polls was that Clinton would beat Dole by 20 percentage points (Gibbs & Duffy, 1996). Although the

Table 14.3
General Election Results

Candidate	Popular Vote	States Won	Electoral Votes
Clinton	49%	31*	379**
Dole	41%	19	159
Perot	8%	0	0

*Plus the District of Columbia.
**270 electoral votes needed to win.

Source: CNN/*Time* (1996).

margin of victory was not that wide, Clinton did amass 49% of the popular vote compared to Dole's 41% and Perot's 8%. Green Party candidate, Ralph Nader, and Libertarian Party candidate, Harry Browne, each managed 1%. With 270 electoral votes needed to win, Clinton won with a comfortable margin of 379 votes in 31 states[2] (and District of Columbia) while Dole won 159 votes in 19 states.[3] See Table 14.3.

Policy Issues

The reason for such an outcome can be explained partly by the candidates' perceived stands on the most salient election policy issues. The top campaign issues and percentage of voters who rate them as important include: economy/jobs (21%), Medicare (15%), federal deficit and education (tied, 12%), taxes (11%), and crime/drugs (7%) (CNN/*Time*, 1996). We examined how Clinton and Dole fared among voters according to these categories. Using the exit polling data, we consider the percentage totals for the candidates among voters who made each policy issue their top voting priority. This information is contained in Table 14.4.

Economy/Jobs (21%). The exit poll indicates that 55% of the voters thought the economy in November was "good" or "excellent." A minority 36% said the economy was "not good" and a mere 7% called the country's economy "poor." As the incumbent, Clinton could effectively take at least partial credit for the economy.[4] Clinton acclaimed his success in improving our economy throughout the campaign. For example, in his acceptance address, he declared that

4.4 million Americans are now living in a home of their own for the first time; hundreds of thousands of women have started their own businesses; more minorities own businesses than ever before; record numbers of new small businesses and exports.... We have the lowest combined rates of unemployment,

Table 14.4
Top Policy Issues in Voting Decision

Policy Issue	All Voters	Clinton Voters	Dole Voters
Economy/Jobs	21%	61%	27%
Medicare	15%	67%	26%
Deficit	12%	27%	52%
Education	12%	78%	16%
Taxes	11%	19%	73%
Crime/Drugs	7%	40%	50%

inflation, and home mortgages in 28 years. . . . Ten million new jobs, over half of them high-wage jobs.

Clinton's campaign discourse consistently acclaimed his accomplishments in strengthening America's economy. Of those who described the economy as "excellent," 78% voted for Clinton, and only 17% for Dole. Likewise, 62% of those who thought the economy was "good" voted for Clinton, and only 31% for Dole.

On the other hand, Dole argued that the economy was not as rosy as Clinton claimed, attacking the incumbent's record. In Dole's acceptance address, for example, he declared that "By any measure, the trade policy of the Clinton administration has been a disaster: trade deficits are skyrocketing, and middle-income families are paying the price." Accordingly, among people who described the economy as "not good," Dole gained 52% of the vote to Clinton's 34%. Those who described the economy as poor supported Dole over Clinton, 51% to 23%. Thus, Clinton argued that he had presided over a healthy economy, and to the extent that the economy was perceived as healthy Clinton was the beneficiary. Conversely, Dole argued that our economy was faltering, and to the extent that the economy was perceived as poor Clinton suffered. In our reading, the economy overall was in generally good shape during the campaign; Clinton's rhetoric made the most of this situation.

Medicare (15%). The Medicare issue provided more problems for Dole. Clinton repeatedly attacked Dole for attempting to cut Medicare while in the Senate. In the spot "Tell," viewers were told that "Dole's campaign co-chair, Senator D'Amato, says he'd look at raising Medicare premiums to help pay for Dole's promises." Among voters who considered Medicare the top issue in the campaign, Clinton carried a 67% to 26% lead. Significantly, by a 38% to 23% margin, voters considered Dole more likely to cut this popular program. We can argue about whether a reduction in the projected growth of Medicare is a cut. However, Clinton apparently convinced many voters that Dole might cut Medicare if elected, and this issue favored Clinton.

Deficit (12%). Voters who were most concerned about federal deficit spending could have provided one bloc of support for Dole as they favored him over Clinton 52% to 27%. Clinton repeatedly charged that Dole's 15% tax cut would "blow a hole in the deficit." However, there seemed little doubt that Clinton proposed more spending initiatives than Dole (for connecting classrooms to the information superhighway, for example). This may have led voters to believe that Dole would be more likely to reduce the deficit than Clinton.

The poll asked voters whether Dole could "cut the deficit and taxes" simultaneously and whether Clinton could "cut the deficit and save programs" simultaneously. The data shows overwhelmingly that voters rejected the budgetary claims that the candidates made. Concerning Clinton's promise to cut the deficit and save programs, 65% said it could not be done, while 31% said it could. Similarly, concerning Dole's promise to cut the deficit and taxes, 66% said it could not be done, while 30% said it could. However, of the 31% who thought Clinton could cut the deficit and save programs, 86% voted for Clinton. Likewise, of the 30% who thought Dole could cut the deficit and taxes, 84% voted for Dole.

Education (12%). This was a topic on which Clinton campaigned frequently. Clinton spoke of the importance of education, connecting classrooms to the Internet, and tax credits for higher education. He also attacked Dole for wanting to eliminate the Department of Education. To those voters most concerned about education, Clinton was by far the favorite, 78% to 16%. Again, his discourse seemed well-designed to attract voters concerned about education.

Taxes (11%). Dole repeatedly stressed his proposed 15% tax cut proposal during campaign '96. Although Clinton doubted that Dole could pay for it (it would "blow a hole in the deficit," Clinton repeatedly claimed), there was no denying that if Dole were elected, he would push for a tax cut. Not surprisingly, then, voters who mentioned taxes as the most important election issue voted overwhelmingly for Dole over Clinton, 73% to 19%.

Crime/Drugs (7%). During the campaign Dole charged that Clinton had been soft on crime, and especially on teenage drug abuse. Dole made the most of footage from Clinton's appearance on MTV in 1992, where he confessed to trying marijuana. Clinton reacted by appointing a new drug czar (and stressing the Brady Bill and 100,000 more police on the streets), reclaiming some lost ground. The fifth most important issue to the voters, crime and drugs, also benefitted Dole over Clinton by a 50% to 40% margin.

It is interesting to note that Clinton did exceedingly well among voters concerned with the two most salient issues: economy/jobs and Medicare. The two issues tied for third place in voter salience, the deficit and education, were taken by Dole and Clinton respectively. Dole did not begin to gain any advantage until issues four and five, taxes and crime/drugs respectively (and these issues were most important to only 18% of the voters). As such, we would argue that Clinton was preferred by voters in the most important policy issue areas. Clinton spent more time on issues that were important to voters, and apparently he took positions that were preferable to Dole's stands for many voters.

Personal Factors

Just as we addressed the top five policy issues in the campaign, so will we explain the top personal factors influencing the election (of course, we should keep in mind that roughly two-thirds of voters rated issues as more important than character). In order of exit poll voter-salience data, they are: (1) "view of government" and (2) "honest/trustworthy" (tied, 20%), (3) "vision for future" (16%), (4) "stand up for beliefs" (13%), (5) "in touch" (10%), and (6) "cares about people" (9%). Keep in mind, though, that two-thirds of the voters considered policy more important than character throughout the campaign.

Voters most concerned about "view of government" constituted a 46% to 41% majority for Dole. Moreover, those most concerned that the president be honest and trustworthy voted for Dole by an 84% to 8% margin. These two categories, which represent 40% of all voters, should have contributed greatly to Dole's success. However, Clinton had more appeal where the other factors were concerned. He even edged out Dole 42% to 40% among those whose chief voting factor was standing up for one's beliefs. Moreover, when it came to primary voting factors of "vision for the future" (77% to 13%), "in touch" (89% to 8%), and "cares about people" (72% to 17%). Clinton's lead was uniformly strong. See Table 14.5.

Demographic Factors

While Clinton won the general election 49% to 41% across the entire voting population, some discrepancies even larger than that lead emerged. This section notes just a few of those demographic differences in the voting outcome. See Table 14.6.

The first demographic feature to note is the gender gap. Among men, Dole was a slight winner by a 45% to 44% margin. However, Clinton's lead among women voters was so strong (54% to 38%) that it more than offset his male voter deficit. Considering race, Dole again had a relatively

Table 14.5
Top Factors in Voting Decision

Factor	All Voters	Clinton Voters	Dole Voters
View of Government	20%	41%	46%
Honest/Trustworthy	20%	8%	84%
Vision for Future	16%	77%	13%
Stands Up for Beliefs	13%	42%	40%
In Touch	10%	89%	8%
Cares about people	9%	72%	17%

Source: CNN/*Time* (1996).

small margin among whites with 46% to Clinton's 44%. Among blacks, Clinton dominated with an 84% to 12% margin over Dole. Hispanics also favored Clinton, 70% to 22%. Asians were the only racial minority to favor Dole, showing him a 49% to 41% preference.

Clinton won every breakdown by age groups, showing particular strength among young (18–29-year-old) voters with a 53% to 35% lead. Likewise, Clinton won among voters at income levels up to $50,000 annually. Dole won handily among those making more than $75,000 a year. The $50,000 to $75,000 bracket was a draw. Concerning educational level, Clinton won among those voters with graduate educations and those voters with no high school, high school, and some college. Dole won among voters with college degrees (but no advanced degrees). Clinton stressed education throughout the campaign, while Dole stood by his statement that we should eliminate the Department of Education. Broken down by religion, Clinton won heavily among Catholics (53% to 38%) and Jews (80% to 16%). Dole had a comfortable lead among Protestants (50% to 41%). Religion was not an issue in the campaign discourse.

In concluding our examination of the election outcomes, it is clear that Clinton had more support among voters in the most salient policy issue categories. While Dole managed to outpace Clinton among some groups and regarding some issues, his appeal was not deep enough to defeat Clinton. Importantly, these results are generally in accord with the acclaims and attacks advanced by the candidates throughout the campaign. Of course, we cannot prove that their messages caused these results (or are more important than factors such as political party affiliation, the state of the economy, or incumbency). Campaigns—and the electorate—are too complex to reduce to a single cause, no matter what that pur-

Table 14.6
Demographic Factors

Demographic	Clinton	Dole
Men	44%	45%
Women	54%	38%
White	44%	46%
Black	84%	12%
Hispanic/Latino	70%	22%
Asian	41%	49%
Other	60%	23%
18-29 year olds	53%	35%
30-44 year olds	49%	41%
45-59 year olds	47%	43%
over 60	50%	43%
<$15,000 per year	60%	26%
$15-30,000	54%	36%
$30-50,000	49%	40%
$50-75,000	46%	46%
$75-100,000	44%	49%
>$100,000	40%	54%
No High School	58%	29%
High School Graduate	51%	35%
Some College	48%	41%
College Graduate	43%	48%
Graduate School	53%	39%
Protestants	41%	50%
Catholics	53%	38%
Other Christians	49%	38%
Jewish	80%	16%
Other	62%	25%
None	57%	26%

Source: CNN/*Time* (1996).

ported cause might be. Still, the election outcomes in 1996 are clearly consistent with the messages produced by the candidates throughout the campaign. It would be more difficult, in our opinion, to try to make the opposite case, that the campaign messages were irrelevant to the outcome.

NOTES

1. All of the major news organizations collaborated on one cooperatively run exit poll. Although some organizations might choose to name the exit polls after their facilities, they are in fact only making use of a shared commodity. Unless referred to otherwise, all of the exit polling information comes from that source.

2. Geographically (moving west to east) Washington, Oregon, California, Nevada, Arizona, New Mexico, Minnesota, Iowa, Missouri, Arkansas, Louisiana, Wisconsin, Illinois, Kentucky, Tennessee, Ohio, Michigan, Pennsylvania, West Virginia, Maryland, Delaware, New Jersey, New York, Connecticut, Rhode Island, Massachusetts, Vermont, New Hampshire, Maine, Florida, and Hawaii.

3. Geographically (moving west to east) Idaho, Montana, Wyoming, Utah, Colorado, North Dakota, South Dakota, Nebraska, Kansas, Oklahoma, Texas, Indiana, Mississippi, Alabama, Georgia, South Carolina, North Carolina, Virginia, and Alaska.

4. We do not address the question of how much credit Clinton deserved for the state of the economy.

Chapter 15

Implications: What Have We Learned?

GENERAL OBSERVATIONS

The results we have obtained for our functional analysis of political campaign discourse reveals that such discourse is replete with acclaims and attacks. Acclaims (66%) are over twice as common as attacks (31%). While both groups of speakers acclaimed more than they attacked, in campaign '96 the Democratic, incumbent party speakers consistently engaged in more acclaiming than the Republican, challenger party speakers (76% to 54%). In contrast, the Republican, challenger party rhetors attacked more than the Democratic, incumbent speakers (44% to 21%). These relative proportions occurred in every message form. Defense occurs much less frequently (3%), and not in all contexts (none in keynotes; none in Clinton's acceptance address or radio addresses; none in Dole's free television remarks). These data are displayed in Table 15.1 (given that we analyzed but a single campaign, we cannot be sure whether these results are best attributed to political party, or incumbency, or both—but we take up this question later).

These findings are readily understandable. Acclaims, if accepted by the audience and if they occur on topics that matter to them, improve the source's apparent preferability. Given that voters choose the candidate who appears to be the better choice, acclaims help the candidate secure election. Attacks function—again, if accepted by the audience and if on salient topics—by decreasing the apparent preferability of the opponent. This should create a *relative* improvement in the source's apparent preferability. However, many voters express a dislike for mudslinging, so the risk of a backlash from attacks seems greater than for acclaims (a candidate could acclaim a deed that offends part of the

Table 15.1
Campaign '96: Acclaims, Attacks, Defenses

Medium	Candidate	Acclaims	Attacks	Defenses
Keynotes	Bayh	33 (77%)	10 (23%)	--
	Molinari	25 (54%)	21 (46%)	--
Acceptances	Clinton	205 (90%)	23 (10%)	--
	Dole	115 (74%)	39 (25%)	2 (1%)
TV Spots	Clinton	268 (58%)	190 (41%)	2 (0.4%)
	Dole	110 (45%)	135 (55%)	1 (0.4%)
Debates	Clinton	371 (71%)	98 (19%)	57 (11%)
	Dole	250 (48%)	249 (48%)	21 (4%)
Free TV Remarks	Clinton	296 (87%)	46 (13%)	1 (0.3%)
	Dole	161 (65%)	87 (35%)	--
Radio Addresses	Clinton	146 (100%)	--	--
	Dole	69 (53%)	60 (46%)	2 (2%)
	Democrats	1319 (76%)	367 (21%)	60 (3%)
Total	Republicans	730 (54%)	591 (44%)	26 (2%)
	Grand Total	2049 (66%)	958 (31%)	86 (3%)

electorate, but in general the risk seems greater for attacks than for acclaims). Thus, both acclaims and attacks can help a candidate win an election, and because acclaims have somewhat less risk than attacks, it seems reasonable to find more acclaims than attacks.

Defenses have risks as well. It is possible that some voters may not have been exposed to the attack of a candidates's opponent. To defend against that attack, the candidate must identify it (e.g., Dole must say "Clinton has asserted that my 15% tax cut will 'blow a hole in the budget'" before he can deny it). Defending against an attack may remind voters of an accusation they had forgotten. Defending against an attack could encourage voters to give more credence to an attack, thinking, "Well, perhaps there *is* something to that accusation if it is serious enough to provoke a response." However, some attacks may be so serious that they demand a response (as noted earlier, Dukakis stated that he waited too long to respond to Bush's attacks). Also, surely it is easier to resist the temptation to defend against an attack when writing a speech or filming a spot than in the heat of a debate. Thus, it is reasonable to find some defense, but much less defense than acclaims and attacks. It is also understandable to find that more defense occurs in the face-to-face confrontation of debates than in other more highly scripted messages.

We also analyzed topics of the utterances in these messages, dividing acclaims, attacks, and defenses into utterances that addressed policy or character. These campaign messages devoted 72% of their utterances to policy matters and 28% to character. Furthermore, the Democratic, incumbent party speakers devoted more of their remarks to policy than the Republican, challenger party speakers (79% to 62%). Of course, this means that the Republican, challenger rhetors spent more time on character than did the Democratic, incumbent rhetors (38% to 21%). These relative proportions occurred in every message form we studied (again, because this is a single campaign, we cannot determine the relative importance of party and incumbency on these resuts). See Table 15.2.

These results also make sense. As noted above, approximately two-thirds of the voters indicated that policy was a more important determinant of their vote, while about one-third reported that character was more important. It appears that the rhetors in the '96 campaign also stressed policy more than character. It is possible that character has become more of a "Republican issue" than a "Democratic issue," even though it seems that character emerged as a particularly salient issue after Nixon resigned and Ford pardoned him. It is also possible that in 1996, Clinton was more susceptible to character accusations than Dole.

The remainder of this chapter's organization reflects the larger divisions of the book thus far, discussing our analyses of the primaries, the nominating conventions, and the general election. We will look for both similarities and differences in the candidates' use of acclaiming, attacking, and defending in these diverse campaign contexts. Because earlier chapters are replete with excerpts from the various texts we analyze, we will include few such examples here.

THE REPUBLICAN PRIMARY CAMPAIGN

We discuss the three functions of political campaign discourse, the relative emphasis of policy and character, strategies for elaborating acclaims and attacks, and issues addressed by the candidates.

Table 15.2
Campaign '96: Policy versus Character

Medium	Candidate	Policy	Character
Keynotes	Bayh	34 (79%)	9 (21%)
	Molinari	30 (65%)	16 (35%)
Acceptances	Clinton	166 (73%)	62 (27%)
	Dole	61 (42%)	84 (58%)
TV Spots	Clinton	365 (80%)	93 (20%)
	Dole	153 (62%)	92 (38%)
Debates	Clinton	373 (80%)	96 (20%)
	Dole	321 (64%)	178 (36%)
Free TV Remarks	Clinton	289 (85%)	53 (15%)
	Dole	158 (64%)	90 (36%
Radio Addresses	Clinton	112 (77%)	34 (23%)
	Dole	87 (67%)	42 (33%)
	Democrats	1339 (79%)	347 (21%)
Total	Republicans	810 (62%)	502 (38%)
	Grand Total	2149 (72%)	849 (28%)

The Functions of Political Campaigns

In all three of the primary campaign media we examined—debates, television spots, and talk radio—acclaiming was the most common form of utterance. Self-praise accounted for between 54% and 66% of the candidates' remarks, uniformly over 50%. Attacking was the second most common function. These candidates devoted 29–39% of their statements to attacks. Defensive utterances comprised the smallest group of comments, ranging from 2% to 9%. Thus, all three functions of political campaign discourse were found in analyses of these utterances, with a fairly consistent allocation of function across contexts. See Table 15.3.

There are some differences, albeit not huge ones, between these three contexts. The candidates acclaimed the most (two-thirds of their comments) and attacked the least (29%) on talk radio. They attacked most frequently (39%) in their television spots. Note that TV ads can rely on

Table 15.3
Functions of Campaigning in the Republican Primary

	Acclaims	Attacks	Defenses
Debates	54%	37%	9%
TV Spots	59%	39%	2%
Talk Radio	66%	29%	6%

others (narrators; the man or woman "on the street") to deliver attacks, while on talk radio every utterance is made by the candidates themselves. Research on television spots indicate that attacks from independent sponsors are better for the candidate (more positive feelings for the candidate, greater likelihood of voting for the candidate, more negative feeling toward the target, less likelihood of voting for the target) than attacks from the candidate himself or herself (Garramone, 1985; Garramone & Smith, 1984). Thus, it is possible that candidates attack more frequently in spots (which can distance the candidate somewhat by using narrators or "people in the street" instead of the candidates to deliver attacks). It is not possible to have surrogate "sponsors" on talk radio candidate forums, so candidates may use less attack in that kind of forum. This could account for the presence of more acclaims on talk radio and more attacks in television commercials. Of course, attacks are common in debates, but candidates may find it more difficult to refrain from attacking in such direct confrontations than when speaking only with the host on talk radio.

Primary debates, which feature face-to-face confrontation by one's opponents, elicited the most defense (9%). Surely it is difficult to resist the temptation to respond to taunts in the heat of debate. On the other hand, television spots contained the least defense (2%). It may well be that candidates tend to be reluctant to spend money to air their opponents' views (which they must describe at least minimally to refute them), even if those views are mentioned only to refute them. Defense occurred at an intermediate level during the talk radio appearances.

In the primary debates Gramm had more acclaiming (74%) than any of the other five leading candidates (who ranged from 45% to 58%; Table 4.1). Alexander devoted more of the statements in his TV ads to acclaiming (78%; the other four leading candidates varied between 59–61%). Dole acclaimed most often on talk radio (76%) and Alexander was a close second (72%). The other three candidates devoted 59–61% of their utterances to acclaiming. Thus, there was no consistent leader in acclaiming during these three primary formats.

In the primary debates we analyzed, Forbes attacked more than the other five leading candidates, at 52% (Table 4.1). The other four candidates ranged from 22% to 41% attacks. Dole attacked the least at 22%. In the primary television spots, most candidates devoted 40–45% of their comments to attacks (Buchanan, 47%; Dole, 47%; Gramm, 38%; and Forbes, 43%; Table 5.1). Alexander had the fewest negative statements in his ads (21%). On talk radio, Buchanan (36%) and Gramm (36%) attacked the most (Table 6.1). Dole only attacked 15% of the time. Thus, there is no clear pattern in who attacks the most, although Dole tends to attack the least.

In the three Republican primary debates we analyzed, the most common target of their attacks was other Republicans, their opponents in the primaries (58%; Table 4.4). As noted above, Dole was the object of attack over twice as much as any other candidate. The establishment bore the brunt of the candidates' ire 25% of the time, while Clinton was attacked in but 17% of the utterances. In their televised primary advertisements, other Republicans were attacked even more often than in the debates, targets for 71% of the attacks (Table 5.3). The establishment was attacked 25% of the time, and Clinton served as the target in a mere 4% of primary ads. Finally, in the Iowa talk radio appearance, other Republicans were the targets of 55% of the attacks, the establishment received 35% of the attacks, and 10% of the attacks were aimed at Clinton (Table 6.2). Thus, there is a consistent pattern of attacking their immediate opponents (other Republicans) most often, their ultimate opponent (Bill Clinton) the least, and the establishment about one-quarter of the time.

While Clinton is the Republicans' ultimate opponent—and thus the ultimate target—these Republicans must win the nomination in order to earn the right to face Clinton. Only by appearing preferable to the *other Republican* candidates can one contender emerge victorious. Attacking the other Republican candidates can contribute more to that victory than attacking Clinton. So, it makes perfect sense for Republican candidates to attack each other more than Clinton in the primaries (and it makes sense to acclaim and defend as well).

Dole defended the most of the leading candidates in these primary debates: 21% of Dole's utterances were defensive (see Table 4.1). The other four candidates spent less than 5% of their time defending. In the television spots, Dole and Forbes jointly defended the most (3%). Neither Buchanan nor Gramm used any defensive remarks in the television ads we analyzed (Table 5.1). On talk radio, Dole and Forbes again tied for most defense (9%), while the other three candidates allocated 4% of their remarks to defense (Table 6.1). Here, Dole and Forbes consistently defended the most in these primary campaign contexts.

Although it was not part of our initial plan for analyzing the 1996 campaign, we decided to conduct analyses of the targets of persuasive attacks when these targets were other Republican candidates. In the primary debates we analyzed (Table 4.5), Dole was the most frequent target of attacks from other Republicans (39%), followed by Gramm (16%), Alexander (14%), Forbes (12%), and Buchanan (7%). In primary television spots (Table 5.4), Dole was the target of 40% of the attacks aimed at other Republicans, Forbes received 29% of the attacks, Alexander was the target of 23% of such attacks, and Gramm (5%) and Buchanan (3%) were attacked relatively infrequently. On talk radio, Forbes was the Republican attacked most often (30%), followed by Buchanan (22%) and Gramm (21%). Dole was attacked 17% of the time, and Alexander 10% (Table 6.3). Although there is not a perfect correlation between being the target of attack and the producer of defense, it is clear that Dole and Forbes defended themselves and their policies frequently because they were attacked frequently. Benoit and Wells' (1996) analysis of the 1992 presidential debates found that George Bush was the most frequent target of attack, and he produced the most defense of the three contenders.

The most common form of defense employed in the Republican debates we studied was denial, accounting for 54% of the defenses (Table 4.2). Defeasibility (16%), transcendence (12%), differentiation (7%), and shift the blame (6%) occurred fairly frequently. Provocation (2%), mortification (2%), and good intentions (1%) were rarely used. Only denial was used in Republican primary spots (Table 5.2). During the talk radio appearances (Table 6.6), denial accounted for 63% of the defenses, followed by differentiation (21%) and shifting the blame (13%). Defeasibility was used once. Simple denial is clearly the defense of choice. It is direct, easy to use and comprehend, and—if accepted by the audience—an effective response to an attack (much better than other options; for example, minimization admits the offensive act but tries to reduce its apparent offensiveness).

Policy versus Character

In the Republican primary debates, candidates were more likely to discuss policy (58%) than character (42%). Primary television advertisements were split almost equally, with 48% of the remarks concerning policy and 52% on character. On talk radio, the candidates allocated more time to policy (57%) than character (43%). Thus, policy was stressed more than character in the debates and on talk radio, compared with television spots (where character had a slight edge). See Table 15.4.

An emphasis on policy occurred for all five of the leading candidates (in fact, only Keyes spent more time on character than policy; Table 4.6). Gramm (74%) and Forbes (71%) spent much more time on policy than on character. In their TV spots (Table 5.5), Forbes (61%) and Alexander (61%) dealt with character more than policy, while Buchanan (60%), Dole

Table 15.4
Policy versus Character in the Republican Primary

	Policy	Character
Debates	58%	42%
TV Spots	48%	52%
Talk Radio	57%	43%

(59%), and Gramm (54%) focused on policy more than character in their ads. During the talk radio appearances, Dole and Forbes (68%) and Alexander (54%) addressed policy more often. Gramm's remarks were split evenly between policy and character, and only Buchanan spent more time discussing character (60%) than policy.

Dole was the only candidate to spend more time on policy in all three contexts; Gramm emphasized policy in two contexts and split his remarks equally on talk radio. The other three candidates focused more on policy in two contexts and on character in one (Alexander and Forbes stressed character in their TV spots; Buchanan on talk radio). All five candidates spent more time on policy than character in the debate.

Thus, in two contexts (debates and talk radio) these candidates allocated more time to policy than character, and in the third (TV spots) utterances slightly favored character over policy. It seems interesting that the two more spontaneous forms of discourse—debates and talk radio—favored policy, while the tightly scripted television spots did not. This could mean that the candidates tended to emphasize policy, while their campaign advisors wanted more emphasis on character.

Strategies for Developing Acclaims and Attacks

Extent was the preferred method of elaborating attacks and acclaims, in the debates, followed by effects on the audience and consistency (Table 4.7). Stressing how those affected were vulnerable only occurred rarely. In primary spots, extent was the most frequent method of elaboration, followed by effects on the audience, persistence, and consistency (Table 5.6). On talk radio, extent was used most often, followed closely by effects on the audience. Persistence, consistency, and vulnerability of victims were rarely used (Table 6.5). In these three contexts, extent and effects on the audience were most common, consistency and persistence also occurred fairly often. Extent, often operationalized with statistics, is a direct and easy way to intensify an attack or an acclaim, and it is generally wise to relate one's arguments to the audience.

Issues Addressed

In the primary debates (Table 4.8), Forbes (33%) and Alexander (31%) devoted the largest percentage of candidates' remarks to the issue that was most important to voters—jobs and the economy. Alexander spent the most time on education (38%). Dole led on the third most important issue, the deficit (63%). Forbes spent more time than his opponents on Medicare and health (52%). Alexander and Dole tied (38%) on welfare. Forbes (32%) and Dole (30%) talked about taxes more than their competitors. Finally, Dole (30%) and Alexander (25%) spent the most time on crime and drugs. In televised advertisements (Table 5.7), Buchanan devoted more utterances to jobs and the economy (72%) than any other candidate. Forbes led the pack on education (62%). Dole spent more time in his ads on the budget deficit (71%). Forbes dominated talk about Medicare and health (80%). Dole (50%) and Gramm (42%) constituted most of the remarks on welfare reform. Forbes spent more time in his ads on taxes than anyone else (51%). Finally, Dole talked more about crime and drugs than his opponents. On talk radio (Table 6.7), Buchanan spent the most time on jobs and the economy (the most important issue), Alexander led on education, Dole and Gramm talked most about welfare, Forbes and Dole devoted more remarks to taxation, and Dole, Gramm, and Alexander talked about the deficit (no one talked about Medicare and health or crime in these appearances). So, no candidate consistently spent most time on the most important issues, but Forbes, Alexander, and Buchanan tended to devote the most remarks to top-ranked issues (Dole and Gramm were more likely to lead on the lower-ranked issues).

Dole secured his party's nomination for the office of president. How did he do in the primaries? He tended to attack less than the other contenders and he defended more often (he was the most common target of attacks). He discussed policy more than character—a preference shared by most voters (see Table 3.1). However, he did not spend the most time on the particular issues rated as most important to voters. Thus, his primary campaign was adequate—he did maintain his position as front-runner and win his party's nomination—but it was not outstanding.

NOMINATING CONVENTIONS

In this section, we take up the topics of the functions of campaign discourse, the relative focus on policy and character, strategies for elaboration of acclaims and attacks, and the issues addressed by the candidates when they discussed policy matters. Two studies have analyzed nominating convention keynote speeches and acceptance addresses from

1960–1996, providing a benchmark for comparing the speeches by Molinari, Bayh, Dole, and Clinton.[1]

Previous research on keynote speeches (Benoit, Blaney, & Pier, 1996) has analyzed this kind of discourse in order to understand it. Such speeches were split almost equally between acclaims (51%) and attacks (48%). Defense was relatively infrequent (1%). Republicans acclaimed (56%) more than they attacked (44%), while Democrats attacked (53%) more than they acclaimed (47%). Even sharper distinctions between keynotes occurred when one considers which party inhabited the White House: incumbents acclaimed much more often (61%) than they attacked (39%), while challengers attacked considerably more (58%) than they acclaimed (42%). This study also found that earlier keynotes tended to direct more comments to the party than to the specific candidates, although in recent years—as candidates became more central to the process and parties somewhat less important—this trend reversed. These speeches focused on policy (61%) more often than they addressed character (39%).

A separate study examined the nominees' acceptance addresses (Wells, Pier, Blaney, & Benoit, 1996) to help understand this form of discourse. Unlike keynoters, these speakers engaged in far more acclaiming (72%) than attacking (27%). Like keynotes, instances of defense were rare (1%). Democratic nominees used acclaiming more (77%) than Republicans (68%). Conversely, Republicans engaged in more attacking (30%) than Democrats (23%). As in the keynotes, incumbents engaged in more acclaiming (77%) than challengers (67%), while challengers were more likely to attack (32%) than incumbents (22%). References to the political parties were more common in the first five sets of acceptance addresses than in the last five. Over half (56%) of all utterances in acceptance addresses concerned policy rather than character (44%).

The Functions of Political Campaigns

The two keynotes emphasized acclaiming (65%) more than attacking (35%), and contained no defenses. Thus, they employed acclaiming quite a bit more (65%) than previous keynotes (51%). Defense has never been common in keynote speeches, and did not occur in these speeches at all. Molinari's Republican keynote devoted 54% of her remarks to acclaiming, while Bayh's Democratic keynote acclaimed in 77% of his utterances (Table 7.1). Historically, Republicans engaged in more praise than attack, while Democrats attacked a bit more than they acclaimed. Thus, these speeches do not reflect the partisan trend established in previous keynotes. See Table 15.5.

Challengers in past keynotes tended to attack more than they acclaimed, while incumbents acclaimed more than they attacked. While

Table 15.5
Functions of Campaigning at the Nominating Conventions

	Acclaims	Attacks	Defenses
Keynotes	65%	35%	0
Acceptances	83%	16%	0.5%
Spouses	95%	5%	0

both of these speakers devoted more than 50% of their remarks to acclaiming (Table 7.1), the speaker of the incumbent party (Bayh) acclaimed
more than the speaker from the challenging party (Molinari). Thus, results for incumbents versus challengers are generally consistent (incumbents praise more than challengers, who attack more than incumbents),
except that both speakers acclaimed more than they attacked.

Consistent with previous speeches, the two nomination acceptance addresses also focused more on self-praise (83%) than attacking. Only
Dole's speech contained defenses (1%). Previous acceptance addresses
also contained relatively little defense. Clinton's Democratic acceptance
acclaimed 90% of the time, while the Republican acceptance address by
Dole acclaimed 74% of the time (Table 8.1). Similarly, Democrats in the
past also acclaimed more than Republicans. Clinton (the incumbent) and
Dole (the challenger) both spent more time acclaiming than attacking, as
was the case in the past. Furthermore, the incumbent (Clinton) engaged
in even more self-praise than the challenger (Dole), again consistent with
previous acceptance addresses.

The two spousal speeches also emphasized acclaiming. Elizabeth
Dole's and Hillary Rodham Clinton's convention speeches both almost
exclusively engaged in acclaiming, praising their spouses 95% of the
time. Neither spouse offered defenses; they may not have wanted to risk
creating the impression that they thought the candidates depended on
their spouses for defense (Table 9.1).

Thus, speeches at the two nominating conventions mostly contained
acclaims and rarely provided defenses. Despite conventional wisdom
that recent campaigns are highly negative, the 1996 conventions were
relatively positive. The keynote and acceptance speeches showed a pattern in which the Republican challengers attacked more than the Democratic incumbents. Historically, incumbents acclaimed more in keynotes
and acceptance addresses, while challengers attacked more. On the other
hand, the influence of party affiliation was not consistent: Republicans
attacked more in acceptance addresses, while Democrats attacked more
in keynotes. Interestingly, the percentages for acclaiming and attacking
for both spouses were identical. See Table 15.5.

Next, we would like to draw some generalizations from a consideration of the six individual nominating convention speeches we examined. Bayh acclaimed somewhat more often (33 times) than Molinari (25 times; Table 7.1). Clinton acclaimed almost twice as many times (205) as Dole (115; Table 8.1). Elizabeth Dole acclaimed almost twice as many times (37) as Hillary Rodham Clinton (21; Table 9.1). Thus, the trend in the keynote and acceptance speeches (more acclaims from the Democratic incumbent) was reversed in the spouses' speeches (more acclaims from the Republican challenger).

Molinari attacked over twice as many times (21) as did Bayh (10; Table 7.1). Dole attacked more often (39 times) than Clinton (23 times; Table 8.1). Neither spouse used much attack: Hillary Rodham Clinton attacked once and Elizabeth Dole twice (Table 9.1). There was a pattern of greater attack by the Republican challengers than from the Democratic incumbents.

Molinari's and Bayh's keynote speeches were relatively similar in their approach to acclaims, with 72% of Molinari's praise directed to the candidate and 67% of Bayh's praise aimed at the candidate (Table 7.2). In the acceptance addresses, both Dole (90%) and Clinton focused their acclaims more on themselves (99% for Clinton, 90% for Dole) than on their parties (Table 8.3). In both cases, Hillary Rodham Clinton's and Elizabeth Dole's praise was aimed solely at their spouse and not their party. Thus, the target of acclaims is heavily tilted toward the candidates, rather than the party. Research on keynotes (Benoit, Blaney, & Pier, 1996) and acceptance addresses (Wells, Pier, Blaney, & Benoit, 1996) reports that the party is less of a target for acclaiming than candidates at more recent conventions, consistent with the declining influence of the party and the increase in importance of individual candidates.

Molinari's speech attacked only the Democratic candidate, never the party. Bayh's speech attacked the Republican party and candidate equally (Table 7.2). In the acceptance addresses, both Dole (90%) and Clinton (70%) attacked their opponent more than the opposing party (Table 8.3). Elizabeth Dole attacked the opposing candidate (twice) and Hillary Rodham Clinton attacked the opposing party (once). In both cases, their praise was aimed solely at their spouse and not their party. Thus, the target of attacks is more likely to be the candidates, rather than the party (Bayh's attacks were divided equally; Hillary Rodham Clinton only attacked once). As with acclaims, studies of attacks (Benoit, Blaney, & Pier, 1996) and acceptance addresses (Wells, Pier, Blaney, & Benoit, 1996) report that the party is less frequently the target for attacking and candidates are more often the target at more recent conventions, consistent with the declining influence of the party and the increase in importance of individual candidates.

Table 15.6
Policy versus Character at the Nominating Conventions

	Policy	Character
Keynotes	72%	28%
Acceptances	61%	39%
Spouses	34%	66%

Policy versus Character

As Table 15.6 indicates, both keynote speeches were more likely to stress policy (72%) than character (28%). This is consistent with past keynotes, in which policy (61%) was discussed much more than character (39%). This tendency was somewhat more pronounced for the Democratic incumbent, because Bayh devoted 79% of his remarks to policy, while Molinari talked about policy in 65% of her utterances (Table 7.3). These data are displayed in Table 15.6.

In 1996, the nominees spent more time on policy (61%) than character (39%). This is similar to past acceptance addresses, which also focused more on policy (56%) than character (44%). However, the contrast between political parties is even sharper in the acceptance addresses than in keynotes, because Clinton devoted more time to policy (73%) than character (27%), while Dole emphasized character (58%) more than policy (42%; Table 8.4). In the past, Democrats and incumbents (like Clinton) as well as Republicans focused more on policy, while challengers (like Dole) discussed character more than policy.

Hillary Rodham Clinton spent 52% of her time on policy, while Elizabeth Dole focused on character in 78% of her remarks (Table 9.2). Thus, there is a clear tendency for the speakers we analyzed at the 1996 nominating convention to stress policy over character, with the Doles being the exception. While these speakers may not have gone into great detail as they discussed policy, there is no question that policy was a more common topic than character—especially for incumbent Democrats.

Strategies for Developing Acclaims and Attacks

The most popular strategies for developing acclaims and attacks in the two keynote speeches were extent and effects on the audience. Consistency, vulnerability of victims, and persistence were used occasionally (Table 7.4). The acceptance addresses were more likely to use extent, followed by effects on the audience (there was one instance of persistence; Table 8.5). Clinton elaborated his utterances more often (39 times) than Dole (18 times). The spouses elaborated most often with extent (Table 9.3). Vulnerability of victims and effects on audience also occurred in their speeches. Thus, extent and effects on audience are the most common forms of elaborating acclaims and attacks.

Issues Addressed

In the keynote speeches (Table 7.5), Bayh devoted more of his remarks to the top three issues (jobs and the economy, education, and the budget deficit. Molinari spent more time on taxes, and the other three issues were roughly equal. In the acceptance addresses (Table 8.6), Clinton (who simply offered more utterances than Dole), dominated every issue but taxes (and still Clinton talked half as much as Dole on that issue). In the spouses' speeches (Table 9.4) both speakers addressed education in one remark. Hillary Rodham Clinton discussed Medicare and health much more often than her counterpart. Elizabeth Dole made the only comment about taxation. Most of the topics important to voters (e.g., jobs and the economy, budget deficit) were not addressed in either speech. Thus, the Democratic incumbent speakers tended to discuss the topics important to voters more often than the Republican challenger rhetors.

These speeches—despite all of the posturing by the speakers—had much in common. There was no decisive outcome from the convention phase of the campaign—both camps received a post-convention bounce, leaving matters about where they were before the two conventions (but this means that the Republican campaign failed to diminish the Democratic lead, and that the Democrats managed to maintain their lead). All of these candidates acclaimed a good deal, giving voters reasons to improve their assessment of the speakers' preferred nominee. All of the speeches contained some attack (although there was very little in the spouses' speeches), giving voters reasons to downgrade their assessment of the speakers' targets. All of the speeches tended to direct comments toward the candidates themselves, rather than to the party (consistent with the trend toward candidate-centered campaigns and a diminished role of the party in selecting nominees). There was virtually no defense in these highly partisan moments. Finally, the Democrats tended to discuss the issues that were most important to voters, giving them a slight edge. However, nothing in the speeches seemed likely to provoke a huge advantage for either candidate.

GENERAL ELECTION CAMPAIGN

Here, we address the functions of political campaign discourse, the discussion of policy and character, strategies used to elaborate acclaims and attacks, and policy issues discussed by the two candidates. Previous research has examined presidential television spots and the presidential debates in 1992, providing some indication of what we might expect in the 1996 campaign.

Benoit, Pier, and Blaney (1997) analyzed televised presidential advertisements from 1980–1996.[2] The utterances in these spots were 49% acclaims, 50% attacks, and 1% defenses. The Democrats praised (54%) more than they attacked (46%), while the Republicans attacked (55%) more than they acclaimed (45%). The ads from challengers attacked (55%) more than they acclaimed (45%), while incumbents' ads acclaimed (54%) more than they attacked (46%). The spots discussed policy (67%) about twice as often as character (33%).

Benoit and Wells (1996) examined the 1992 presidential debates. While they did not break out acclaims separately, we can combine their categories of bolstering and corrective action to provide that information (however, there is no way to derive contrasts between policy and character from their work). They found that 56% of the utterances acclaimed, 30% attacked, and 14% defended. However, the Republican incumbent defended more and attacked less, while the Democratic challenger defended less and attacked more.

The Functions of Political Campaigns

Each of these message forms privileged acclaims over attacks, and attacks over defenses. Television spots (54%) and debates (59%) devoted somewhat over half of their remarks to self-praise. Radio addresses (78%) and free television time (77%) spend over three-quarters of their time acclaiming. Television spots had the most attacks (46%), while radio addresses (22%) and free television time (23%) devoted just over one-fifth of their time to attacks. The amount of attack in debates fell between these figures at about one-third (33%). Debates spent far more time defending (7%) than the other three forms (which ranged from 0.2% to 1% defenses). See Table 15.7 for these data.

It is clear that acclaims predominated in the general campaign: no message form had more attacks than acclaims. Still, television advertisements were the most negative form. Surely it is no coincidence that these messages are the only kind of message we studied that permits other speakers besides the candidate to speak (narrators/announcers, ordinary people, endorsers). Thus spots may be more negative because the candidate is not the only source. Furthermore, debates, a situation with direct confrontation, produced the most defenses. There is no question that the audience is aware of an opponent's attack during the debate, and so the candidates do not have to spend limited time and money to describe an attack before refuting it. It is also human nature to respond immediately to such attacks.

Table 15.7
Functions of Campaigning in the General Election

	Acclaims	Attacks	Defenses
TV Spots	54%	46%	0.4%
Radio Addresses	78%	22%	1%
Debates	59%	33%	7%
Free TV Time	77%	23%	0.2%

In their general campaign television advertisements, Clinton acclaimed (58%) more than he attacked (41%). He also acclaimed more than Dole, who attacked (55%) more than he acclaimed (45%; Table 10.1). This finding is consistent with previous research on party and incumbency (Democrats and incumbents tended to acclaim more while Republicans and challengers favored attacking). Neither candidate relied heavily on persuasive defense: only 3 out of 703 utterances in their television spots were defenses. Again, defenses historically account for only 1% of presidential spot utterances.

Clinton only engaged in acclaiming in his radio addresses—none of the radio speeches we examined from Clinton contained a single attack (Table 11.1). Dole acclaimed (53%) more than he attacked (46%). Dole used defense in 2 out of 131 utterances.

In the two debates (Table 12.1), Clinton acclaimed (71%) much more than he attacked (19%). Dole's nondefensive utterances were split virtually evenly between acclaims (48%) and attacks (48%). Clinton defended (11%) more than Dole (4%) in the debates. Similarly in 1992, both major party candidates acclaimed more than they attacked, the challenger attacked more than the incumbent, and the incumbent defended more than the challenger.

In their free television time statements (Table 13.1), both acclaimed more than they attacked (and only Clinton defended, and he did so but once). However, Clinton (87%) acclaimed more than Dole (65%), and therefore Dole attacked (35%) more often than Clinton (13%).

Thus, Clinton—the Democratic incumbent—consistently acclaimed more often than he attacked. Dole—the Republican challenger—attacked more than he acclaimed in his television spots; he used acclaiming and attacking equally in the debates, and he acclaimed more in his radio addresses and free TV time than he attacked. Neither candidate defended much except in the debates, where Clinton defended twice as much as Dole.

Table 15.8
Policy versus Character in the General Election

	Policy	Character
TV Spots	74%	26%
Radio Addresses	72%	28%
Debates	72%	28%
Free TV Time	76%	24%

Policy versus Character

The candidates in the general campaign showed a marked preference for discussing policy rather than character. There was also remarkable consistency here: no message devoted less than 72% of utterances to policy (radio addresses, debates), and no message form spent more than 76% of the time on policy (free television time; television spots were 74%). Thus, character (images) did not overshadow policy (issues) in 1996. See Table 15.8 for these data.

Clinton discussed policy (80%) more than character (20%) in his television spots (Table 10.3). Dole revealed the same pattern (policy: 62%; character 38%), but he addressed policy less often than Clinton. Consistent with this finding, Democrats stressed policy even more than Republicans in past television spots (Benoit, Pier, & Blaney, 1997).

In the radio addresses (Table 11.2), Clinton talked about policy (77%) much more often than character (23%). Again, Dole followed the same pattern (policy: 67%; character 33%), although he did not discuss policy quite as much as Clinton. In the debates (Table 12.3), Clinton mainly discussed policy (80%). Dole spent more time on policy (64%) than character (36%), but not as much as Clinton. Finally, their free television time remarks (Table 13.2) exhibit exactly the same tendency. Clinton mentioned policy (85%) more than character, as did Dole (64%), but Dole spent less time on policy than Clinton. Thus, in every kind of message we examined from the general campaign, both candidates devoted more time to policy than to character, although Dole spent less time on policy (and more on character) than Clinton.

We hasten to add that while these candidates devoted more time to policy than to character, we do not claim that the candidates' discussion of policy matters means that they go into great depth on the issues. Almost all of the general campaign spots in 1996 were 30 seconds long. The length of their answers to questions in the debates was strictly limited by format rules. Neither candidate presented lengthy radio addresses. Free television remarks were also limited in length—the most generous format (CBS) permitted only two and a half minutes a day for four days. Thus, we do not claim the candidates discussed policy in depth. Still, they do not dwell primarily on character or image.

Three other patterns emerged from our analysis of specific forms of policy and character utterances. First, Clinton tended to use a mixture of attacks and defenses on both past deeds and future plans. Acclaims and attacks were not equal (he did consistently acclaim more than he attacked, and in his radio addresses he never attacked once), but both were generally represented in his utterances on past deeds and future plans. Dole, on the other hand, tended to attack on past deeds and acclaim future plans, but relatively rarely acclaimed his own past deeds or attacked Clinton's future plans. In the television spots, Dole attacked Clinton's past deeds 96 times but praised his own past deeds only 5 times; he praised his own future plans 26 times but attacked Clinton's future plans only 3 times (Table 10.3). In Dole's radio addresses he attacked Clinton's past deeds 42 times but praised his own accomplishments only twice (Table 11.2). He acclaimed his proposals 21 times, while attacking Clinton's future plans only once. In the debates, he attacked Clinton's past deeds over three times as often as he acclaimed his own. He boasted of his future plans over four times as often as he criticized Clinton's plans (Table 12.3). Finally, in the free television remarks, Dole again attacked Clinton's past deeds over three times as often as he acclaimed his own accomplishments. Dole praised his proposals 49 times but never attacked Clinton's plans (Table 13.2). Thus, Dole did not make full use of the options available to him.

For example, Clinton attacked Dole's past deeds (opposing Social Security) and acclaimed his own (creating jobs). He attacked Dole's proposals (the 15% tax cut would blow a hole in the deficit) and praised his own (wanted to connect all classrooms to the Internet). Dole, in contrast, attacked Clinton's past deeds (increasing taxes instead of giving a middle-class tax cut) but rarely touted his own accomplishments. Dole boasted of his proposed 15% tax cut, but rarely attacked Clinton's plans. In other words, Clinton repeatedly (1) acclaimed his own past deeds, (2) attacked Dole's past deeds, (3) acclaimed his future plans, and (4) attacked Dole's proposals. Dole, however, tended to use only half of the four options available to him, eschewing the first and last options.

A second finding is that both candidates tended to acclaim more than to attack on general goals. This is true in the general spots (Clinton 52/8; Dole 21/2; Table 10.3), radio addresses (Clinton 20/0; Dole 17/4; Table 11.2), general debates (Clinton 8/5; Dole 46/9; Table 12.3), and free TV time (Clinton 84/4; Dole 37/3; Table 13.2). General goals tend to sound good (balance the budget; maintain a strong defense) and are therefore easier to acclaim than to attack. One can, of course, criticize specific (future) plans for achieving those goals, but it is not as easy to attack the goals themselves.

Third, we found a similar phenomena occurred with their personal ideals: more acclaims than attacks for both candidates. This is true in the television spots (Clinton 32/6; Dole 20/8; Table 10.3), radio addresses (Clinton 18/0; Dole 20/6; Table 11.2), debates (Clinton 55/7; Dole 52/16; table 12.3), and free TV remarks (Clinton 45/5; Dole 35/16; Table 13.2). This contrasts fairly dramatically with, for example, personal qualities, where the numbers are not as skewed (TV spots 41 acclaims and 49 attacks; radio addresses 6 attacks and 13 acclaims; debates 55 attacks and 74 acclaims, or free TV remarks 11 attacks and 19 acclaims). Ideals are general personal characteristics, and like general (policy) goals, they are easier to acclaim than to attack.

Strategies for Elaborating Acclaims and Attacks

The same pattern of elaboration strategies appeared in each of the four general campaign message forms. The two candidates were most likely to develop acclaims and attacks by stressing extent, followed by effects on the audience, vulnerability, consistency, and persistence. Although statistics are not the only way to demonstrate extent (of either problems in attacks or benefits in acclaims), they are an easy and common method. Given the importance of voters in a campaign, it is not surprising to see that the candidates talked frequently of effects on the audience when developing acclaims and attacks.

Issues Addressed

In general television spots (Table 10.5), Clinton discussed the top five topics (and the seventh topic) substantially more than Dole. Dole led only on one topic, taxation. We were able to obtain copies of almost twice as many ads from Clinton (and the DNC) as from Dole (and the RNC). However, even taking that into consideration, Clinton devotes *more than twice as many* utterances to each of these six categories as Dole. Thus, while Clinton's utterances may be more concise, the fact that he discussed more of the topics important to voters more frequently than Dole is not just an artifact of the number of ads we located. In the radio addresses (Table 11.4), Clinton devoted substantially more comments to the highest-rated issue (jobs and the economy) and to the third, fourth, and fifth issues. Dole devoted more remarks to education, taxes, and crime and drugs. In the debate (Table 12.5), Clinton talked more than Dole about the second (education), third (deficit), fourth (Medicare and health) and seventh (crime) issues. Dole led on taxes (the sixth most important issue) (and welfare and jobs and the economy were roughly tied). In the free television remarks (Table 13.4), Clinton spent more time on the first two issues (jobs and the economy, education) and on the fourth and fifth (Medicare and health, welfare). Dole led on only one, taxation (Clinton had a slight edge on the deficit). Thus, Clinton led on more issues than Dole, and Clinton tended to dominate the issues that were more important to voters. In fact, the only topic on which Dole consistently led is taxation, considered sixth most important of these issues to voters (in three contexts it was the only topic Dole dominated).

Of course, the fact that Clinton showed a clear tendency to spend more time on issues that were important to voters is not necessarily decisive. It is possible that what Clinton said when he addressed those topics alienated voters (actually we would argue that there is nothing that either candidate could say to secure the support of all voters). However, at least he was talking more often about things that, according to public opinion polls, voters thought were important in the election.

COMPARISONS OF THE PARTS OF THE CAMPAIGN

Two message forms occurred in both primary and general campaigns—debates and television spots—and so are directly comparable. We will compare the totals for each (all primary candidates and both general election candidates) and Dole's performance in each phase of the campaign. (We do not compare Clinton's primary spots with his general spots because, as noted earlier, Clinton did not face a contested primary. His television spots never attacked other Democratic figures, and his spots only targeted Dole. Thus we considered all of Clinton's spots to be "general" spots regardless of the time period in which they aired.)

Functions

The functions of political campaign discourse were relatively stable across campaign phases. Acclaiming accounted for between 54–59%, attacks for 33–37%, and defenses for 7–9%. Dole's performance, in contrast, varied considerably. He engaged in much more acclaiming in the primary than the general debates (57%; 48%), more attacking in the general debates than the primary debates (48%; 22%), and more defense in the primary than the general debates (21%; 4%). This shift could well be due to the fact that he switched from being front-runner in the primary to second-place in the general campaign. See Table 15.9.

Functions in television spots were relatively consistent between the primary and general phases of the campaign. Acclaims were most common, ranging from 55–59%; attacks followed at from 39–44%; and defense was infrequent at from 0.5–2%. Dole's percentages hovered roughly

Table 15.9
Primary versus General Debates: Functions

	Acclaims	Attacks	Defenses
Primary	54%	38%	9%
General	59%	33%	7%
Dole Primary	57%	22%	21%
Dole General	48%	48%	4%

around 50%, but his emphasis shifted from somewhat more acclaiming than attacking in the primary (50%; 47%) to more attacking than acclaiming in the general campaign (54%; 45%). This difference could also reflect his changed standing in the polls. His defenses were infrequent, but even less likely in the general campaign than the primary (0.5%; 3%). This may have occurred because his fellow Republicans subjected him to more attack than did Clinton (Clinton attacked 41% of the time, while in the Republican primaries attacks constituted 39% of the utterances—but attacks were 39% of *multiple* candidates in the primaries). These data can be found in Table 15.10.

Policy versus Character

In television commercials, policy was discussed much more often in the general campaign than in the primary (71%; 48%). Character was addressed more frequently in the primary than the general campaign (52%; 29%). This might reflect the notion that character tends to be more of a Republican than a Democratic issue, as suggested earlier, and these primaries were exclusively Republican. Dole's discourse was relatively consistent, devoting 59% of the remarks in his advertisements to policy in the primary, and 61% in the general campaign. See Table 15.11.

If we consider relative emphasis on policy and character, the opposite picture emerges. The debates were not stable across campaign phases, with more emphasis on policy in the general than the primary debates (72%; 58%) and more emphasis on character in primary than general debates (42%; 28%). Dole remained quite consistent in his emphasis, devoting about two-thirds of his remarks to policy in primary and general debates (63%; 64%), and one-third to character (37%; 36%). This may have happened because other Republican debaters stressed character more than Clinton. These data are displayed in Table 15.12.

Table 15.10
Primary versus General TV Spots: Functions

	Acclaims	Attacks	Defenses
Primary	58%	40%	2%
General	54%	46%	0.4%
Dole Primary	50%	47%	3%
Dole General	45%	55%	0.4%

CONCLUSION

We take up several topics in our conclusion. First, we discuss the functional approach to political campaign discourse. Second, we discuss stages of the campaign. Third, we consider various message forms. Then we discuss political party. Fifth, we take up the difference between incumbents and challengers. Finally, we contrast our analysis of campaign '96 with generic studies of discourse.

The Functional Approach to Political Campaign Discourse

We believe the functional approach to political campaign discourse was very useful to our investigation of campaign '96. Of course, past research on television spots has frequently looked at positive and negative ads. At least one study (Benoit & Wells, 1996) investigated attack and defense in presidential debates. No one has examined all three functions—acclaiming, attacking, and defending—or done so throughout an entire campaign. We found messages were replete with acclaims and attacks. Defense was relatively infrequent, but it occurred in every kind of message except for the spouses' convention speeches. Acclaims are a discursive means of persuading voters to perceive a candidate as preferable, as more worthy of the citizens' vote. Attacks are a way to convince citizens that an opponent is less deserving of their vote. Defenses are a way to try to restore desirability that might be lost from such an attack. Regardless of party (Republicans and Democrats used acclaims, attacks, and defenses), incumbent/challenger status, primaries or general campaign, and message types, acclaiming, attacking, and defending are important components of campaign discourse.

Primary versus General Election Campaigns

As noted above, relatively little research has investigated campaign primaries. A few studies of primary debates and primary advertising

Table 15.11
Primary versus General TV Spots: Policy and Character

	Policy	Character
Primary	48%	52%
General	74%	26%
Dole Primary	59%	41%
Dole General	62%	38%

can be found, but not many of either and little else. This is an important gap in our understanding of political campaign discourse. The primaries were contested in at least one party in all recent campaigns. Sometimes other candidates challenged incumbents (Buchanan challenged Bush in 1992; Edward Kennedy challenged Jimmy Carter in 1980). The primary race is important because it determines at least one of the nominees, and possibly both. It may be said that the general campaign is most important because it decides who will be elected president, but it is the primaries that determine who will contest for that office.

Furthermore, we found that there are some differences between primary and general messages. The targets of attack certainly differ in the two stages of the campaign: the principal targets of attack in the primary, quite understandably, are other party members—not the presumed nominee of the opposing party. There is more discussion of policy in the general campaign than the primary in 1996, in both television spots and debates. There is more defense in primary television spots and debates than general spots and debates. There is more attack in general television spots than primary spots, but more attack in general debates than primary debates. It is not clear whether these differences are attributable entirely to the stage of the campaign, because we did not have a contested Democratic primary in 1996. Nevertheless, these data demonstrate that we should not assume that primary messages are just like general messages. Primary messages deserve study along with general messages (and preferably, contrasts between primary and general messages of the same types).

Message Forms

Although there are some consistencies throughout all of the message forms we studied (acclaiming tended to be more common than attacking, and attacks were more frequent than defenses; policy tended to overshadow character), there are also important and systematic differences

Table 15.12
Primary versus General Debates: Policy and Character

	Policy	Character
Primary	58%	42%
General	72%	28%
Dole Primary	63%	37%
Dole General	64%	36%

between the various message types. For example, in the direct confrontation of debates, defenses are more common. In television spots (which may not always feature the candidate), attacks are more common. The spousal speeches had relatively few attacks and no defenses at all. These kinds of differences are not shocking, but they do matter.

Most research on political campaign messages focuses on two message forms: debates and television spots. However, these message forms are different in systematic and readily explicable ways from other kinds of messages. That means that our knowledge of these message forms cannot be assumed to transfer readily to other kinds of messages. Debates and television spots might be the two most important message forms, but they are not the only kinds of campaign discourse. Our understanding of political campaign rhetoric would be enhanced by attention to other message forms. We studied several other forms in this study (e.g., radio addresses, talk radio appearances, free television time remarks). We urge scholars to study these as well as other forms, like radio spots, printed brochures, direct mail, and World Wide Web sites, in future research.

Political Party and Campaign Discourse

It is difficult to disentangle the potential effects of political party on campaign discourse from the effects of incumbency in a study like this. In campaign '96 there was only one incumbent, who was a Democrat, and one challenger, who was a Republican. It is difficult to know whether characteristics of Clinton's discourse are more likely to stem from his ideology or his situation—and the same it is true of Dole. However, given the fact that there is some benchmark research done across many campaigns in three contexts—keynotes from 1960–1996 (Benoit, Blaney, & Pier, 1996), acceptance addresses from 1960–1996 (Wells, Pier, Blaney, & Benoit, 1996), and television spots from 1980–1996 (Benoit, Pier, & Blaney, 1997)—we can advance a few tentative conclusions.

In two of the three contexts in which there is a baseline—acceptance addresses and television spots—Republicans attacked more than Democrats, while Democrats acclaimed more than Republicans. In keynote speeches, on the other hand, Republicans praised more than Democrats, while Democrats attacked more than Republicans. There are two possible explanations for this state of affairs. First, the constraint of political party on production of acclaims and attacks may be relatively weak. Second, it is possible that many of the party members selected to present keynote speeches did not present speeches that were consistent with the party's predilections. Modest support for the second explanation can be found in research on effects of political television advertising. Ansolabehere and Iyengar (1995) found that Republican viewers were more persuaded by negative than positive spots (by attacking than acclaiming ads), while Democrats were more persuaded by positive than negative spots. There may be a tendency for members of the Republican Party to be susceptible to attacks. For example, Democrats—even the so-called "New Democrats"—may be more likely than Republicans to look to governmental programs as solutions to problems. If so, that might give Republicans an incentive to attack more, being critical of the governmental solutions proposed by Democrats. Because Republicans favor less governmental regulation and "interference," they may propose fewer programs for Democrats to attack. In any event, it appears as if there might be some tendency, albeit not a powerful one, for Republicans to attack more than Democrats.

Incumbents versus Challengers

As mentioned above, in a study of a single campaign it is difficult to unravel the effects of party and situation. Here, however, the evidence for the possible effects of incumbents and challengers on political campaign discourse is more consistent (see Trent & Friedenberg, 1995; Trent & Trent, 1995). In all three areas in which there are baseline data—keynotes, acceptance addresses, and television spots—incumbents acclaim more than they attack, while challengers attack more than they acclaim. We believe this is true because the incumbent's record in office is, in general, the most potent source of information about that candidate's likely performance in the future. As such, the incumbent's record is a source of acclaims by the incumbent and attacks by the challenger.

Of course, this generalization requires some qualification. First, the effects of incumbency are probably stronger for sitting presidents who are seeking a second term, like Nixon in 1972, Carter in 1980, Reagan in 1984, Bush in 1992, and Clinton in 1996. The effects of incumbency are probably about as powerful for those who were not elected to office (Johnson in 1964 and Ford in 1976). We suspect the effects of incumbency are weaker for vice presidents who seek to ascend to the presidency

(Nixon in 1960; Bush in 1988). Second, there are other places to look for information about a candidate's likely performance in office. Business-people like Perot or Forbes may tout their records in the corporate world. Governors like Dukakis or Clinton may boast of their records in Mas-sachusetts and Arkansas—and an opponent like Bush may attack their records in that office. However, we believe that an incumbent's record in the office being sought is a particularly powerful source of evidence about their likely future performance. This explains why there is a con-sistent finding that incumbents acclaim more than they attack, while challengers attack more than they acclaim.

It is also possible that this finding is influenced by another set of fac-tors. Incumbents do not always win (e.g., Carter in 1980 or Bush in 1992), and they are not always the front-runner. However, incumbents have many indisputable advantages. In 1996, although surely most voters knew who Bob Dole was (Senate majority leader), most voters probably knew more about Clinton. The president is the epicenter of media cov-erage of the government, national affairs, and international relations. Thus, it may be important for challengers to do something dramatic to attract attention and counteract some of the incumbent's advantage. This may encourage challengers to attack. If indeed incumbents tend to have an advantage, they may be less willing to risk a potential backlash from voters who profess to dislike mudslinging. Thus, there could be other factors which impel incumbents to favor acclaiming, while challengers are prone to attack.

Trent and Trent (1995; see Trent & Friedenberg, 1995; Trent & Trent, 1974) offer an insightful discussion of incumbents versus challengers. They describe several incumbent strategies (e.g., creating pseudo-events, making presidential appointments, spending federal money), including "emphasizing his accomplishments" (p. 74). They argued that near the end of the 1992 campaign, Bush "abandoned the strategies common to an incumbent, recognizing that he did not have the presumption of vic-tory, assumed the role of the challenger, and attacked" (p. 76). It is cer-tainly possible that Bush increased the relative proportion of his attacks toward the end of his campaign. We have found that, in general, incum-bents acclaim more than challengers and challengers attack more than incumbents. However, acclaiming is done by *both* kinds of candidates, just as *attacks* are used by incumbents as well as challengers. While they presumably do not mean to argue that incumbents never attack and chal-lengers do nothing but attack, this passage could be taken to imply just that. We would be more comfortable saying that Bush began to devote a higher proportion of his utterances to attacking than incumbents usu-ally produce than to say that he abandoned the incumbent strategy of acclaiming and took up the challenger strategy of attacking.

Genre Studies

We want to end our investigation into campaign '96 by addressing the question of how our analysis differs from a generic analysis. Genre criticism operates from the assumption that "rhetorical forms that establish genres are stylistic and substantive responses to perceived situational demands" (Campbell & Jamieson, 1978, p. 19; cf. Black, 1978). This kind of search for a set of similar rhetorical features which describe the essence of a distinctive type of discourse has led to a variety of studies. Many studies focus on situational features as defining characteristics: the gallows speech (Aly, 1969), resignation addresses (Martin, 1976), inaugural addresses (Campbell & Jamieson, 1985), or *apologia* (Ware & Linkugel, 1973). Other studies take the rhetor and/or characteristics of the rhetor as foundational: ambassador's speeches (Wooten, 1973) or political ideology (Clark, 1979). Some analyses focus on the purpose of the discourse: polarization (King & Anderson, 1971; Raum & Measell, 1974), diatribe (Windt, 1972), or opposition to war (Murphy, 1992a). In some areas of inquiry (although perhaps not self-described as genre studies), the type of message (medium) seems to be an important consideration, as studies of presidential debates (Carlin & McKinney, 1994; Hellweg, Pfau, & Brydon, 1992; Jamieson & Birdsell, 1988) are quite distinct from studies of presidential television spots (Jamieson, 1996; Kern, 1989). Thus, a "genre" seems to be able to spring from a variety of factors that influence the production of discourse.

Our analysis of campaign '96 revealed that this discourse was influenced by—or is best explained by—several factors. Obviously, our study has prominently featured the *purpose* or functions of campaign messages. Second, there are differences that stem from the *situation* or scene. For example, we found that incumbents were more likely to praise and challengers were prone to attack. We also found some differences between discourse produced in the primary race and the general campaign. Third, other differences stem from contrasts among the *candidates* or agents. Most prominent here are differences between Republicans and Democrats. Furthermore, Buchanan and Forbes, who have never held elective office, were more prone to attack the establishment than Senators Dole and Gramm. Finally, there are important differences in the *medium* or agency of these messages. We found, for example, that debates had the most defense, while television spots had the most attacks in the general campaign.

These findings support the view of the genesis of rhetorical action articulated by Benoit (1994): "Use of all four of the ratios—scene-act, agent-act, purpose-act, and agency-act—contribute to a full understanding of rhetorical action" (p. 353). Campaign discourse is produced or influenced by a number of related factors: purpose, situation, agent, and agency. Rhetorical scholarship, therefore, may not be best served by attempts to identify "the" genre of political campaign discourse (or even, say, of presidential debates or of television spots), lumping together messages which possess important systematic differences (e.g., incumbents versus challengers, Republican versus Democrat). It may well be that we are ready to move onto another stage of rhetorical scholarship in which we attempt to identify a congeries of factors that come together at the point of rhetorical invention to jointly shape discourse.

Thus, an approach to understanding rhetorical discourse that goes beyond identification of "observations which indicate that one group of entities shares some important characteristic which differentiates it from all other entities" (Harrell & Linkugel, 1978, p. 263) could be an important advance in rhetorical theory and criticism. Providing a single generic description of political campaign discourse would ignore these important and interesting factors which we have uncovered in this study. Of course, it is possible that the rhetorical constraints of some situations (e.g., papal encyclicals; Jamieson, 1975) are so powerful that other factors in the rhetorical equation become inconsequential. However, we believe it is unlikely that most discourse is so highly constrained. Of course, our point is *not* that identification of genres is a useless or misguided task; only that there may well be a way to extend generic analyses by identifying factors that jointly shape these discourses (like agent, purpose, situation, and agency).

NOTES

1. This research, including keynotes and acceptance addresses from 1960 to 1996, includes the nominating convention speeches from 1996. Thus, we must assume that the 1996 speeches would have points of commonality with the two baseline studies because they contributed to those generalizations. However, nine other campaigns are also included in those historical studies, so we do not believe the comparison is useless.

2. Again, this research includes the 1996 campaign as one of the six presidential campaigns studied. Thus, we should expect some similarity between the 1996 campaign and the study that includes the 1996 campaign. However, because there are five other campaigns included—and thus ten other candidates—we do not believe this renders the comparison useless.

References

Abramowitz, A. (1978). The impact of a presidential debate on voter rationality. *American Journal of Political Science, 22,* 680–90.

Adato, K. (1993). *Picture perfect: The art and artifice of public image making.* New York: Basic Books.

Alexander, H. E., & Margolis, J. (1980). The making of the debates. In G. F. Bishop, R. G. Meadow, & M. Jackson-Beeck (Eds.), *Presidential debates: Media, electoral, and policy perspectives* (pp. 18–32). New York: Praeger.

Allen, R. E. (1993, September 23). Apologies are not enough. *New York Times,* p. C3.

AllPolitics CNN/*Time.* (1996). National presidential exit poll questions and results. http://www.allpolitics.com/elections/-natl.exit.poll/index.html.

Aly, B. (1969). The gallows speech: A lost genre. *Southern Speech Communication Journal, 34,* 204–13.

Ansolabehere, S., & Iyengar, S. (1995). *Going negative: How attack ads shrink and polarize the electorate.* New York: Free Press.

Associated Press Wire. (1996, March 19). Dole sweeps midwest; Clinches Republican nomination in third try.

Associated Press Wire. (1996, August 21). Vice president's wife calls Dole's bounce "predictable."

Associated Press Wire. (1996, August 30). Clinton gets convention bounce despite aide's resignation.

Atkin, C., & Heald, G. (1976). Effects of political advertising. *Public Opinion Quarterly, 40,* 216–28.

Baker, R. W. (1989, June 14). Critics fault Exxon's "PR campaign." *Christian Science Monitor,* p. 8.

Barefield, P. A. (1970). Republican keynotes. *Speech Monographs, 37,* 232–39.

Basil, M., Schooler, C., & Reeves, B. (1991). Positive and negative political advertising: Effectiveness of ads and perceptions of candidates. In F. Biocca

(Ed.), *Television and political advertising* (vol. 1, pp. 245–62). Hillsdale, NJ: Erlbaum.

Bayh, E. (1996, September 1). We have an obligation. *Vital Speeches of the Day, 62,* 715–16.

Becker, L. B., Sobowale, I. A., Cobbey, R. E., & Eyal, C. H. (1978). Debates' effects on voters' understanding of candidates and issues. In G. F. Bishop, R. G. Meadow, & M. Jackson-Beeck (Eds.), *The presidential debates: Media, electoral, and policy perspectives* (pp. 126–39). New York: Praeger.

Benedetto, R. (1996, November 4). One constant in race has been Clinton's lead. *USA Today,* p. 8A.

Bennett, J. (1996, July 30). Steaming, Buchanan spurns 15-second taped-message spot. *New York Times,* p. A9.

Benoit, P. J. (1997). *Telling the success story: Acclaiming and disclaiming discourse.* Albany: State University of New York Press.

Benoit, W. L. (1982). Richard M. Nixon's rhetorical strategies in his public statements on Watergate. *Southern Speech Communication Journal, 47,* 192–211.

Benoit, W. L. (1994). The genesis of rhetorical action. *Southern Speech Communication Journal, 59,* 342–55.

Benoit, W. L. (1995a). *Accounts, excuses, and apologies: A theory of image restoration strategies.* Albany: State University of New York Press.

Benoit, W. L. (1995b). Sears' repair of its auto service image: Image restoration discourse in the corporate sector. *Communication Studies, 46,* 89–105.

Benoit, W. L. (1997a). Hugh Grant's image restoration discourse: An actor apologizes. *Communication Quarterly 45,* 251–67.

Benoit, W. L. (1997b). Image restoration discourse and crisis communication. *Public Relations Review, 23,* 177–86.

Benoit, W. L. (1998). *A functional approach to televised political spots: Acclaiming, attacking, defending, 1952–1996.* Chicago: Central States Communication Convention.

Benoit, W. L., & Anderson, K. K. (1996). Blending politics and entertainment: Dan Quayle versus Murphy Brown. *Southern Speech Communication Journal, 62,* 73–85.

Benoit, W. L., Blaney, J. R., & Pier, P. M. (1996). *Attacking, defending, and acclaiming: A functional analysis of nominating convention keynote speeches, 1960–96.* San Diego, CA: Speech Communication Association.

Benoit, W. L., & Brinson, S. L. (1994). AT&T: Apologies are not enough. *Communication Quarterly, 42,* 75–88.

Benoit, W. L., & Czerwinski, A. (1997). A critical analysis of USAir's image restoration discourse. *Business Communication Quarterly, 60,* 38–57.

Benoit, W. L., & Dorries, B. (1996). *Dateline NBC's* persuasive attack on Wal-Mart. *Communication Quarterly, 44,* 463–77.

Benoit, W. L., Gullifor, P., & Panici, D. (1991). President Reagan's discourse on the Iran-Contra affair. *Communication Studies, 42,* 272–94.

Benoit, W. L., & Gustainis, J. J. (1986). An analogic analysis of the keynote addresses at the 1980 presidential nominating conventions. *Speaker and Gavel, 24,* 95–108.

Benoit, W. L., & Hanczor, R. S. (1994). The Tonya Harding controversy: An analysis of image restoration strategies. *Communication Quarterly, 42,* 416–33.

Benoit, W. L., Pier, P. M., & Blaney, J. R. (1997). A functional approach to televised political spots: Acclaiming, attacking, and defending. *Communication Quarterly, 45*, 1–20.

Benoit, W. L., & Wells, W. T. (1996). *Candidates in conflict: Persuasive attack and defense in the 1992 presidential debates.* Tuscaloosa: University of Alabama Press.

Benze, J. G., & Declercq, E. R. (1985). Content of television political spot ads for female candidates. *Journalism Quarterly, 62*, 278–83, 288.

Bishop, G. F., Oldendick, R. W., & Tuchfarber, A. J. (1978). The presidential debates as a device for increasing the "rationality" of electoral behavior. In G. F. Bishop, R. G. Meadow, & M. Jackson-Beeck (Eds.), *The presidential debates: Media, electoral, and policy perspectives* (pp. 179–96). New York: Praeger.

Black, E. (1978). *Rhetorical criticism: A study in method.* Madison: University of Wisconsin Press.

Blaney, J. R., & Benoit, W. L. (1997). The persuasive defense of Jesus in the Gospel according to John. *Journal of Communication and Religion, 20*, 25–30.

Blankenship, J., Fine, M. G., & Davis, L. K. (1983). The 1980 Republican primary debates: The transformation of actor to scene. *Quarterly Journal of Speech, 64*, 25–36.

Blankenship, J., Robson, D. C., & Williams, M. S. (1997). Conventionalizing gender: Talk by and about women at the 1996 national political conventions. *American Behavioral Scientist, 40*, 1020–47.

Blumenthal, S. (1980). *The permanent campaign: Inside the world of elite political operatives.* Boston: Beacon Press.

Bradley, B. (1992). Keynote address. *Vital Speeches of the Day, 58*, 655–56.

Bradley, B. E. (1960). Back to the red clay hills. *Southern Speech Communication Journal, 52*, 199–204.

Bradley, B. E. (1983). Jefferson and Reagan: The rhetoric of two inaugurals. *Southern Speech Communication Journal, 48*, 119–36.

Breglio, V. (1987). Polling in campaigns. In L. P. Devlin (Ed.), *Political persuasion in presidential campaigns* (pp. 24–34). New Brunswick, NJ: Transaction Books.

Brennen. W. (1992, June 14). An open letter to Sears' customers. *New York Times,* p. A56.

Brinson, S. L., & Benoit, W. L. (1996). Dow Corning's image repair strategies in the breast implant crisis. *Communication Quarterly, 44*, 29–41.

Brydon, S. R. (1985). *Reagan versus Reagan: The incumbency factor in the 1984 presidential debates.* Denver, CO: Speech Communication Association.

Burgoon, M., Pfau, M., & Birk, T. S. (1995). An inoculation theory explanation for the effects of corporate issue/advocacy advertising campaigns. *Communication Research, 22*, 485–505.

Burke, K. (1970). *Rhetoric of religion.* Berkeley: University of California Press.

Burke, K. (1973). *The philosophy of literary form.* 3rd ed. Berkeley: University of California Press.

Bush, G. (1992). A new crusade to reap the rewards of our global victory. *Vital Speeches of the Day, 58*, 706–10.

Campbell, K. K., & Jamieson, K. H. (1978). Form and genre in rhetorical criticism: An introduction. In K. K. Campbell & K. H. Jamieson (Eds.), *Form and genre: Shaping rhetorical action* (pp. 9–32). Falls Church, VA: Speech Communication Association.

Campbell, K. K., & Jamieson, J. H. (1985). Inaugurating the presidency. *Presidential Studies Quarterly, 15,* 394–411.

Capella, J. N., Turow, J., & Jamieson, K. H. (1996). Call-in political talk radio: Background, content, audiences, and portrayal in mainstream media. http://www.asc.upenn.edu.

Carlin, D. B. (1994). A rationale for a focus group study. In D. B. Carlin & M. S. McKinney (Eds.), *The 1992 presidential debates in focus* (pp. 3–19). Westport, CT: Praeger.

Carlin, D. B., & McKinney, M. S. (Eds.). (1994). *The 1992 presidential debates in focus.* Westport, CT: Praeger.

Chaffee, S. H. (1978). Presidential debates—Are they helpful to voters? *Communication Monographs, 45,* 330–46.

Chaffee, S. H. (1979). Approaches of U.S. scholars to the study of televised political debaies. *Political Communication Review, 4,* 19–33.

Clark, T. D. (1979). An analysis of recurrent features of contemporary American radical, liberal, and conservative political discourse. *Southern Speech Communication Journal, 44,* 399–422.

Claussen, E. N. (1965). John Sharp Williams: Pacesetter for Democratic keynoters. *Southern Speech Journal, 31,* 1–9.

Claussen, E. N. (1966). "He kept us out of war": Martin H. Glynn's keynote. *Quarterly Journal of Speech, 52,* 23–32.

Clinton, B. (1996, September 15). A bridge to the future. *Vital Speeches of the Day, 52,* 706–12.

Clinton, H. R. (1996, August 27). *Remarks at the Democratic National Convention.* Chicago.

CNN/*Time.* (1996). http://www.cnn.comm/allpolitics.

Collier, J., & Collier, M. (1986). *Visual anthropology: Photography as a research method.* Albuquerque: University of New Mexico Press.

Congressman paid self for office space: report: Rostenkowski used campaign funds. (1992, December 14). *Columbia Daily Tribune,* p. 5A.

Cragen, J. F., & Cutbirth, C. W. (1984). A revisionist perspective on political ad hominem argument: A case study. *Central States Speech Journal, 35,* 228–37.

Crawford, D. (1996, August 28). Wives enjoy new roles in presidential politics: When Hillary Clinton and Elizabeth Dole speak, the voters listen and like what they hear. *The Orlando Sentinel,* p. A1.

Crittendon, J. (1971). Democratic functions of the open mike radio forum. *Public Opinion Quarterly, 35,* 467–79.

Crotty, W., & Jackson, J. S. (1985). *Presidential primaries and nominations.* Washington, DC: Congressional Quarterly Press.

C-SPAN. (1996). http://www.c-span.org/campaign.

Cundy, D. T. (1986). Political commercials and candidate image: The effect can be substantial. In L. L. Kaid, D. Nimmo, & K. R. Sanders (Eds.), *New perspectives on political advertising* (pp. 210–34). Carbondale: Southern Illinois Press.

Cuomo, M. (1984, August 15). Keynote address. *Vital Speeches of the Day, 50,* 646–49.

Davis, D. K. (1979). Influence on vote decisions. In S. Kraus (Ed.), *The great debates: Carter versus Ford 1976* (pp. 331–47). Bloomington: Indiana University Press.

Davis, M. H. (1982). Voting intentions and the 1980 Carter-Reagan debate. *Journal of Applied Social Psychology, 12*, 481–92.

Democratic convention '96: Ratings check. (1996, August 29). *Los Angeles Times,* p. A19.

Denton, R. E., & Woodward, G. C. (1990). *Political communication in America,* 2d ed. New York: Praeger.

Desmond, R. J., & Donohue, T. R. (1981). The role of the 1976 televised presidential debates in the political socialization of adolescents. *Communication Quarterly, 29*, 302–8.

Devlin, L. P. (1977). Contrasts in presidential campaign commercials of 1972. *Central States Speech Journal, 28*, 238–49.

Devlin, L. P. (1986). An analysis of presidential television commercials, 1952–1984. In L. L. Kaid, D. Nimmo, & K. R. Sanders (Eds.), *New perspectives on political advertising* (pp. 21–54). Carbondale: Southern Illinois Press.

Devlin, L. P. (1987). Campaign commercials. In L. P. Devlin (Ed.), *Political persuasion in presidential campaigns* (pp. 208–16). New Brunswick, NJ: Transaction Books.

Devlin, L. P. (1989). Contrasts in presidential campaign commercials of 1988. *American Behavioral Scientist, 32*, 389–414

Devlin, L. P. (1993). Contrasts in presidential campaign commercials of 1992. *American Behavioral Scientist, 37*, 272–90.

Devlin, L. P. (1995). Political commercials in American presidential elections. In L. L. Kaid & C. Holtz-Bacha (Eds.), *Political advertising in western democracies: Parties & candidates on television* (pp. 186–205). Thousand Oaks, CA: Sage.

Devlin, L. P. (1997). Contrasts in presidential campaign commercials of 1996. *American Behavioral Scientist, 40*, 1058–1084.

Diamond, E., & Bates, S. (1993). *The spot: The rise of political advertising on television.* 3rd ed. Cambridge, MA: MIT Press.

Dole, E. (1996, August 14). *Remarks at the Republican National Convention.* San Diego, CA.

Dole, R. (1996, September 1). The best days are yet to come. *Vital Speeches of the Day, 52*, 674–79.

Dover, E. D. (1994). *Presidential elections in the television age: 1960–1992.* Westport, CT: Praeger.

Dow, B. J., & Tonn, M. B. (1993). "Feminine style" and political judgment in the rhetoric of Ann Richards. *Quarterly Journal of Speech, 79*, 286–302.

Downs, A. (1957). *An economic theory of democracy.* New York: Harper and Row.

Drew, D., & Weaver, D. (1991). Voter learning in the 1988 presidential election: Did the debates and the media matter? *Journalism Quarterly, 68*, 27–37.

Duin, J. (1996, August 17). TV audience way off: Boredom gets partial blame. *The Washington Times,* p. A12.

Eisenberg, E. (1984). Ambiguity as strategy in organizational communication. *Communication Monographs, 51*, 227–42.

Ellsworth, J. W. (1965). Rationality and campaigning: A content analysis of the

1960 presidential campaign debates. *Western Political Quarterly, 18,* 794–802.

Felknor, B. L. (1992). *Political mischief: Smear, sabotage, and reform in U.S. elections.* New York: Praeger.

Fiorina, M. P. (1981). *Retrospective voting in American national elections.* New Haven, CT: Yale University Press.

Fisher, W. R. (1970). A motive view of communication. *Quarterly Journal of Speech, 56,* 131–39.

Fleiss, J. L. (1981). *Statistical methods for ratios and proportions.* New York: Wiley.

Flight 427 flew shorter routes to avoid overhaul: Jet was part of cost-cutting effort, source says. (1994, September 21). *Columbia Daily Tribune,* p. 3A.

Free TV for Straight Talk Coalition. (1996, October 18). Let the running debate begin. . . . *New York Times,* p. A8.

Frenette, C. A. (1991, April 28). Open letter. *Nation's Restaurant News,* p. 24.

Friedenberg, R. V. (1994). Patterns and trends in national political debates, 1960–1992 (pp. 235–59). In R. V. Friedenberg (Ed.), *Rhetorical studies of national political debates, 1960–1992,* 2d ed. New York: Praeger.

Frye, J. K., & Krohn, F. B. (1977). An analysis of Barbara Jordan's 1976 keynote address. *Journal of Applied Communications Research, 5,* 73–82.

Gallup Poll. (1996). Trial heats. http://www.gallup.com/election/trialheats/.

Garramone, G. M. (1985). Effects of negative political advertising: The roles of sponsor and rebuttal. *Journal of Broadcasting and Electronic Media, 29,* 147–59.

Garramone, G. M., Atkin, C. K., Pinkleton, B. E., & Cole, R. T. (1990). Effects of negative political advertising on the political process. *Journal of Broadcasting and Electronic Media, 34,* 299–311.

Garramone, G. M., & Smith, S. J. (1984). Reactions to political advertising: Clarifying sponsor effects. *Journalism Quarterly, 51,* 771–75.

Geer, J. G. (1988). The effects on presidential debates on the electorate's preference on candidates. *American Politics Quarterly, 16,* 486–501.

Gibbs, N., & Duffy, M. (1996, November 4). Two men, two visions. *Time,* 31–36.

Gold, E. R. (1978). Political *apologia*: The ritual of self-defense. *Communication Monographs, 46,* 306–16.

Goodman, E. (1992, March 14). Old Joe Camel might have met his match. *Columbia Daily Tribune,* p. 4A.

Graber, D. A., & Kim, Y. Y. (1978). Why John Q. Voter did not learn much from the 1976 presidential debates. In B. Rubin (Ed.), *Communication yearbook 2* (pp. 407–21). New Brunswick, NJ: Transaction Books.

Gramm, P. (1992). Had Congress said yes: More opportunity, more government. *Vital Speeches of the Day, 58,* 721–23.

Gronbeck, B. E. (1978). The functions of presidential campaigning. *Communication Monographs, 45,* 268–80.

Gronbeck, B. E. (1992). Negative narrative in 1988 presidential campaign ads. *Quarterly Journal of Speech, 78,* 333–46.

Gustainis, J. J., & Benoit, W. L. (1988). Analogic analysis of the presidential candidates' acceptance speeches at the 1980 national nominating conventions. *Speaker and Gavel, 25,* 14–23.

Hagner, P. R., & Rieselbach, L. N. (1978). The impact of the 1976 presidential debates: Conversion or reinforcement? In G. F. Bishop, R. G. Meadow, & M. Jackson-Beeck (Eds.), *The presidential debates: Media, electoral, and policy perspectives* (pp. 157–78). New York: Praeger.

Hallin, D. (1992). Sound bite news: Television coverage of elections, 1968–1988. *Journal of Communication, 42(2)*, 5–24.

Harrell, H., & Linkugel, W. A. (1978). On rhetorical genre: An organizing perspective. *Philosophy & Rhetoric, 11*, 262–81.

Hart, R. P., & Jarvis, S. E. (1997). Political debate: Forms, styles, and media. *American Behavioral Scientist, 40*, 1095–123.

Hatfield, M. O. (1964, July 13). Keynote address. *Vital Speeches of the Day, 30*, 652–54.

Hellweg, S. A., Pfau, M., & Brydon, S. R. (1992). *Televised presidential debates: Advocacy in contemporary America.* New York: Praeger.

Hellweg, S. A., & Phillips, S. L. (1981). A verbal and visual analysis of the 1980 Houston Republican primary debate. *Southern Speech Communication Journal, 47*, 23–38.

Henry, D. (1988). The rhetorical dynamics of Mario Cuomo's 1984 keynote address: Situation, speaker, metaphor. *Southern Speech Communication Journal, 53*, 105–20.

Hickman, R. H. (1984/85). Presidential election debates: Do they matter? *Election Politics, 2*, 10–14.

Hill, R. P. (1989). An exploration of voter responses to political advertisements. *Journal of Advertising, 18*, 14–22.

Hilts, P. J. (1989, March 31). Environment may show spill's effects for decade. *Washington Post*, p. A6.

Hinck, E. A. (1993). *Enacting the presidency: Political argument, presidential debates, and presidential character.* Westport, CT: Praeger.

Hofstetter, C. R., Donovan, M. C., Klauber, M. R., Cole, A., Hue, C. J., & Yuasa, T. (1993). Political talk radio: A stereotype reconsidered. *Political Research Quarterly, 47*, 467–79.

Hofstetter, C. R., & Zukin, C. (1979). TV network news and advertising in the Nixon and McGovern campaigns. *Journalism Quarterly, 56*, 106–15, 152.

Holbrook, T. M. (1996) *Do campaigns matter?* Thousand Oaks, CA: Sage.

Hollander, B. (1995/1996). The influence of talk radio on political efficacy and participation. *Journal of Radio Studies, 3*, 23–31.

Hollander, B. (1996). Talk radio: Predictors of use and effects on attitudes about government. *Journalism Quarterly, 73*, 102–13.

Holsti, O. R., Loomba, J. K., & North, R. C. (1968). Content analysis. In G. Lindsey & E. Aronson (Eds.), *Handbook of social psychology* (vol. 2, pp. 596–692). Reading, MA: Addison-Wesley.

Inouye, D. K. (1968). Commitment: Keynote address. *Vital Speeches of the Day, 34*, 709–11.

Interim Secretary of State sworn in: Impeached Moriarty awaits court edict. (1994, October 7). *Columbia Daily Tribune*, p. 1A.

Iyengar, S., & Kinder, D. R. (1987). *News that matters: Television and American opinion.* Chicago: University of Chicago Press.

Jacoby, J., Troutman, T. R., & Whittler, T. E. (1986). Viewer miscomprehension of the 1980 presidential debate: A research note. *Political Psychology, 7,* 297–308.

Jamieson, K. H. (1975). Antecedent genre as rhetorical constraint. *Quarterly Journal of Speech, 61,* 406–15.

Jamieson, K. H. (1987). Television, presidential campaigns, and debates. In J. L. Swerdlow (Ed.), *Presidential debates 1988 and beyond* (pp. 27–33). Washington, DC: Congressional Quarterly Inc.

Jamieson, K. H. (1992). *Dirty politics: Deception, distraction, and democracy.* New York: Oxford University Press.

Jamieson, K. H. (1996). *Packaging the presidency: A history and criticism of presidential campaign advertising.* 3rd ed. New York: Oxford University Press.

Jamieson, K. H., & Birdsell, D. S. (1988). *Presidential debates: The challenge of creating an informed electorate.* New York: Oxford University Press.

Johnson-Cartee, K. S., & Copeland, G. (1989). Southern voters' reactions to negative political ads in the 1986 election. *Journalism Quarterly, 66,* 888–93, 986.

Johnson-Cartee, K. S., & Copeland, G. (1991). *Negative political advertising: Coming of age.* Hillsdale, NJ: Erlbaum.

Johnson-Cartee, K. S., & Copeland, G. (1997). *Manipulation of the American voter: Political campaign commercials.* Westport, CT: Praeger.

Joslyn, R. A. (1980). The content of political spot ads. *Journalism Quarterly, 57,* 92–98.

Joslyn, R. A. (1981). The impact of campaign spot advertising on voting defections. *Human Communication Research, 7,* 347–60.

Joslyn, R. A. (1986). Political advertising and the meaning of elections. In L. L. Kaid, D. Nimmo, & K. R. Sanders (Eds.), *New perspectives on political advertising* (pp. 139–83). Carbondale: Southern Illinois Press.

Judd, W. H. (1960). The best way to achieve good objectives and keep them: Keynote address. *Vital Speeches of the Day, 26,* 647–51.

Just, M., Crigler, A., & Wallach, L. (1990). Thirty seconds or thirty minutes: What viewers learn from spot advertisements and candidate debates. *Journal of Communication, 40,* 120–32.

Kaid, L. L. (1991). The effects of television broadcasts on perceptions of presidential candidates in the United States and France. In L. L. Kaid, J. Gerstle, & K. R. Sanders (Eds.), *Mediated politics in two cultures: Presidential campaigning in the United States and France* (pp. 247–60). New York: Praeger.

Kaid, L. L. (1994). Political advertising in the 1992 campaign. In R. E. Denton (Ed.), *The 1992 presidential campaign: A communication perspective* (pp. 111–27). Westport, CT: Praeger.

Kaid, L. L. (1997). Effects of the television spots on images of Dole and Clinton. *American Behavioral Scientist, 40,* 1085–94.

Kaid, L. L., & Ballotti, J. (1991). *Television advertising in presidential primaries and caucuses.* Atlanta: Speech Communication Association.

Kaid, L. L., & Boydston, J. (1987). An experimental study of the effectiveness of negative political advertisements. *Communication Quarterly, 35,* 193–201.

Kaid, L. L., & Davidson, D. K. (1986). Elements of videostyle: Candidate presentation through television advertising. In L. L. Kaid, D. Nimmo, & K. R. Sanders (Eds.), *New perspectives on political advertising* (pp. 184–209). Carbondale: Southern Illinois Press.

Kaid, L. L., & Johnston, A. (1991). Negative versus positive television advertising in U.S. presidential campaigns, 1960–1988. *Journal of Communication, 41,* 53–64.

Kaid, L. L., Leland, C. M., & Whitney, S. (1992). The impact of televised political ads: Evoking viewer responses in the 1988 presidential campaign. *Southern Speech Communication Journal, 57,* 285–95.

Kaid, L. L., Nimmo, D., & Sanders, K. R. (Eds.). (1986). *New perspectives on political advertising.* Carbondale: Southern Illinois Press.

Kaid, L. L., & Sanders, K. R. (1978). Political television commercials: An experimental study of type and length. *Communication Research, 5,* 57–70.

Kane, T. (1987). The Dewey-Stassen primary debate of 1948: An examination of format for presidential debates. In J. Wenzel (Ed.), *Argument and critical practices* (pp. 249–53). Annandale, VA: Speech Communication Association.

Kaplan, A., & Goldsen, J. M. (1965). The reliability of content analysis categories. In H. D. Lasswell et al. (Eds.), *The Language of politics: Studies in quantitative semantics* (pp. 83–112). Cambridge, MA: MIT Press.

Kean, T. H. (1988). Keynote address. *Vital Speeches of the Day, 55,* 7–10.

Kelley, S. (1983). *Interpreting elections.* Princeton, NJ: Princeton University Press.

Kendall, K. A. (1997). The 1996 Clinton-Dole presidential debates: Through media eyes. In R. V. Friedenberg (Ed.), *Rhetorical studies of national political debates—1996* (pp. 1–29). Westport, CT: Praeger.

Kennedy, K. A., & Benoit, W. L. (1997). The Newt Gingrich book deal controversy: A case study in self-defense discourse. *Southern Speech Communication Journal, 63,* 197–216.

Kern, M. (1989). *30-second politics: Political advertising in the eighties.* New York: Praeger.

King, A. A., & Anderson, F. D. (1971). Nixon, Agnew, and the "Silent Majority"; A case study in the rhetoric of polarization. *Western Speech, 35,* 243–55.

Kirk, P. (1995, October 28). Presidential debates and democracy. C-SPAN.

Kraus, S. (Ed.). (1979). *The great debates: Carter versus Ford 1976.* Bloomington: Indiana University Press.

Lamoureaux, E. R., Entrekin, H. S., & McKinney, M. S. (1994). Debating the debates. In D. B. Carlin & M. S. McKinney (Eds.), *The 1992 presidential debates in focus* (pp. 55–67). Westport, CT: Praeger.

Lang, A. (1991). Emotion, formal features, and memory for televised political advertisements. In F. Biocca (Ed.), *Television and political advertising* (vol. 1, pp. 221–43). Hillsdale, NJ: Erlbaum.

Lang, G. E., & Lang, K. (1978). The formation of public opinion: Direct and mediated effects of the first debate. In G. F. Bishop, R. G. Meadow, & M. Jackson-Beeck (Eds.), *The presidential debates: Media, electoral, and policy perspectives* (pp. 61–80). New York: Praeger.

Lang, K., & Lang, G. E. (1977). Reactions of viewers. In S. Kraus (Ed.), *The great debates: Carter versus Ford, 1976* (pp. 313–30). Bloomington: Indiana University Press.

Lanoue, D. J. (1991). The "turning point": Viewers' reactions to the second 1988 presidential debate. *American Politics Quarterly, 19,* 80–95.

Lanoue, D. J., & Schrott, P. R. (1989). Voters' reactions to televised presidential debates: Measurement of the source and magnitude of opinion change. *Political Psychology, 10,* 275–85.

Leff, M. C., & Mohrmann, G. P. (1974). Lincoln at Cooper-Union: A rhetorical analysis of the text. *Quarterly Journal of Speech, 60,* 346–58.

Lemert, J. B. (1993). Do televised presidential debates help inform voters? *Journal of Broadcasting and Electronic Media, 37,* 83–94.

Levine, M. A. (1995). *Presidential campaigns and elections: Issues and images in the media age.* Itasca, IL: Peacock Publishers.

Lewis, N. A. (1996a, September 18). Panel on debates bars Perot, calling him unelectable: Texan's camp quickly vows to file suit. *New York Times,* pp. A1, A12.

Lewis, N. A. (1996b, October 2). Judge rejects suit by Perot to join presidential debates. *New York Times,* pp. A1, C23.

Lichter, S. R., & Noyes, R. E. (1995). *Good intentions make bad news: Why Americans hate campaign journalism.* Lanham, MD: Rowman & Littlefield.

Lichtman, A. J. (1996). *The keys to the White House, 1996: A surefire guide to predicting the next president.* Lanham, MD: Madison.

Louden, A. D. (1989). Political advertising bibliography. *Political Communication Review, 14,* 19–46.

Lubell, S. (1977). Personalities versus issues. In S. Kraus (Ed.), *The great debates: Carter versus Ford, 1976* (pp. 151–62). Bloomington: Indiana University Press.

Lucas, S. E. (1986). Genre criticism and historical context: The case of George Washington's first inaugural address. *Southern Speech Communication Journal, 51,* 354–70.

Martin, H. W. (1976). A generic exploration: Staged withdrawal, the rhetoric of resignation. *Central States Speech Journal, 27,* 247–57.

Mathews, J., & Peterson, C. (1989, March 31). Oil tanker captain fired after failing alcohol test: Exxon blames government for cleanup delay. *Washington Post,* pp. A1, A6.

McClure, R. D., & Patterson, T. E. (1974). Television news and political advertising: The impact of exposure on voter beliefs. *Communication Research, 1,* 3–21.

McGee, M. C. (1978). "Not men, but measures": The origins and impact of an ideological principle. *Quarterly Journal of Speech, 64,* 141–54.

McLeod, J. M., Bybee, C. R., & Durall, J. A. (1979). Equivalence of informed political participation: The 1976 presidential debates as a source of influence. *Communication Research, 6,* 463–87.

McLeod, J., Durall, J., Ziemke, D., & Bybee, C. (1979). Reactions of young and older voters: Expanding the context of effects. In S. Kraus (Ed.), *The great debates: Carter versus Ford 1976* (pp. 348–67). Bloomington: Indiana University Press.

Meadow, R. G., & Sigelman, L. (1982). Some effects and non-effects of campaign commercials: An experimental study. *Political Behavior, 4,* 163–75.

Merritt, S. (1984). Negative political advertising: Some empirical findings. *Journal of Advertising, 13,* 27–38.

Middleton, R. (1962). National TV debates and presidential voting decisions. *Public Opinion Quarterly, 26,* 426–29.

Mifflin, L. (1996, September 28). CBS to give Clinton and Dole free air time on radio and TV. *New York Times*, p. A11.

Miles, E. A. (1960). The keynote speech at national nominating conventions. *Quarterly Journal of Speech, 46*, 26–31.

Miller, A. H., & MacKuen, M. (1979). Learning about the candidates: The 1976 presidential debates. *Public Opinion Quarterly, 43*, 326–46.

Molinari, S. (1996, September 15). A legacy of hope and opportunity. *Vital Speeches of the Day, 62*, 681–83.

Moore, M. T. (1996, September 12). Clinton, Dole get air time on Fox TV. *USA Today*, p. 11A.

Mulder, R. (1979). The effects of televised political ads in the 1975 Chicago mayoral election. *Journalism Quarterly, 56*, 335–41.

Murphy, J. M. (1992a). Epideictic and deliberative strategies in opposition to wars: The paradox of honor and expediency. *Communication Studies, 43*, 65–78.

Murphy, J. M. (1992b). Presidential debates and campaign rhetoric: Text within context. *Southern Speech Communication Journal, 57*, 219–28.

NBC/*Wall Street Journal* (1997; March 1–5, May 10–14, June 20–25, August 2–6, September 12–17, October 19–22). *Roper Center at the University of Connecticut: Public Opinion Online.*

Neilsen Media Research. (1993). *Neilsen tunes into politics: Tracking the presidential election years (1960–1992).* New York: Neilsen Media Research.

Newell, S. A., & King, T. R. (1974). The keynote address of the democratic national convention, 1972: The evolution of a speech. *Southern Speech Communication Journal, 39*, 346–58.

Newhagen, J. E., & Reeves, B. (1991). Emotion and memory responses for negative political advertising: A study of television commercials used in the 1988 presidential election. In F. Biocca (Ed.), *Television and political advertising* (vol. 1, pp. 197–220). Hillsdale, NJ: Erlbaum.

Niedowski, E. (1996, October 16). It's a family affair: Spouses, kids prove invaluable campaign resources in '96 races. *The Hill*, p. 12.

Nimmo, D., Mansfield, M., & Curry, J. (1978). Persistence and change in candidate images. In G. Bishop, R. Meadow, & M. Jackson-Beech (Eds.), *The presidential debates: Media, electoral, and policy perspectives* (pp. 140–56). New York: Praeger.

Nixon, R. M. (1970). Cambodia: A difficult decision. *Vital Speeches of the Day, 37*, 450–52.

Nixon, R. M. (1972). The Republican candidate for president: Acceptance speech. *Vital Speeches of the Day, 38*, 706–9.

North, R. C., Holsti, O. R., Zaninovich, M. G., & Zinnes, D. A. (1963). *Content analysis: A handbook with applications for the study of international crisis.* Evanston, IL: Northwestern University Press.

Norvold, R. O. (1970). Rhetoric as ritual: Hubert H. Humphrey's acceptance address at the 1968 Democratic National Convention. *Today's Speech, 18*, 34–38.

Ortega, K. D. (1984). Keynote address. *Vital Speeches of the Day, 50*, 12–13.

Owen, D. (1996). Who's talking? Who's listening? The new politics of talk radio.

In S. C. Craig (Ed.), *Broken contract? Changing relationships between Americans and their government* (pp. 127–46). Boulder, CO: Westview Press.

Palda, K. S. (1973). Does advertising influence votes? An analysis of the 1966 and 1970 Quebec elections. *Canadian Journal of Political Science, 6,* 638–55.

Pastore, J. O. (1964). The Democratic record: Keynote address. *Vital Speeches of the Day, 30,* 706–8.

Patterson, T. E. (1980). *The mass media election: How Americans choose their president.* New York: Praeger.

Patterson, T. E. (1994). *Out of order.* New York: Random House, Vintage Books.

Patterson, T. E., & McClure, R. D. (1973). Political advertising on television: Spot commercials in the 1972 presidential election. *Maxwell Review,* 57–69.

Patterson, T. E., & McClure, R. D. (1976). *The unseeing eye: The myth of television power in national politics.* New York: Putnam.

Payne, J. G., Marlier, J., & Barkus, R. A. (1989). Polispots in the 1988 presidential primaries. *American Behavioral Scientist, 32,* 365–81.

Pepsi-Cola. (1991, March 11). Accounts payable/receivable. *Nation's Restaurant News,* p. 34.

Petrozello, D. (1994, November 21). The name of the game is sports. *Broadcasting & Cable,* 52–53.

Pfau, M. (1984). A comparative assessment of intra-party political debate formats. *Political Communication Review, 8,* 1–23.

Pfau, M. (1988). Intra-party political debates and issue learning. *Journal of Applied Communication Research, 16,* 99–112.

Pfau, M., & Eveland, W. P. (1994). Debates versus other communication sources: The pattern of information and influence. In D. B. Carlin & M. S. McKinney (Eds.), *The 1992 presidential debates in focus* (pp. 155–73). Westport, CT: Praeger.

Pfau, M., & Kenski, H. C. (1990). *Attack politics: Strategy and defense.* New York: Praeger.

Pitt, C. A. (1968). Judd's keynote speech: A congruous configuration of communication. *Southern Speech Communication Journal, 23,* 278–88.

Politicsnow. http://www.politicsnow.com.

Pomerantz, A. (1987). Attributions of responsibility: Blamings. *Sociology, 12,* 266–74.

Popkin, S. L. (1994). *The reasoning voter: Communication and persuasion in presidential campaigns.* Chicago: University of Chicago Press.

Popkin, S. L., Gorman, J., Smith, J., & Phillips, C. (1976). Comment: toward an investment theory of voting behavior: What have you done for me lately? *American Political Science Review, 70,* 779–805.

Prostitution sting nets St. Louis city prosecutor. (1992, March 13). *Columbia Daily Tribune,* p. 3A.

Putnam, L. R., & Sorensen, R. L. (1982). Equivocal messages in organizations. *Human Communication Research, 8,* 114–32.

Ragsdale, G. (1997). The 1996 Gore-Kemp vice presidential debates. In R. V. Friedenberg (Ed.), *Rhetorical studies of national political debates—1996* (pp. 31–60). Westport, CT: Praeger.

Raum, R. D., & Measell, J. B. (1974). Wallace and his ways: A study of the rhetorical genre of polarization. *Central States Speech Journal, 25,* 28–35.

Rawl, L. G. (1989, April 3). An open letter to the public. *New York Times*, p. A12.

Reagan, R. (1984). Acceptance speech. *Vital Speeches of the Day, 50*, 706–10.

Rebuffed moviegoers get apology. (1992, March 31). *Columbia Daily Tribune*, p. 3A.

Riley, P., & Hollihan, T. A. (1981). The 1980 presidential debates: A content analysis of the issues and arguments. *Speaker and Gavel, 18*, 47–59.

Ritter, K. W. (1980). American political rhetoric and the jeremiad tradition: Presidential nomination acceptance addresses, 1960–1976. *Central States Speech Journal, 31*, 153–71.

Ritter, K. (1996). The presidential nomination acceptance speech since 1980: An evolving American jeremiad. In D. D. Cali (Ed.), *Generic criticism of American public address* (pp. 201–10). Dubuque, IA: Kendall/Hunt.

Roper Center. (1996). Poll of Republican voters, January 27–30, 1996.

Roper, E. (1960, November). Polling post-mortem. *Saturday Review*, 10–13.

Rosenthal, P. I. (1966). The concept of ethos and the structure of persuasion. *Speech Monographs, 33*, 11–26.

Rudd, R. (1986). Issues as image in political campaign commercials. *Western Journal of Speech Communication, 50*, 102–18.

Rudd, R. (1989). Effects of issue specificity, ambiguity on evaluations of candidate image. *Journalism Quarterly, 66*, 675–82, 691.

Ryan, H. R. (1982). *Kategoria* and *apologia*: On their rhetorical criticism as a speech set. *Quarterly Journal of Speech, 68*, 256–61.

Ryan, H. R. (1988). (Ed.). *Oratorical encounters: Selected studies and sources of twentieth-century political accusations and apologies*. Westport, CT: Greenwood.

Sabato, L. (1981). *The rise of political consultants*. New York: Basic Books.

Sabato, L. J. (1997a). The conventions: One festival of hope, one celebration of impending victory. In L. J. Sabato (Ed.), *Toward the millennium: The elections of 1996* (pp. 93–120). Boston: Allyn and Bacon.

Sabato, L. J. (1997b). The November vote: A status quo election. In L. J. Sabato (Ed.), *Toward the millennium: The elections of 1996* (pp. 143–61). Boston: Allyn and Bacon.

Sabato, L. J. (1997c). Presidential nominations: The front-loaded frenzy of '96. In L. J. Sabato (Ed.), *Toward the millennium: The elections of 1996* (pp. 37–91). Boston: Allyn and Bacon.

Safer cigarette developed, not marketed. (1992, September 9). *Columbia Daily Tribune*, p. 4A.

Same drugs cost far more in U.S. than in Britain. (1994, February 2). *Columbia Daily Tribune*, p. 7A.

Scheele, H. Z. (1984). Ronald Reagan's 1980 acceptance address: A focus on American values. *Western Journal of Speech Communication, 48*, 51–61.

Schlenker, B. R. (1980). *Impression management: The self-concept, social identity, and interpersonal relations*. Monterey, CA: Brooks/Cole.

Scott, M. H., & Lyman, S. M. (1968). Accounts. *American Sociological Review, 33*, 46–62.

Scouts files suggest group is "Magnet for pedophiles." (1993, October 14). *Columbia Daily Tribune*, p. 12A.

Sears to drop incentives in auto service centers. (1992, June 23). *Columbia Daily Tribune*, p. 5B.

Sepstrup, P. (1981). Methodological development in content analysis? In K. E. Rosengren (Ed.), *Advances in content analysis* (pp. 133–58). Beverly Hills, CA: Sage.

Shyles, L. (1986). The televised political spot advertisement: Its structure, content, and role in the political system. In L. L. Kaid, D. Nimmo, & K. R. Sanders (Eds.), *New perspectives on political advertising* (pp. 107–38). Carbondale: Southern Illinois Press.

Smith, C. A. (1990). *Political communication.* San Diego, CA: Harcourt Brace Jovanovich.

Smith, C. R. (1971). Richard Nixon's 1968 acceptance speech as a model of dual audience adaption. *Today's Speech, 19,* 15–22.

Smith, C. R. (1975). The Republican keynote address of 1968: Adaptive rhetoric for the multiple audience. *Western Speech, 39,* 32–39.

Smith, R. L. (1962). A keynoter's dilemma: A new dimension. *The Forensic, 47,* 9–11, 13.

Steele, C. A., & Barnhurst, K. G. (1996). The journalism of opinion: Network news coverage of U.S. presidential campaigns, 1968–1988. *Critical Studies in Mass Communication, 13,* 187–209.

Stewart, C. J. (1975). Voter perception of mud-slinging in political communication. *Central States Speech Journal, 26,* 279–86.

Stuckey, M. E., & Antczak, F. J. (1995). The battle of issues and images: Establishing interpretive dominance. In K. E. Kendell (Ed.), *Presidential campaign discourse: Strategic communication problems* (pp. 117–34). Albany: State University of New York Press.

Swerdlow, J. L. (1984). *Beyond debate: A paper on televised presidential debates.* New York: Twentieth Century Fund.

Swerdlow, J. L. (1987). The strange—and sometimes surprising—history of presidential debates in America. In J. L. Swerdlow (Ed.), *Presidential debates 1988 and beyond* (pp. 3–16). Washington, DC: Congressional Quarterly.

Thompson, W. N. (1979a). Barbara Jordan's keynote address: Fulfilling dual and conflicting purposes. *Central States Speech Journal, 30,* 272–77.

Thompson, W. N. (1979b). Barbara Jordan's keynote address: The juxtaposition of contradictory values. *Southern Speech Communication Journal, 44,* 223–32.

Thorson, E., Christ, W. G., & Caywood, C. (1991). Effects of issue-image strategies, attack and support appeals, music, and visual content in political commercials. *Journal of Broadcasting and Electronic Media, 35,* 465–86.

Tiemens, R. K., Hellweg, S. A., Kipper, P., & Phillips, S. L. (1985). An integrative verbal and visual analysis of the Carter-Reagan debate. *Communication Quarterly, 33,* 34–42.

Times-Mirror Center (1993). *The vocal minority in American politics.* N.p.

Toner, R. (1996, March 17). In this race, it's the center against the middle. *New York Times,* p. 4.3.

Trent, J. D., & Trent, J. S. (1974). The rhetoric of the challenger: George Stanley McGovern. *Central States Speech Journal, 25,* 11–18.

Trent, J. D., & Trent, J. S. (1995). The incumbent and his challengers: The problem of adapting to prevailing conditions. In K. E. Kendall (Ed.), *Presidential campaign discourse: Strategic communication problems* (pp. 69–92). Albany: State University of New York Press.

Trent, J. S., & Friedenberg, R. V. (1995). *Political campaign communication: Principles and practices.* 3rd ed. Westport, CT: Praeger.

TV ministry to seek return of $9.3 million from Bakkers. (1988, January 2). *New York Times*, p. A9.

Valley, D. B. (1974). Significant characteristics of Democratic presidential nomination acceptance speeches. *Central States Speech Journal, 25,* 56–62.

Valley, D. B. (1988). *A history and analysis of Democratic presidential nomination acceptance speeches to 1968.* Lanham, MD: University Press of America.

Wanat, J. (1974). Political broadcast advertising and primary election voting. *Journal of Broadcasting, 18,* 413–22.

Ware, B. L., & Linkugel, W. A. (1973). They spoke in defense of themselves: On the generic criticism of *apologia. Quarterly Journal of Speech, 59,* 273–83.

Wayne, S. J. (1992). *The road to the White House 1992: The politics of presidential elections.* New York: St. Martin's Press.

Weber, R. P. (1985). *Basic content analysis.* Newbury Park, CA: Sage.

Weisberg, H. F., & Kimball, D. C. (1993). *The 1992 presidential election: Party identification and beyond.* Paper presented at the American Political Science Association, Washington, DC. (Quoted in M. A. Levine [1995], *Presidential campaigns and elections: Issues and images in the media age.* Itasca, IL: Peacock Publishers.)

Weithoff, W. E. (1981). "I accept your nomination": Carter, Reagan, and classical obscurantism. *Indiana Speech Journal, 16,* 33–40.

Wells, W. T., Pier, P. M., Blaney, J. R., & Benoit, W. L. (1996). *Acclaiming, attacking, and defending in nominating convention acceptance addresses, 1960–96.* San Diego, CA: Speech Communication Association.

West, D. M. (1993). *Air wars: Television advertising in election campaigns 1952–1992.* Washington: Congressional Quarterly.

West, D. M. (1997). *Air wars: Television advertising in election campaigns 1952–1996.* 2d ed. Washington: Congressional Quarterly.

Williams, M. L. (1980). The effect of deliberate vagueness on receiver recall and agreement. *Central States Speech Journal, 31,* 30–41.

Windt, T. O. (1972). The diatribe: Last resort for protest. *Quarterly Journal of Speech, 17,* 299–328.

Wooten, C. W. (1973). The ambassador's speech: A particularly Hellenistic genre of oratory. *Quarterly Journal of Speech, 59,* 209–12.

Wright, L. (1993, November 26). Retailer hit with ad violations: Attorney General cites Show-Me Furniture. *Columbia Daily Tribune,* p. 1A.

Zerbinos, E. (1995/1996). The talk radio phenomenon: An update. *Journal of Radio Studies, 3,* 10–22.

Author Index

Subject Index

About the Authors

WILLIAM L. BENOIT is Professor of Communication at the University of Missouri. He has published numerous articles and three books: *Candidates in Conflict: Persuasive Attack and Defense in the 1992 Presidential Debates* (1996, with William T. Wells), *Accounts, Excuses, and Apologies: A Theory of Image Restoration Strategies* (1995), and *Readings in Argumentation* (1992, with Dale Hample and Pamela J. Benoit). His Ph.D. is from Wayne State University.

JOSEPH R. BLANEY is a doctoral candidate in the Department of Communication at the University of Missouri. He has published in *The Journal of Communication and Religion* (with Benoit). His M.A. is from Saint Louis University.

P. M. PIER is a doctoral candidate in the Department of Communication at the University of Missouri. She has published in *Communication Quarterly* (with Benoit and Blaney). Her M.A. is from Southwest Missouri State University.

ISBN 0-275-96361-6

90000>

EAN

9 780275 963613

HARDCOVER BAR CODE